John Stuart Blackie

Lay Sermons

John Stuart Blackie

Lay Sermons

ISBN/EAN: 9783337159641

Printed in Europe, USA, Canada, Australia, Japan

Cover: Foto ©Lupo / pixelio.de

More available books at **www.hansebooks.com**

BY

JOHN STUART BLACKIE

PROFESSOR OF GREEK
IN THE UNIVERSITY OF EDINBURGH

NEW YORK

CHARLES SCRIBNER'S SONS

743 AND 745 BROADWAY

1881

TO

ARTHUR MITCHELL

M.D., LL.D.

FELLOW OF THE ROYAL SOCIETY OF ANTIQUARIES SCOTLAND,

COMMISSIONER OF LUNACY FOR SCOTLAND,

AN EFFICIENT PUBLIC SERVANT, A SOUND ARCHÆOLOGIST,

AND A MAN WISE IN THE BEST WISDOM OF LIFE,

THESE DISCOURSES

ARE WITH SINCERE ESTEEM DEDICATED

BY

THE AUTHOR

PREFACE.

THESE Discourses originated in a series of Sabbath evening Addresses, which, at the request of the late excellent Maurice Lothian, I delivered to the Young Men's Association connected with Dr. Guthrie's congregation. One or two of the Discourses delivered there, written out after delivery, appear here; others were delivered on other occasions to different audiences; some published in *Good Words*, one in the *Contemporary Review;* and all of them submitted to a severe process of thorough study, revision, and, where necessary, enlargement. I have called them Sermons, not Lectures, because, though some of them were delivered in the form of popular lecture, they have all a direct practical drift, and are intended either to apply Christian Ethics or to expound Christian doctrine in reference to matters of special interest in the present age of theological disturbance and religious transition.

I may mention that I am in no wise walking out of the proper sphere of my studies in taking up theological subjects, having been educated for the Church, and habitually prosecuted the study of the Scriptures in the original tongues as one of the most fruitful fields of scholarly activity.

COLLEGE, EDINBURGH,
October 1881.

CONTENTS.

I.
                                                              PAGE
THE CREATION OF THE WORLD .   1

II.
THE JEWISH SABBATH AND THE CHRISTIAN LORD'S DAY .   81

III.
FAITH   113

IV.
THE UTILISATION OF EVIL   . 138

V.
LANDLORDS AND LAND LAWS   .   .   157

VI.
THE POLITICS OF CHRISTIANITY   .   .   .   191

VII.

The Dignity of Labour . 221

VIII.

The Scottish Covenanters 236

IX.

On Symbolism, Ceremonialism, Formalism, and the
  New Creature 299

APPENDIX.

The Metaphysics of Genesis I. 333

I.

THE CREATION OF THE WORLD.

(GENESIS i. 1-31 ; ii. 1-3.)

I HAVE often thought of that strange misfortune of human nature—or wonderful condition of all nature, should we not rather say?—by which a high power of a good thing so readily becomes a bad thing, and the superlative degree of a great advantage turns over, by a slight touch, into a great disadvantage. Without light, for instance, as we all know, no picture is possible; but much light certainly spoils the picture; nay, the greatest skill of the greatest artists is shown in nothing so much as in the cunning management of darkness. Money, again, is a good thing, a very good thing, an indispensable thing: so Aristotle taught on the banks of the Ilissus more than two thousand years ago; so venerable and thoughtful pundits teach on the banks of the Ganges at the present hour; so cunning Greeks, and canny Scots, and vigorous Englishmen, always have believed, and always will believe, with a most persistent orthodoxy. Yet mountains of money, we see every day, often serve no other purpose than to smother and to bury the best humanity of the man who has made it; and as for those who do not make it, but only get it, there is no surer receipt for riding post-haste to perdition than to give a young man of a certain average quality of blood, at a certain stage of his existence, a thousand pounds or two in his pocket. So it has often struck me, in reference to Christianity, that a great many people at the present day really do not know how good a thing it is, merely for this reason, that they have got so much of it that their eyes are over-flooded and their ears over-echoed with it; that they are constantly living in the very atmosphere and breath of it; so that, as the German proverb says, they "cannot see the wood for trees." The first Christians had unquestionably this grand advantage over us, which arose out of their great disadvantage; they saw the gospel directly confronted with idolatry; the God-man Christ Jesus against a sensual Bacchus and a carnal Venus; light in miraculous radiance made more manifest by the pitchy darkness through which it shot. It is difficult for some of us in these latter days to get a glimpse of Christianity as the grandest phenomenon in the history of the moral world; we take out our sectarian spectacles and microscopes, and we scan our special form of Christianity— our Episcopacy, our Presbyterianism, our Independency, our Popery—most minutely; but we find the utmost difficulty in getting out of this habit of over-nice inspection, and adapting our eye to a larger range of vision. We become, so to speak, short-sighted in spiritual matters, and we see only the fingers and the nails of the great statue of divine Truth, not the whole figure. Nay, worse; there are some of us who have got into an evil habit of looking exclusively at the small spots and scratches which our microscopic habits have taught us to discover on the fair nails of the statue; and we seem vastly conceited with this discovery. There is nothing which seems to delight a certain class of minds so much as finding faults in beautiful things; as Coleridge tells a story of a smart Cockney who could see nothing in Dannecker's beautiful statue of Ariadne at Frankfort, but a few blue spots in the marble, "very like Stilton cheese"! Comments not very different in spirit, I fear, are often made on the Divine image of moral beauty presented to us in the gospel, and on some of the more prominent passages of the Bible. Among others, the first chapter of Genesis, which has always appeared to me a perfect model of sublime and simple wisdom, has come in for its fair share of microscopic inspection, and of short-sighted misconception. It has been curiously dissected in parts, but not looked at as a whole, or comprehended in its grand drift and universal significance; it has been tortured into all shapes by all sorts of impertinent scientific appliances, instead of being looked at as a revelation of the great lines of theological and philosophical truth; it has been confronted with Playfair and Hutton, and the minute shell-fish of Murchison's

Silurian rocks, not, as it ought to have been, with Homer, and Hesiod, and Thales, and Heraclitus, or the portentous cosmogonies of the Indian Puranas. It is my intention, in the present paper, to present the Mosaic account of the creation in its natural grand points of contrast with the heathen mythologies and philosophies which it supplanted; to show by what profound, though plain, statements of eternal wisdom, it has declared for all times and all places a philosophy of the divine architecture of the world, beyond which the human mind can never reach; and to accustom the thoughtful reader to look seriously upon this most venerable of all documents, in its own natural aspect and attitude, placed where it properly stands in the moral and intellectual history of the world, not, as it may appear, after having been forced into all sorts of unnatural positions, by curious speculations of merely physical science, which, whether true or false, do not in the slightest degree affect its theological import.

What, then, I ask, are the grand truths, philosophical or theological (for philosophy and theology at the fountain-head are one), which this document reveals? It appears to me that they naturally arrange themselves under the following heads:—

I. In the first place we have the philosophy of CREATION. And here we must first ask what the Mosaic record means by this word. It is a word, as commonly used, which goes into depths which a man with human thought can no more fathom, than with human legs he can tread the pathless air. Creation, we say, is "to make something out of nothing;" and this is the meaning of the word which, with a few exceptions, we believe, has always been accepted by the Christian Church. But the creation of something out of nothing, though it may be concluded from speculative reasons, and is generally supposed to be enunciated in the words of the Apostle (Hebrews xi. 3), is an abstract metaphysical truth, and does not naturally lie in the scope of the Scriptures, given as they were mainly for the purposes of practical piety, and for intellectual enlightenment only so far as this is necessary to achieve that end. We shall not, therefore, be surprised to find that the idea of creation out of nothing, however it may have entered the system of Christian doctrine, certainly does not lie in the words or in the scope of the Mosaic account of creation. By creation, Moses means only the creation of order out of confusion: this is certain, both from the whole drift of the document, and from the meaning of the Hebrew word *bara* (identical with our word *bear*; Greek, $\phi\acute{\epsilon}\rho\omega$; Latin, *fero, pario*; Sanscrit, *bhri*), as expounded by Gesenius and other lexicographers. Sanscrit scholars tell us that there is not in the whole vocabulary of the Brahmanic language, copious as it is, a single word answering to our word *matter*;[1] this I believe. Equally

---

[1] See the learned and ingenious exposition of the first three chapters of Genesis, lately published by Dr. Ballantyne.

certain is it to me that in the Hebrew language there is no word answering to our idea of "to create out of nothing;" for this plain reason, that the grand excellence of the Hebrew theology lies in its avoidance of all subtle and unprofitable questions, and founding godly action on the faith of those unquestioned divine truths which every soundly-constituted intellect can comprehend. If there is one point more than another which distinguishes the theology of Moses from that of the Vedas, and some of the Greek philosophers, it is this—its essential and pervading practicality. Theological truths exciting only to subtle speculation, and leading to no practical result, are not propounded by Moses. Creation out of nothing, however true, is a barren truth for us; for, with our finite faculties, we cannot comprehend it, and even if we did, we could make no use of the conception. But the other meaning of creation, which Moses enunciates, though it does not puzzle our idle wit, tells us something which, while it is absolutely and eternally true, is clearly comprehensible by every rational being, and is capable of being turned to use by us at every moment of our existence. Creation is the production of order. What a simple, but at the same time comprehensive and pregnant principle is here! Plato could tell his disciples no ultimate truth of more pervading significance. Order is the law of all intelligible existence. Everything that exists in the world, everything that has either been made by God, or has been produced by man, of any permanent value, is only some manifestation of order in its thousandfold possibilities. Everything that has a shape is a manifestation of order; shape is only a consistent arrangement of parts; shapelessness is found only in the whirling columns that sweep across African Saharas; but even these columns have their curious balance, which calculators of forces might foretell, and the individual grains of sand of which they are composed reveal mathematical miracles to the microscope. Every blade of grass in the field is measured; the green cups and the coloured crowns of every flower are curiously counted; the stars of the firmament wheel in cunningly calculated orbits; even the storms have their laws. In human doings and human productions we see everywhere the same manifestation. Well-ordered stones make architecture; well-ordered social regulations make a constitution and a police; well-ordered ideas make good logic; well-ordered words make good writing; well-ordered imaginations and emotions make good poetry; well-ordered facts make science. Disorder, on the other hand, makes nothing at all, but unmakes everything. Stones in disorder produce ruins; an ill-ordered social condition is decline, revolution, or anarchy; ill-ordered ideas are absurdity; ill-ordered words are neither sense nor grammar; ill-ordered imaginations and emotions are madness; ill-ordered facts are chaos. What then is this wonderful enchanter called ORDER? What exactly do we mean by it? If we look into it more narrowly we shall find that it implies the separation, division, and distribution of things according to their qualities, in certain definite well-calculated times and spaces. Number and measure are of the essence of it. The sands of the desert cannot be numbered—at least not by us; relatively to our faculties they are mere chaos. But the soldiers of a well-ordered army, arranged in rank and file, can be numbered, and their thousands told, with as much ease as the units of a small sum, if only the arrangement be completed. So then order consists in dividing a confused multitude of individual elements into groups that bear a natural resemblance to one another in kind, in number, and in measure. A squad of full-grown soldiers, five in front, and three in depth, like the band of the old Greek chorus, is perfect order; each unit being like the other, and the whole being composed of parts that bear a definite relation of equality or proportion to the whole; the many under the controlling power of order have become one, and with that unity have acquired a distinct character, and are capable of answering a definite purpose. This, and this only, is the difference between an avalanche of shattered rocks on the storm-battered sides of Mont Blanc or Ben Muic-Dhuibh, and the stable piles of the Memphian pyramids, or the chaste columns of the Parthenon; between what the great Scotch poet paints as

> "Crags, knolls, and mounds, confusedly hurled,
> The fragments of an earlier world,"

and the beautiful procession of things which Moses describes as marching forth into existence at the fiat of the Omnipotent. So it is with forms. Forces also are subject to the same law. Take a kettle of boiling water. Look at the steam coming out of its neck; how it bubbles and blows and puffs and whiffs and wheezes, and makes all sorts of irregular inorganic movements and noises. The atoms of which that vapour is composed are, as the chemist well knows, composed of elements that come not together at random, but are subject to a calculation as nice and exact as those which measure the orbits of the stars, and the flux and reflux of the tides; but the vapoury mass itself, as it issues from the kettle, is a blind force, not produced with any object other than that of disengaging itself, and not productive of any result such as well-ordered forces are daily seen to produce. Well! take that same hot vapour, spitting and spurting in its wild unlicensed way, and confine it in a cylinder; then by the calculated injection of cold water, cause it to contract and expand at certain intervals; and the originally blind force, made subject now to calculation and order and law, becomes a serviceable power, which, acting on a series of pistons, beams, and wheels, becomes a steam-engine!—a machine which, like a Briareus with a hundred arms, can achieve all sorts of weighty work, with a touch as light as the hand of a little child playing with a hoop. And thus an idle puff of evanescent vapour becomes the great wonder and wonder-worker of the age; the greatest mechanical wonder, perhaps, of all ages that have been since the world began. Such are the triumphs of order.

II. In the second place, we have the CAUSE of CREATION. If all things, knowable and cognisable, are only different forms of ORDER, the question arises, *How is order produced?* Now, in order to look with proper reverence at the profound simplicity with which Moses has answered this question, the best thing we can do is to inquire, first, how the great popular oracles of ancient times answered it. What does Homer say?—

"Ocean the prime generator of gods, and Tethys the mother." [1]

What does Hesiod say, who was a greater authority in these matters with the Greeks, because he was a doctor of divinity—or all that the good Bœotians had for one—about eight hundred years before Christ, and wrote a genealogy of the gods, meant to instruct the Greeks in those very matters in which we are now instructed by the first chapter of Genesis. Well, this Bœotian theologer says:—

"In the beginning was CHAOS: and after Chaos primeval EARTH broad-breasted, the firm foundation of all that existeth; Murky TARTARUS then in the broad-wayed Earth's abysmal Deep recesses; then LOVE, the fairest of all the Immortals, LOVE, that loosens the firm-knit limb, and sweetly subdueth Wisest of men to her will, and gods that rule in Olympus. Then from Chaos was EREBUS born, and the sable-vested

---

[1] *Iliad*, xiv. 201.

NIGHT; from NIGHT came ETHER, and glorious DAY into being,
Born from Night, when Erebus knew her with kindly embrace-
ment.
Earth, then, like to herself in breadth produced the expanded
Starry HEAVEN, to curtain the Earth, and provide for Immortals
Lucid seats on the brazen floors of unshaken Olympus;
Also from Earth the MOUNTAINS came forth, the lofty, the
rugged,
Dear to OREAD NYMPHS who haunt the rocky retirement.
Then the billowy SEA, the bare, the briny, the barren,
Fatherless, born of herself; but after, in kindly embracement
She to HEAVEN brought forth the vast deep-eddying OCEAN;
Likewise CŒUS, and CRIUS, IAPETUS, and HYPERION,
THEIA, RHEA, and THEMIS, and MEMORY, mother of MUSES,
PHŒBE, with golden diadem bound, and beautiful TETHYS."

Along with this specimen of cosmogonic speculation from the most intellectual people of the West, we shall wisely set down the corresponding conclusions of the most celebrated people of the early East—the Babylonians. Their doctrine concerning the creation of the world we have from three sources,—from the works of Berosus, a learned Chaldean historian, who flourished in the time of Alexander the Great; from the report of Damascius, a subtle Greek speculator, who wrote a work about the principles of things some four hundred years after our era; and, lastly, from certain tablets of the ancient Cuneiform writing, the decipherment of which has encircled with such a halo of glory the philology of the nineteenth century. I set them down here in this order.

BEROSUS.

"There was a time in which what existed was mere darkness and water; and in the darkness and the water animals of strange and monstrous forms were produced. Men were born, some with two wings, and some with four wings and two faces, and with one body and two heads, one of a man, and one of a woman.

"And there were other men, with goats' legs and goats' horns; others with horses' hoofs; others had the hinder part of their bodies as the body of horses, and the front of men, like what the Greeks call Hippocentaurs; and there were also produced bulls with the heads of men, and dogs with four bodies, but with fishes' tails; also dog-headed horses, and men and other animals with the heads and bodies of horses, and the tails of fish; and other animals, of all kinds of strange shapes. In addition to these there were fish and creeping things and serpents. There were other animals of strange and mysterious form, as they are to be seen represented in the temple of Belus. They say, further, that a woman ruled over all these, whose name was Omorca, or, as it is called in the Chaldean language, Thalatth, which in Greek is Θάλαττα, *the sea*.

"Things being in this condition, Belus came and clove the woman through the middle in two. Of the one half of her he made the earth, and of the other half he made the heavens, and caused all the animals to perish. Then the annalist goes on to say that these things were allegories of what exists in nature: the whole of things being water, and animals being produced in it. This god, he further declares, cut off his own head; and the other gods mingled the blood with the clay, and therewith formed men; and from this cause they are intelligent, and participate in the Divine mind. Further, they say that Belus, which they interpret as Ζεὺς or Jove, separated the earth from the heavens, and arranged the universe, but that the animals, not being able to endure the power of the air, perished; whereupon, seeing the world waste and uninhabited, he ordered one of the gods to produce other animals, able to endure the light; and Belus created the sun and the moon and the five planets." [1]

Damascius.

"Of the Barbarians the Babylonians seem to make no mention of one original first cause of the universe, but give us two—TAUTHE and APASON, the latter the husband of the former, and this female power they call the mother of the gods. From this pair they say a son was born, called MOUMIN, which I conceive to be the intelligible world, proceeding from two principles. From the same pair another offspring came forth, named LACHE and LACHOS; and again, from the same another pair, KISSARE and ASSOROS, from whom were born three,

---

[1] Berosi quæ supersunt. Edit. Richter. Lips. 1825, p. 49.

Anos, and Illinos, and Aos; from which Aos and Dauke a son was born, Belus, whom they call the demiurge or artificer of the universe." [1]

Chaldean Account of the Creation.

The First Tablet.

1. When the upper region was not yet called Heaven,
2. And the lower region was not yet called Earth,
3. And the abyss of Hades had not yet opened its arms,
4. Then the Chaos of Waters gave birth to all of them,
5. And the waters were gathered into one place.
6. No men yet dwelt together; no animals yet wandered about;
7. None of the gods had yet been born.
8. Their names were not spoken; their attributes were not known.
9. Then the eldest of the gods—
10. Lakhma and Lakhama—were born,
11. And grew up.
12. Assar and Kissar were born next,
13. And lived through long periods.
14. ANU.

The Fifth Tablet.

1. He constructed dwellings for the great gods.
2. He fixed up constellations, whose figures were like animals.
3. He made the year; into four quarters he divided it.
4. Twelve months he established, with their constellations, three by three.
5. And for the days of the year he appointed festivals.

---

[1] *Damascii* quaestiones de principiis. Edit. Kopp., 1826, p. 384.

CREATION OF THE WORLD.

6. He made dwellings for the planets, for their rising and setting.
7. And that nothing should go amiss, and that the course of none should be retarded,
8. He placed with them the dwellings of BEL and HEA.
9. He opened great gates on every side ;
10. He made strong the portals, on the left hand and on the right ;
11. In the centre he placed Luminaries.
12. The Moon he appointed to rule the night,
13. And to wander through the night until the dawn of day.
14. Every month without fail he made holy assembly days.
15. In the beginning of the month, at the rising of the night,
16. It shot forth its horn to illuminate the Heavens.
17. On the seventh day he appointed a holy day,
18. And to cease from all business he commanded.
19. Then arose the Sun in the horizon of Heaven in glory.[1]

Now, these are curious, and in some views beautiful, passages; but when we reflect seriously, and begin to ask what wisdom they contain, we feel a terrible void—a void as terrible as the chaos which is the first link in this strange genealogy. Our pious desire to know what may be known of things supersensible is rudely baffled ; and

---

[1] *Records of the Past*, vol. ix. Assyrian texts. Translator—H. Fox Talbot, F.R.S. This translator, however, is not confirmed by Smith and Sayce in the indication of the *Jewish Sabbath*, which he flatters himself to have discovered in the 17th and 18th lines. These lines appear thus in Sayce's edition of Smith's Chaldean account of Genesis, London, 1880 :—(17) "On the seventh day thy circle—the moon's—begins to fill ; (18) but open in darkness will remain the half on the right ;" and on this 18th line Professor Sayce remarks that the version given is Dr. Oppert's, but the line is so mutilated as to make any attempt at translation extremely doubtful.

we see plainly that we have been fooled in expecting wisdom from this quarter; certainly they from whom we asked bread have given us a stone. Let us take the Greek first; and at the first glance it becomes plain that the old doctor of Bœotian theology does not touch the important question at all which we have now raised—What is the *cause* of order? He only tells you that before order was chaos, and that light was evolved out of darkness. This is all very true as a historical sequence—just as true as that a chicken comes out of an egg, or a child out of the womb. But the point of cause is not touched on at all; for the egg is certainly not the cause of the chicken, as we all know that it required a hen previously to produce the egg. As little, when I take a phosphorus match, and by rubbing it on the hearthstone, produce light, can it be said that this darkness, out of which the light came, caused the light; it only preceded it. Hesiod and Homer, it will be observed, do not at all agree in the first link that they set forth in the great chain of existing things. The secular poet says that all the gods are produced from Ocean and Tethys—the male and female powers of water; the theological doctor, that Chaos and Earth were first; that Chaos had no productive power; but that from Earth were produced Tartarus, Night, Day, Heaven, Ocean, etc., and by descent from them, as the sequel of the poem teaches, Jove, Apollo, Juno, Venus, and all the heavenly Powers. But in one thing they both agree: they speak of an evolution and a development by the ordinary method of generation, which, as we all know, is not a cause but a process. When grain is put into the hopper of a mill, it will certainly be drawn in, and by a constant action of wisely-arranged machinery come out changed into well-ground meal. But the clear perception of this process does not help me a single step to the comprehension of that other question, How came the mill to be so curiously contrived, and whence came the grain that was put into the hopper? Or again, if in a large manufactory you see a little wheel which takes its motion from the teeth of a big wheel, and that big wheel takes its motion from a yet bigger wheel, and that wheel again from a rolling cylinder, and that cylinder from a perpendicular shaft, and that shaft from a horizontal beam; in such a case you would never dream for a moment of confounding the different steps by which the motion is conveyed with the source of the motion; you must go on till you come to the steam and the water, and the boiler and the fire, and beyond that also you must go till you come to James Watt. The cause of the motion of the little wheel with which you commenced is the mind of James Watt, directing, for a certain purpose, the elastic force of the aëriform water, which we call steam. So we say to wise old Homer, whose writings the Greeks fondly conceited themselves to contain all wisdom, What do you mean when you say that Ocean is the prime generator of gods? Do you mean only that, according to the old adage, "WATER IS BEST," not because the inventors of that proverb were total abstainers, but because that without water no living organism can exist (turn water into a solid—as at the poles—and all vegetation ceases); and, therefore, that the existence of water is the first condition of all vital being on this earth? This we willingly believe; but it is only one important fact connected with a great process; for when you are singing the praises of water, Heraclitus, the son of Blyson, a grave old gentleman who philosophised at Ephesus about four hundred years after Homer, bethinks himself that as all water becomes solid by the abstraction of heat, so the existence of water is possible only under the supposition that Fire previously exists. Fire, therefore, or heat, or, if you prefer a learned Latin word, caloric, is the first principle or cause of all things. Well, this seems to go a little bit farther than either Homer or Hesiod; but, after all, our thinking appetite has got nothing that it can feed on; for what is Fire? And whatever it be, what virtue has it to produce order? Does it not rather, in our experience, tend as much to produce disorder? Is it not one of the great agents of dissolution, destruction, and death? Strange! Nevertheless the chemist comes in and tells me very dogmatically, that whatever heat may be, it acts, in his department at least, in a very orderly way; for the elements to whose mutual action it is necessary, will not unite except in certain fixed and definite proportions, the recognition of which is now necessary to the most rudimentary knowledge of chemistry. Water, to whose atomical composition we previously alluded, is made up of two gases or airs—oxygen and hydrogen—which, in forming that compound, will unite only in the proportion of two bulks of the latter to one of the former. And in the same way of all other bodies. The elements of which they are composed are combined, under the expansive action of heat, in certain curiously calculated proportions. And in this way we seem plainly to arrive at the old doctrine of Pythagoras, promulgated about 550 before Christ, that NUMBER or MEASURE is the first principle of all things. But this also is only a fact, not a cause. For the cause of NUMBER, which indeed is only another name for order, and for that cunning proportion among the atoms of compound bodies which the great Dalton discovered, we must go a step beyond Dalton, a step beyond Pythagoras, a step beyond Heraclitus, a step beyond Homer. Will the Babylonian help us to make this step? Scarcely. Belus, no doubt, is the great plastic artificer—$\delta\eta\mu\iota\text{o}\upsilon\rho\gamma\acute{o}\varsigma$—who disposes the primitive jumble of things into the existing beautiful order, by the action, one must suppose, though it is not expressly said, of a designing intellect; but whence came Belus? Like Zeus in the Greek mythology, he is not a primitive self-existent power, but the product of pre-existent forces; he is more indeed than Jove, whom the Greeks worshipped as the supreme head of the existing order of affairs, physical and moral, but not as the author of that order. Belus seems really, in some sense, to be the author of the world which he governs; but like an heir to an entailed, neglected, mismanaged, and bankrupt estate, he receives it rather as an inheritance to recreate and to remodel, than as a possession lorded from the first by no one but himself. In fact, so far as one can see from our fragmentary notices, the Supreme God of the Babylonians, no less than the Jove of the Greeks, is conceived in the first place as the effective result of a historical sequence, rather than as the prime figure in a chain of metaphysical causation. And we may say generally, I imagine, that in all polytheistic mythologies the purely theological or metaphysical question of the original cause of the creation lies outside of the popular conception of the gods, who demand our fear and our acknowledgment directly as the unseen controlling agents of those mysterious phenomenal forces, on which the happiness of human beings to such a great extent depends. Their earliest cosmogonic poetry, accordingly, would give them no answer to a question which the popular intellect had never raised. The utmost that the Bœotian theologer could do, was to bring in Ἔρως Πόθος, LOVE or DESIRE, as the fourth term in his list of original forces; but Πόθος was not a creative god eminently—only a name to express in a personal figure that miraculous blind instinct by which men are led to the reproduction of their kind. Gods and men, somehow or other, are produced by a transcendental process of generative evolution, of which LOVE or DESIRE is the motive force, as water is the motive force of a mill-wheel. And the dualism of male and female, which lies at the bottom equally of the Babylonian and the Hellenic cosmogony, plainly shows that the whole scheme has been devised after the analogy of the common process of generation in our little dependent world, without ascending to the idea of an independent, self-existent Cause of the Creation, such as we are now seeking for. That they might have found out such a cause without much difficulty, had they been inclined, there seems no reason to doubt; for, as Paul says (Romans i. 20), the visible things of the universe stand out as a living blazon of the invisible excellence behind, which only the blind can fail to perceive. But as a man will sometimes not hear even the sound of a cannon, when his faculties are diverted far off in a different direction; so the people that formed those early cosmogonies, being in a poetical and imaginative, rather than a philosophic and metaphysical stage of being, either allowed the question of the ultimate cause of the cosmic order to drop altogether, or solved it in a half-hearted blundering sort of way, which could satisfy only the half-thinkers. Let us see then how we have to proceed now-a-days, when, brushing aside all those strange cosmogonic imaginations, we essay to find the ultimate cause of the cosmic order from observing carefully what takes place under our own eyes. We have constantly, in every action of life, to do with order and disorder; we are constantly employed in creating either the one or the other; so we cannot be at a loss to discover their cause. A father makes a present of a curious toy to his little boy. Tommy amuses himself with it for a day or two, or it may be a week or more, according to the laws of legitimate sport in youthful gentlemen; but in due season he tires of it, and longs for something new; and to make public proclamation to papa and other powerful patrons that the old toy has served its purpose, he takes it all to pieces some morning before papa is out of bed, and strews the fragmentary pegs and wheels and springs, and various-coloured beads, upon the parlour floor in motley confusion. Here we have an example of the creation of disorder. How? In the simplest way possible! By utter thoughtlessness, and a restless, impatient activity on the part of a witless child. The boy needed no wisdom to achieve this deed. He did not purposely wish to do anything; he only wished to undo a thing that another had done. What was necessary for the accomplishment of such a purely negative result? Nothing but blind force. A monkey in sport, as readily as a man with a reasoning purpose, could do a business of this kind; a maundering idiot, an unreasoning madman, as easily as an Aristotle, a Newton, or a Gioberti. Blind force, therefore, unreasoning, uncalculating impulse, is the author of disorder. But with the making even of the simplest toy it is quite a different affair. We know that no most assiduous action of blind puffs and strokes will make a toy. Toys are made by ingenious, thinking minds, and by a series of processes, of which ingenious, thinking minds are the authors. We find, therefore, that mind, and mind only, disposes a few pieces of painted wood, flexible steel, and shining studs, into that finely calculated trifle which we call a toy. So we find in all other cases. A wild, raging, passion-stung rabble can pull down a palace in a few hours, which it required years of thoughtful toil in the architect to scheme, and in the builder to erect. A sudden fit of what we call fever, which is a violent irregular action of the blood and venous system, will turn into a chaotic babblement the utterance of a mind, whose words, before this intrusion of a disorderly force, might have hymned the poetry of the universe in a lofty epos, or directed the fate of kingdoms by a salutary ordinance. All that exists without and beyond chaos exists only by virtue of indwelling or controlling mind—mind not cognitive merely and contemplative, but active ; that is to say, intelligent force, as contrasted with blind force. Here, therefore, we have, within the space of our own direct knowledge and experience, the most indubitable proof of the real cause of order. In no branch of the many-armed activity of human life do we see any other principle than this at work—mind constantly the cause of order; disorder as constantly proceeding from the absence of mind. Nor is there the slightest room to suppose that, while we make this conclusion safely with regard to what falls within our human sphere of action, we are making a rash leap into the dark when we say that the presence of a like mind always and everywhere is the cause, and the only cause, of all orderly operations and results in the external universe. For the order which we perceive in the external universe is exactly similar to that which we create by our own activity; and to suppose different or contrary causes for effects altogether similar and identical is unphilosophical. Nay, more; the most curious machines which we can make, with the highest power of our most highly cultivated reason, have already been made, and are already constructed in the world over which we exercise no control, exactly on the same principles as those which are the product of our thought-directed finger. The eye, as everybody knows, is a telescope. The man who doubts that the power which made the human eye is, in its manner of working, not only similar to, but absolutely identical with, the mind which invented the telescope, may as well doubt whether the little paper boat which young Bobbie or Billy launches upon the pond floats there upon the same principle by which the mighty ocean bears the armadas of England and France and America upon its bosom. Doubters of this description labour under a disease for which argument certainly is not the proper cure.[1]

---

[1] The self-evidential character of the world, as the expression of order and design in a plastic mind, is the reason why this truth has been universally recognised wherever men existed in the normal state, or unsophisticated by the perversity and puzzle-headedness of a later

CREATION OF THE WORLD. 25

We have thus arrived at the cause of order, in a very simple way, by actual experience of the fact, than which nothing,—no, not even the boasted necessity of mathematics,—is more certain. It is not more certain that two and two make four, or that the angle at the centre of a circle is double the angle at the circumference,

generation of sophists, more anxious to show their own cleverness by making petty objections, than to repose on the deep bosom of catholic truth. How different the wretched quibbling of a Hume in this view from the healthy instinct of Aristotle, "the great master of those who know," who assumes the catholic utterance of human instinct in this matter as the postulate of all reasonable thinking with regard to the cause of the order which is the universe. Ἀρχαῖος μὲν οὖν τις λόγος παὶ πάτριός ἐστι πᾶσιν ἀνθρώποις ὡς ἐκ θεοῦ τὰ πάντα καὶ διὰ θεοῦ ἡμῖν συνέστηκεν· οὐδεμία δὲ φύσις αὐτὴ καθ' ἑαυτὴν αὐτάρκης ἐρημωθεῖσα τῆς ἐκ τούτου σωτηρίας (De Mundo, 6), which is just what St. Paul says in Acts xvii. 28. See also the beautiful passage from the great thinker's exoteric works in CICERO, de Nat. deorum, ii. 37. The theology of Aristotle, which has to be collected from various passages of his metaphysics and physical tracts, is thus concisely and distinctly stated by BIESE,—"Neither the universal in separation from the individual, nor the individual for itself, can be the principle of the actual and spiritual world; but the alone absolute principle is GOD, the highest self-thinking REASON, which is unlimited energy; HIS THOUGHT IS DEED; and his deeds are the vital and vivifying principle through which only the world becomes possessed of actuality and truth" (BIESE, Philosophie des Aristoteles, Berlin, 1835, vol. i. p. 611). The self-thinking force is called by Aristotle, νόησις νοήσεως, thinking of which thought is the subject, as an artist thinks of his own self-engendered idea, and not about anything external. He shapes from his shaping thought, and acts as a god so far as the giving of actuality to conception is concerned; only, not having life in himself, he cannot confer vitality on his realised conceptions. But God is not only thought, but life, and His thought is essentially vital.

than it is that a grand exhibition of curiously calculated reasonable results could not have proceeded from the action of a blind, unreasoning force, or the combination of a host of such forces. Yet must we not be surprised if the world and the wise men of the world did not at once arrive at this natural, necessary, and inevitable conclusion. In the secret consciousness of the healthy human intellect, the thought of the eternal, universal cause, no doubt, ever resides, not only as the greatest truth, but as the root of all possible truth. The widespread existence of Polytheistic forms of faith forms no exception to this rule. Every form of Polytheism either acknowledges one Supreme God as the preserver of order in the universe—as Jove among the Greeks; or at least conceives the existence of certain superhuman powers, which, if they do not act always on the noblest principles, nevertheless are there, and do act in some way to preserve the recognised order of the universe, so far as human minds in a very low state of culture are capable of recognising that order. For it must be observed that the order of the physical universe, however cunning and certain, is on so great a scale, and involves so many complex relations, that unthinking and uncalculating minds may often fail to have any very clear perception of it. The cleverest monkey, with all the action of its most clever conceits, will remain at an infinite distance from the possibility of comprehending a steam-engine; and men born without the organ of tune shall have their ears besieged by all the sweet, subtle forces of a Mozart and a Beethoven in vain. As there are individual men deficient in certain faculties and sensibilities, so there may be whole races of men whose faculty of thinking is so little cultivated that they have very little idea of what thought means in their own narrow, meagre life; much less are they able to rise to a clear perception of that thoughtful order of things in the great whole, which made the Greeks designate the visible universe so significantly a κόσμος, or *garniture*. Besides, many things are constantly taking place in the physical and moral world, which, to a superficial view, seem actually the result, not of reasonable calculation, but of blind force. Storms, hurricanes, blights, burnings, volcanic explosions, subterranean quakings of the earth, civil wars, murders, rapines, and the triumphal march of prosperous injustice, as it appears, are phenomena which, even to thoughtful minds, have often suggested horrible forecasts of Atheism and blind Necessity. Deeper thought, no doubt, always teaches the absurdity of fixing our eyes on these irregular, and, to us, incalculable, exhibitions of force, as any foundation for systematic atheism. The connection and ultimate purpose of all the violent and most sweeping movements of the world can no more be comprehended by us than a fish can comprehend the currents of the ocean in which it swims, or a fly the revolutions of the wheel on which it has fixed itself. But the existence of these irregular, and, so far as their immediate and most obvious operation goes, destructive phenomena, may, along with a low state of culture, easily explain the existence of a sort of atheism among various races of men. I do not see, however, any proof that absolute atheism, or the belief in an absolute unreasoning Something, without a name, as the cause of the definite reasonable Something, which we call the world, has ever prevailed extensively among the human race. The Buddhists, it has been said, are atheists. But the atheism which they profess,[1] is, so far as my studies have taught me, not so much a formal denial of intellectual causality in the universe, as a fixture of the feeling of reverence upon a great human preacher of righteousness, to the neglect of the great fountain of all righteousness. This is a very different thing from the perverse scepticism of certain irreverent individuals of highly cultivated intellect, who can bring themselves to believe in no intelligent author of the universe, because, with all their cleverness, they are so shallow as not to know the difference between a cause and a sequence, or because they are so despotic in a certain intellectual selfishness as not to be willing to allow any intellect in the universe superior to their own. Such men require a moral conversion, not a logical refutation. Professed and vainglorious atheists must just be allowed to pass as ghosts which haunt the day, with which a sound living eye can hold no converse—

[1] See the chapter "Buddhism" in my *Natural History of Atheism*. London, 1877.

> "Just are the ways of God,
>   And justifiable to men ;
> Unless there be who think not God at all ;
>   If any be, they walk obscure ;
> For of such doctrine never was there school,
> But the heart of the fool,
> And no man therein doctor but himself."

We have now talked over some twenty-eight pages, and yet are not beyond the breadth of that significant verse : IN THE BEGINNING GOD CREATED THE HEAVEN AND THE EARTH. We have seen how Hesiod and Homer and Heraclitus dealt with this important matter, and how they failed to approach the sublime significance of that enunciation. But let us not believe that all the Greeks who sought after wisdom were so unfortunate as their first pioneers. On the contrary, the wisest Greeks declare the doctrine of the first book of Moses in the plainest terms. Of these pious heathen philosophers, the name is legion ; but we shall content ourselves with three of the most notable—Anaxagoras, Socrates, and Plato. Let their testimony, however, be preceded fitly by something perhaps older than the oldest of them, certainly of a more venerable and hoary pedigree. "The first Being," says the great Indian Epos, "the Mahabharata, is called MANASA,[1] or INTELLECTUAL, and is so celebrated by great sages; he is God without beginning or end, indivisible, immortal, undecaying."[2]

---

[1] Latin, *mens;* Greek, μένος; German, *meinen;* English, *mean,* mind.   [2] Wilson's *Vishnu Purana*, p. 14, note.

So far superior is the theology that grew up on the sacred banks of the Ganges to anything that Helicon, Parnassus, or Olympus could boast of in the earliest ages of Greek wisdom. But, as we have said, the Greeks were a subtle people, whose special mission it was, as St. Paul testifies, to seek wisdom; and that their speculation should long have wandered about without hitting on the grand truth, which is the only possible key-stone of all coherent thought, was not to be expected. That Orpheus, Olen, Linus, and the most ancient worshippers of Apollo, were pious theists and believers, by a healthy, poetic instinct in one original Mind, the cause of the universe, is extremely probable; but the first philosophical speculator that distinctly announced to the Greeks the great truth of the first words of Moses was Anaxagoras. This remarkable man, born at Clazomenæ, in Asia Minor, about the year 500 B.C., was the intimate friend of Pericles, the great Athenian statesman, in whose Life, by Plutarch, we find the statement that "this philosopher was the first who taught that not CHANCE or NECESSITY, but MIND, pure and unmixed (νοῦν ἄκρατον), was the principle of the universe, this mind possessing the virtue of separating the particles in a confused compound, and forming thereby new homogeneous wholes." This is exactly what we described above as the proper definition of order; and the creator of this order, with the clear-sighted old Ionian thinker, is not mere attraction, or repulsion, or elective affinity, or any such juggle of words, serving to conceal ignorance, or to cloak atheism; but simply and directly MIND. For this satisfactory enunciation the pious philosopher had the honour of being accused of impiety by the Athenian mob; which is pretty much like the case of the beer-toper in the humorous German drinking-song, who, coming out of a smoky tap-room into the clear moonlight, and finding the moon looking somewhat asquint, the houses all nodding, and the lanterns staggering about, concludes with great satisfaction that the whole external world is drunk, and goes forthwith back into the beer-shop as the only sober quarter of the world known to him at that moment! But Aristotle, the great encyclopædist, knew better who was drunk and who was sober in this matter. He says distinctly that all those who philosophised before about the first principle appear as mere infantile babblers, compared with the great man who first enounced νοῦς as the alone authorised oracle to answer all the questions of all the philosophers. After Anaxagoras, Socrates appeared on the Athenian stage; a man no less distinguished for sound common sense and genial humour than for profound piety, and a healthy, intelligible philosophy. This great teacher, "the acknowledged master of all eminent thinkers who have since lived,"[1] in an argument with a little dapper gentleman called Aristodemus, reported by Xenophon, states the whole doctrine of Natural Theology, as it has since been taught by Paley and

[1] J. S. Mill on *Liberty*, p. 46, in a splendid passage of one of the finest books in the English language.

other Christian philosophers, with a distinctness of view and a happiness of illustration that leaves little to desire. He exhibits in detail the many instances of exquisite and benevolent design in the structure of the human frame; he shows how the gods, so far from neglecting human beings, have fitted them out with so many gifts, that they do actually live as gods upon the earth, when compared with other animals; he shows that religion is the true sign, badge, and privilege of reasonable, as compared with unreasoning, creatures; and he asserts finally, that as the Divine Being is everywhere present, and everywhere cognisant of whatever takes place, a wise man will take care not only to avoid disreputable actions before men, but will preserve his purity with holy reverence, even in the lonely desert. Not less lofty or less sublime on all questions connected with God and the god-like element in man, was his great disciple Plato, who again and again declares that "Intellect alone is the great first principle," for that " all the wisest men with one voice witness that Mind is king of all things, whether in heaven above, or on the earth below."[1]

III. It may seem scarcely necessary, after the immediately preceding remarks, to assert articulately in a separate proposition that the doctrine of DESIGN or reasonable purpose and plan existing in the world, and in the Creative Mind of which it is the product,

[1] See *Philebus*, 15.

if not in so many words, is certainly implied in every paragraph of the Mosaic account of the creation; but as it has become fashionable with certain professors of physical science, and one or two abstract thinkers since Bacon's time, in this country, to talk slightingly of final causes, and to scout teleology, or the doctrine of design as a manifest deduction from the phenomena of the Universe, we shall be readily excused in making a few special remarks on that point here. If Moses, or whoever it was that wrote the book, does not assert design as a substantive proposition, it is simply because he did not conceive that any reasonable being with his eyes open could have denied it. The cause of the world, according to his account, is the direct action of divine volition in a self-existent plastic mind by its own inherent virtue, bringing order out of confusion; and how this can be done without a design of putting an end to confusion by bringing in order, no sane man can understand. Design is only another word to express the fact that the order of things which we call the world, proceeds according to a marked-out plan—*designare*—without which in the direction of order it manifestly could not proceed at all. How comes it then that men of such high and commanding intellects as Bacon, Spinoza, Goethe, and others of less note, have come to talk contemptuously of final causes? So far as I see, from two reasons, of which the first is a transference of the mental attitude naturally assumed by the students of physical science to the domain of metaphysics, where it is altogether inapplicable. The question *Why* or *What for* is, as Goethe wisely remarked,[1] not a scientific question. The scientific man asks *How*, and with that he is content. How is water made? By the union of oxygen and hydrogen in certain proportions, cries the chemist, and therewith blazons to all the world the singular glory of his peculiarly analytic science. Let all the universe be analysed in the same fashion, and the result is always a series of answers full of most curious interest to the question *How*, but in no case trenching on the independent right of that other question, *Why?* and *to what purpose?* and *with what effect?*—as little in any way touching that deeper question, which may justly be divined to contain the root of the final cause, *Whence* and *from what source?* The question how a salad is made, for instance—a well-known case proposed by Kepler to his wife—may be answered very simply as to the *how*, by saying that it is a certain admixture of green vegetables, vinegar, cream, sugar, and oil; but two important questions still remain behind; first, whether it could make itself as well by a chance jumble as by a careful preparation; to which question Madam Kepler answered, Certainly not; and second, what the purpose was for which in this case the lady scientifically prepared the salad, viz. as a pleasantly-stimulant adjunct to the mid-day meal of a great philosopher. It is plain, therefore, that the hunting out and laying bare of a series of invariable sequences, for a successful series of

[1] See Eckermann's *Conversations*.

answers to the question *How*, does not in the slightest degree supersede, much less render illegitimate, the putting of the question *What for?* On the contrary, the illegitimacy is all the other way. The rejection or ignoring of final causes, because the knowledge of them does not enable us to answer the question *how*, is an illegitimate transference, and an impertinent intrusion into a foreign domain. There is a narrow-mindedness in scientists as well as in theologians; and the narrow-mindedness of the scientists shows itself in a tendency to deny the existence of all forces of which they cannot take cognisance with their microscopes or handle with their pincers. But the highest things are precisely those which are neither measureable nor tangible; and here the scientist ought to stop. But no man likes to be stopped, especially in the full career of triumphant discovery; and so, like our great conquerors, the scientific man plants himself valiantly on the back of the world, with the one LAW which happens to be in vogue at the time, and conceits himself to have explained all, or protests at least that nothing is explicable which happens to be beyond the reach of his formula. But there is another reason which helps us to explain the strange phenomenon that in a world blossoming all over and radiant with divine reason, a certain class of persons, rather above the average in point of culture, should persist in seeing no marks of that design which can nowhere be absent where reason is energetically present. It is a fact that there are persons styling themselves atheists, who, when closely examined, may be brought to confess that what they disbelieve is not the existence of self-existent plastic reason, as the substantial cause of a reasonable world,[1] but the unreasonable God that certain unreasonable, ignorant, and presumptuous persons have created out of their own imaginations. In the same way a well-trained scientist may persistently deny that he sees any signs of design in the structure of the universe,

[1] A notable example of this we have in the poet SHELLEY, who, having in the style of *bravura* natural to a young man, flung forth the startling sentence in his text,

THERE IS NO GOD,

forthwith explains in his note that "this negation must be understood solely to affect a *creative Deity*. The hypothesis of a pervading Spirit co-eternal with the universe remains unshaken"—an atheism consequently meaning only a denial of an impertinent theological interpretation forced upon two innocent phrases of the first verse of the Hebrew Bible! In the same way the atomic atheism of DEMOCRITUS might be made to lose a little of its manifest absurdity, if he could be cross-questioned on the words οὐδὲν Χρῆμα μάτην γίνεται, ἀλλὰ πάντα ἐκ λόγου τε καὶ ὑπ' ἀνάγκης (Mullach, p. 216). For, though λόγος here is neither the *Reason* of Plato nor the νοῦς of Anaxagoras, but only *calculation, proportion, method*, yet, as the great atomist posits κίνησις or *motion*, as indispensable to set his atoms into action, he might well be asked what is λόγος *plus* κίνησις, unless pretty much what theists call God? In truth, the fact that the same word, both in Greek and Latin —λόγος, *ratio*—expresses both *calculation and reason*, shows plainly enough the true instinct of unsophisticated minds, that the two things spring out of one root, and that there can be no calculation, or orderly method of any kind, without *Reason* or MIND. As for ἀνάγκη or *Necessity*, that is not a force or a power in any sense, but only the assertion of the invariable self-consistent method of action, which belongs inherently to the divine Λόγος.

when he merely means to deny some particular object, design, or purpose, which superficial persons have interpolated into the divine scheme; and we should thus have here only another instance of the familiar principle of *reaction* or *revulsion,* which plays such an important part in the play of moral no less than of physical forces in the universe.[1] Under this head fall, of course, all those ready-handed interpretations of judgments, in which certain good people, more pious than wise, are apt to indulge. If the potato crop, for instance, happens to fail, or a boat taking a pleasure trip on Sunday to be swamped, or an eloquent atheist is suddenly struck dumb, and afflicted with incurable aphasia, these pious interpreters of the divine procedure have no hesitation in attributing all such evil chances to the express interposition of the Divine Being, with the design of inflict-

[1] I am glad to find a most judicious and accurate writer on physical science agreeing with me here. "One often hears final causes spoken of with a contempt which is indeed only a revulsion from a style of writing which will not now find many admirers, in which adaptations were found by pointing out what extraordinary consequences would follow some impossible alteration in Nature, and finally were made to do the duty of efficient causes; but in the history of the vertebrate heart may be seen a remarkable instance of the definite evolution of a complex mechanism to perform a particular kind of work. There is no reason to doubt that here we have morphological evolution and final causes combined; just as it is possible to imagine, though we may have little experience of it, a building morphologically belonging to the Gothic order, yet teleologically fitted for the wants of modern life." *Evolution, Expression, and Sensation,* by JOHN CLELAND, M.D., F.R.S., Professor of Anatomy, University, Glasgow. Maclehose, 1881 (p. 30).

ing special castigation, after a human fashion, for some special offence. But notions of this kind, however powerful in the days when augurs and soothsayers might lame the hand of the wisest commander in the conduct of a campaign, exercise such a secondary influence now, that they do not require any serious refutation. Of more relevance to the present point is the habit which certain people have of assuming a special divine intention in any use which they may find it convenient to make of any created object. Things are used not always because the use made of them lay in the design of the maker, but because it lies in the necessities of the user. If any person, with human utilities only in view, should assert that bears, and foxes, and sheep, and other hairy or fleecy animals were provided with such covering with the design of furnishing warm clothing to human beings in cold climates, he would be making a most false conclusion.[1] They were provided with these

---

[1] Not at all an uncommon conclusion, however, I fear; Spinoza at least assumes that it is a general prejudice "*dicunt enim homines et pro certo statuunt Deum* OMNIA PROPTER HOMINEM FECISSE" (*Ethics*, i. 36); and in the same chapter he goes on to complain justly that men have devised systems of theology in such a fashion "*ut Deus illos supra reliquos diligeret, et totam naturam in usum cæcæ illorum cupiditatis et insatiabilis avaritiæ dirigeret;*" and then, of course, if everything in nature exists only to subserve human happiness, if storms and tempests, and potato diseases, and other exhibitions of nature's potency occur, not at all conducive to human comfort or well-being, men forthwith conclude "*quod Dii irati sunt ob injurias sibi ab hominibus factas; et quanquam experientia in dies reclamat et infinitis exemplis ostendat commoda atque incommoda piis æque ac impiis promiscue*

coverings with the design of rendering their own existence possible; and the adaptation of their integuments to the clothing of man is only a secondary purpose, which they accidentally serve, from coming in contact with naked and thinly-clad human beings. As an instrument made expressly for one operation may, in the hands of an expert operator, be made to do efficient service in a foreign sphere, so the fact of a certain purpose being served by a certain contrivance does not in anywise necessarily prove that the contrivance was made with the express design of effecting that purpose. In a rich and various world, any object—as trees, for instance—in the large œconomy of terrene existence may serve various purposes; but their primary purpose is simply to exist. The millions of flowers that, as the poet has it, were born to blush unseen, serve this primary purpose as much as the gayest bouquet that ever was used to adorn fair breast or garnish forth a splendid banquet. We shall, therefore, at once agree with the iconoclasts of design, in so far as they accentuate the important doctrine that human uses are by no means always identical with divine designs, and that in this,

---

evenire non ideo ab inveterato prejudicio desistunt." And Pollock (Spinoza, p. 166) tells of "the *theological* conception of the universe as created and governed by a magnificent human despot, which indirectly makes man the measure of all things"—a passage, the phraseology of which gives us the key, if key were needed, to the strange atheistic proclivities of some of our modern writers, who constantly confound scientific theology with the most crude notions of unthinking anthromorphism.

as in the more serious sphere of the moral government of the world, " His ways are not as our ways, nor His thoughts as our thoughts." But He has thoughts, the pious Hebrew believed, only more wide in their range, and more complex in their operation, than many of our human thoughts ; whereas the dogmatic denouncers of all teleology in our times seem to delight in excluding thought and thinking altogether from the universe, and leaving the most skilful combinations of nicely compacted vital machinery to be explained by unreasoned evolutions and accidental variabilities. That all organisms will be liable to modification from the action of various accidental causes is self-evident. A ship returning from an arctic expedition, after having squeezed its way successfully through floating armies of icebergs, will present some very serious modifications, no doubt, of its external trimmings to the observant eye. A pet cat also, or a pampered lapdog, will be modified not inconsiderably, both in outward appearance and inward disposition, by the peculiar enfeebling treatment to which it has been subjected. But no sane man imagines that the powers which are calculated to modify the appearance or condition of any object, or to adapt it to new circumstances, are the same kind of powers that could plastically form that object. The bowsprit of a ship may be broken off by an iceberg, but only a ship-carpenter could make the ship. In the same way, though the human being is the most adaptable of animals in respect of the various adverse influences under which he can maintain existence, no man ever dreams that this power of adaptation, and the variety of human type thereby produced, has anything to do with the production of the man, or could render the marks of design in the wonderful structure of his body, less eloquent now than they were to Socrates more than two thousand years ago. The variability of type which climatic influences produce may with time possibly assume the form, and be allowed to assert the position of permanent species; but it is the most unwarranted of all assumptions to suppose that any variety of solar or terrene influences could make the seed of a rose grow up into a lily. External influences produce only external differences, and accidental variations can never be the mother of systematic organisations. The virtue that makes the type is internal, and being the more powerful factor of the two, is able to resist successfully any invasion from without that would deprive it of its essential character. It will sooner die than be transmuted. The idea that a mere uncalculated germ of something coming into an accidental conjunction with an uncalculated anything could develop itself in a blind groping sort of way into a curiously constructed living machine, capable of achieving the most difficult ends with the smallest amount of cunningly applied force, can be regarded only as one of those startling paradoxes in which science divorced from philosophy delights, while cradling itself into the pleasant belief of its own infallibility, and endowing despotically the charm of a favourite idea with the virtue of a universal solvent. Such fancies will have their day; there will always be ingenious men doting over their own cogitations, as mothers do over their crazy brats; men who will be willing to spin paradoxes by the yard; and there will always be no less hundreds of persons, willing to receive those flashes of ingenious fancy for authoritative revelations; but it never can be a safe thing in the long run for science to exercise itself, like certain forms of church orthodoxy, in plucking the beard of reason and planting itself in rude antagonism to the common instincts of mankind, and the catholic experience of the world. To all such negative and abnormal self-assertors I feel inclined to give the hint which Cromwell gave to the Presbyterian theologians,—*I do beseech your reverences, for once to think it possible you may be wrong.* And it certainly is in every way more likely that the apostles of unreasoned evolution, like Ixion in the fable, thinking to wed Juno, should have embraced a cloud, than that Moses and David, and Pythagoras and Socrates, and Plato and Aristotle, and Dante and Newton, Kepler and Milton, should have been mistaken in believing design to be the one legitimate exponent of divine wisdom in the cunning framework of the universe.

IV. Another striking principle in the wonderful process of creative energy, which the Mosaic cosmogony sets before us with such simple and dignified dramatic grace, is that of PROGRESSION—gradation from less to greater, and from greater to greatest; and, as indissolubly connected with this, the principle of inferiority and superiority, or, in a single word, subordination. The principle of progression in the life of the cosmos, a principle with which in political history we are all sufficiently familiar, is set forth by Moses under the form of a period of six days of creative activity, with a special act of the divine plasticity put forth in each day, with its specific result of progressive vitality. The progression, of course, is from the more simple to the more complex; from the more easy and obvious to the more difficult achievements of organising energy; from the teeming life of fish in the water, which old wisdom always recognised as the prolific source of the lower forms of vitality, to the more perfect organisation of birds and quadrupeds, up to the king of the mammals, Man. Anything like a concise and minute sequence of the stages of zoological development, as they are pointed out now-a-days by the experts in geological science, no reasonable reader will look for in a writing meant to assert great theological principles, not to indicate the line of detailed scientific research. In the main, however, the coincidence between the ladder of life as constructed in this first chapter of Genesis and the successive stages of the growth of animal life on the globe, as demonstrated by geological science, is sufficiently striking to excite our unqualified admiration. Compared with the Babylonian account, for instance, which we have given above, it asserts a superiority in respect of taste, of science, and of theological dignity, as great as the utterance of a full-grown thinker does above the babblings of a child. But while it thus keeps free from the grotesque confusion of other sacred cosmogonies, it avoids with equal wisdom the opposite extreme of despotic simplicity, a rage for which has taken some of our most ingenious naturalists in these times into a strange captivity. Of evolution, as distinguished from progressive creativeness, Moses knew nothing. Had he been minded to use the phrase, he would certainly have said that all things were evolved out of God, not out of one another. And this phraseology also would have been nearer to the scientific truth; for growth, gradual, slow, and to the vulgar eye scarcely visible from moment to moment, is the eternal miracle of the divine creativeness; and growth is only common colloquial English for what the scientists call evolution, only without the superadded notion that one thing grows or is evolved out of another. Moses, however, was not concerned so much to use scientifically correct as dramatically effective language; and the force of the divine volition, on which radically all divine manifestation depends, was made more apparent by the picturesque representation of single strokes of creation than by a prosaic following of the minute stages of a rising development. We must never forget that all early literature is poetry, and that the earliest form of poetry, so far as it is not pure song, is dramatic narrative. Progression, therefore, by well-marked steps, and each step loyally performed in obedience to a separate act of sovereign divine volition, was the only form that the Mosaic theology, to assure itself of popular comprehension, could assume. The general law of progression thus dramatically indicated does not in the slightest degree conflict with the scientific doctrine of evolution, if that doctrine still prove to be more than a pretty fancy, and if it choose to remain in its natural close attachment to the necessary root of all organic evolution, viz. self-existing, plastic, organising MIND. Without this it is a mere phrase, calculated only to amuse the ingenious, and to confound the superficial; for that one army of blind forces and unpurposed appetencies should lead another army of forces and appetencies equally blind, and not fall into a ditch, is a law of progress which only the bastard philosophy of a one-eyed squinting science can dream that it comprehends; but which must ever remain incomprehensible to the man who knows that in no possible world could the motley multiplicity of disorderly chaotic forces work itself into a well-ordered cosmos without the constant controlling agency of an ordering mind, and that the blind rattle of an infinity of chances, after the lapse of an infinity of years, would be as far from producing a finely proportioned and nicely balanced and nicely adapted scheme of things as it was at the first throw.

The principle of development by progression in an ascending line from lowest to highest brings us directly in face of the antagonist principle of equality, which some political speculators and socialist dreamers have been eager to interpolate into the divine constitution of things. Manifestly, in a world rich in a luxuriant variety of ascending types, subordination, not equality, must be the expression of the law which binds them into a harmonious whole. In such a system of calculated gradation every one must know his place and keep his place, if the harmony is not to be changed into a jar, and the fair association of kindred parts to resolve itself into the original jumble. In the various strata of unreasoning and unspeculating things, whether vegetable or animal, which remain directly under the firm rein of divinely regulated instinct, no attempt to transgress the natural bounds set to the subordinated species is visible. A moss cannot elevate itself into a rose, nor a grass rise into a palm. No amount of straining or striving and appetency for wings would ever allow a worm to become a wren, or a boa constrictor to become an eagle. With all wisdom, therefore, the worm remains a worm, and the serpent a serpent. But with man, in some sense, it has been conceived to be otherwise. And no doubt man is an animal of wide range, wonderful capacity, and special adaptability. Endowed with the perilous gift of liberty and self-direction within certain limits, we see him daily rise, so to speak, above himself, and sink below himself, in a fashion which no brute can emulate; but to him also are bounds set which he cannot pass. The constituent law of the internal type, and the modifying influence of potent external circumstance, equally conspire to prevent the low man from mounting up to the platform of the high, or the high man from usurping the throne of the highest. Equality amongst men is a condition only possible on the postulate that the low shall universally conspire to degrade the high, and that both shall delight to play their parts in a dull drama of the most wearisome monotony. Equality in a political sense only means that all men are men, and are entitled to be treated as such,—that all citizens are citizens, and not to be handled as chattels or slaves; but it cannot mean that they are all equally strong, equally fair, equally good, or equally wise; and if not, they are entitled also to a treatment where such differences come into account, different according to the quantity and quality of the difference. So of liberty and fraternity, the other two pet words of those who, harping on crazy old French harps, set their faces stoutly against the great law of graduated subordination in the universe. Every man ought to be at liberty to use the faculties which God has given him for the purposes which they serve; but he is not at liberty to shake himself free from those thousandfold limitations, partly natural, partly artificial, which render society possible and progress certain. Fraternity, again, is true only in so far as in a bird's-eye view of human nature all men belong to one family, of whom the father is God; but this equality is more a sentiment than a fact. When the brothers of a family which counts by millions are cast in every variety of mould, exhibit every various grade of excellence, and are driven to action by the most diverse, and not seldom the most hostile instincts, the fraternity becomes a phrase of no more practical value than if an orange and a cannon ball should claim fraternity in virtue of the round of a mathematical circle, which is the type of both. The progress which the divine system of things is constantly working out, in the political as in the physical world, tends rather to difference than to equality. The greatest possible variety, under the control of the most stringent unity, and the greatest possible freedom in limited circles, under the firm guidance of a reasonable sovereignty,—this is what the wisdom of Moses teaches us to accept as the formula for the interpretation of the divine order of things under which we live,—not an equality contradicted by every fact of existence, or a lawless liberty which, if allowed full swing, would turn every garden into a wilderness, every harmony into a dissonance, and every most compact organism into dust.

V. In the twenty-sixth verse of the grand roll of creation, the great Hebrew lawgiver announces the last or culminating step of the creative process, with the very peculiar phraseology, "*Let us make* MAN *in our image, after our likeness.*" This leads us at once to inquire into the differential and distinctive features of the great king of the mammals; and brings emphatically before

us the glowing contrast between the lofty wisdom of
Moses and the low fancies of a certain school of ma-
terialising philosophers that have recently been making
broad their phylacteries in the British Isles; and not
here only, but in Germany also, though hatched from a
very different egg. The monistic cosmogony of Haekel,
which is only Darwinianism followed out to its consistent absurdity, is merely the extreme revulsion from
the transcendental spiritualism in which Schiller, Fichte,
Hegel, and other notable Teutonic speculators, had wan-
tonly indulged. Germany, to whom the pathless air
had long been assigned as her peculiar province, and to
whom, careering in metaphysical balloons filled with
inflammable gas had long been a familiar exercitation,
now bethinks herself, for a change, if from no better
motive, of becoming practical; and this she does in two
ways—first, by testing the value of modern theories of
political œconomy under the dictatorial captainship of
Bismarck, and then by flinging herself as far as possible
down from the Platonic throne of imperial Mind ($\beta\alpha\sigma\iota$-
$\lambda\iota\kappa\grave{o}\varsigma$ $No\hat{v}\varsigma$) into the midst of the blind conflict of atoms
in the Epicurean void. But John Bull's recent flirta-
tion with the material cosmogony of Epicurus has a
very different origin. Naturally Bull has no philosophy,
except what he finds embalmed in church creeds, and
which he rarely knows how to reanimate. An instinctive horror for speculative ideas and comprehensive
constructive principles is his boast; and so, as he must
have something to give him an air of wisdom, he

betakes himself to induction from outside phenomena, and deems himself on the sure road to certainty, when he deduces his whole confession of faith from his senses and from his fingers, not from his soul. In this way, of course, all soul, all reason—λόγος, νοῦς—is practically discounted from his philosophy; ingenious attempts are paraded to educe unity from multiplicity, and to interpret everything internal, spiritual, and intellectual, as only the necessary result of an accidental conjunction and co-operation of things external, material, and unreasoning; and then to juggle the unthinking multitude of would-be philosophers, PROTOPLASM, or some other Greek compound,—meaning something or nothing, or anything,—is formally stamped and publicly promulgated as the god of this new scientific world, in whom all men not willing to be thought fools are called upon to believe. To this substitution of Protoplasm for Elohim we have it plainly to attribute the antagonism between the peculiar divinity, written on the front of man by the Hebrew legislator, and the brotherhood of the baboon so ostentatiously proclaimed by some of our modern philosophasters. Man, says Moses, is a creature distinctively and exceptionally created in the image of God. Not at all, says Darwin, he is only a transmuted monkey, as the monkey is a transmuted ascidian, and an ascidian only a fully developed blot or bubble of Protoplasm. To carry out this theory after the favourite Baconian method, by external induction,—that is, by collecting all low external facts and neglecting all high internal factors,—two things seemed extremely serviceable: in the first place, to direct attention to the lowest type of human beings, of whom travellers give any account, and then to parade the wonderful instincts of even the lowest animals, as performing feats indicative of reasoning faculties, not only equal but far superior to the boasted reason of the human being. But both these are illegitimate arguments, and fail altogether to abolish the broad lines of distinction which Nature has traced betwixt reasoning man and the unreasoning brute. As to the savage tribes with whose habits Tylor and Lubbock have done so much to make us familiar, so far as we may creditably believe that they ever present themselves in a form scarcely to be distinguished from the dumb, unthinking, inexpressive brute, we can only say, as fair reasoners, that these are not normal specimens of the type which they are produced to illustrate; and from normal specimens only can the distinctive mark of any natural genus be scientifically concluded. As a bird without wings is not a bird, and a fox without a tail is no just specimen of the classical Reynard of the mediæval stories, so neither is the fatuity or the furiosity of an inmate of a lunatic asylum, nor the rank animal savagery of the inhabitant of some lone, neglected island in the Australian seas, a specimen which can be fairly taken as distinctive of the reasonable featherless biped whom we call Man. As for the instincts of the lower animals, there is nothing new in teaching us to admire them; nothing more true than that they possess powers of divination, let us call them, or of transcendental intuition, acting within a prescribed sphere, which surpass the most subtle achievements of human reason, and are, in fact, so far as our faculty of exposition goes, miraculous.[1] But this only proves that they are divine. All Nature is divine; and what we call life, with its treasure of secret potencies, and its array of magnificent functions, is only the constant, abiding operation of the plastic energy of the self-existent, all-causative Reason which we call GOD,—a power which to us weak, dependent creatures, is always in its nature essentially miraculous, and only not so called because it is common. There is as much miracle in the regular beating of the heart, the index of life, as in the wanderings of a home-seeking cat, the migrations of a tropical bird, or the nosings of a venatorial hound. All animals are constantly doing things which defy and transcend all reason, but do not therefore give the slightest ground to suspect that they either use reason in what they do, or possess any germ of speculation that could possibly —with the help of millions of years—be developed into reason. You ask why the lower animals do these miraculous things? Simply because they are in the hand of God; because He leads them, and they may go, and must go, with a miraculous unconscious guidance, to any goal which for them, by His presiding forethought

---

[1] "In brutis plura observantur quae humanam sagacitatem longe superant."—SPINOZA, Ethics, III. 2.

purpose, may be set. They are tools in the hand of God, and therefore they do their work more surely than man; but not, therefore, are they superior to man, or in any way commensurate with him; for they have not been elevated into the throne of conscious liberty and possible blunder, which is at once the privilege and the penalty of the sons of Adam. Let us look, then, at man in his broad aspects, on the highroad of his career, not on those devious and dim byways where speculators, more anxious for novelty than for truth, pick up the exceptional facts out of which they spin their perverse philosophies. There are two undisguisable forms of expression in virtue of which the human creature emphatically marks himself out as generically different from the brute—Language [1] and Laughter. Let us inquire what these mean. By language of course we cannot mean here the language of gesticulation, or of ejaculation, or of any sort of sounds that any voiceful creatures may make to express their wants, to give vent to their sorrow, or to revel in their joy. Such language may exist in many animals considerably below the model monkey soon to be a man, or the model ascidian in whose heart the dream of eventual monkeyhood is beginning to germ. But by language we mean in this argument that cunningly articulated system of articulate sounds, expressing

[1] Ἐκ σοῦ γὰρ γένος ἐσμὲν ἴης μίμημα λαχόντες
Μοῦνοι, ὅσα ζώει τεκαὶ ἕρπει θνητ' ἐπὶ γαῖαν.
    CLEANTHES, *Hymn to Jove.*

ideas, which of all animals man only is known to have evoked and to possess. What are ideas? Our scholastic teachers tell us that they are conventional terms denoting not individual objects, apprehended by sensation, but genera or families of objects created by thought; and they are right. An orange, and the idea of an orange, may seem in some senses very cognate things; nevertheless, they are not only different things, but things formed from a different centre, and placed by nature in irreconcileable antagonism to one another. Not one orange, or two, or two score, or two millions of oranges, could give rise to the idea of an orange, unless some composing, combining, and discriminating faculty were present to separate the accidental from the essential of the phenomenon, and stamp the word to the intelligence with the features that belong to the genus, to the exclusion of what may belong to the individual. Jaffa oranges, for instance, are of large size, and have thick skins; but neither their size nor their thickness has anything to do with the significance of the word ORANGE. Of the sensations which bring individual oranges to our perceptive faculty, externality and multiplicity are the characteristics; in the creation of the idea, notion, or concept of an orange, internality and unity are the indispensable factors. We may fitly compare the individual notices supplied by sense to the evidence given in a court of law by the various witnesses: these form the materials on which the case is to be decided; but the decision comes from the judge;

and the judge is one; and his judgment collects and includes, and by wonderful alchemy of construction and assimilation, works into a harmonious unity, the conflicting variety of the evidence. Or again, we may say, as his thousands of soldiers who fight the battle are to the great general who schemes the campaign, so are the sensations of a reasoning being like man to his ideas, essential to one another, and incapable of separate action, but different, nevertheless, and distinct, energising from opposite centres, antagonistic in their attitude, and sometimes, as in the case of a mutiny, even hostile in their action. Of these ideas, language is the natural bearer and exponent; and not only natural, but necessary, we may surely say; for the sum of Nature is made up everywhere of inward forces, which reveal themselves in outward forms; and an internal world of ideas without any external form for making itself manifest would be an anomaly in the constitution of things which we have no right to assume. If, when an extruded cat moans woefully through a frosty night, or a stray dog whimpers piteously at your gate, you are entitled to conclude that he is expressing in his way the feelings which a poor human child would experience in the same circumstances, the absence of all articulate signs expressive of ideas in the brute creation affords a just ground for denying their existence altogether in the lower platform of life. Nature is not wont to be defeated of her object in this stupid sort of way. If she has put a well of ideas into the breast of any of her creatures, they will find their way to manifestation in some adequate form, we may depend on it. The brutes, therefore, have no language which is the body of ideas ; have no ideas such as claim that body as their natural concomitant ; labour plainly under the want of that God-like faculty distinctive of man, which, according to Moses, marks his superiority in the scale of created beings. And not only is there here a marked inferiority in degree, but a marked difference in kind ; not only is the difference one of ascending steps in a slope, but rather a gap such as that which exists between a crystal of mica and a lichen crust, or between a lichen crust and a sheep's fleece. And this will the more appear if we consider further the culmination of ideas in what are called Ideals. Man may well be defined an animal that delights in conceiving and is destined to find his highest happiness in struggling after the realisation of Ideals. What does this mean? What are Ideals? Whence do they come? and how do they specially assert their existence in the distinctively human scenes of the grand drama of human life? The ideal of a thing is just the most perfect type of the thing ; and its genesis is clearly traceable to the innate God-implanted aspiration after excellence in the human soul operating upon the materials supplied by the senses to the generalising and unifying action of the understanding. Now, the ideal of a circle is the concrete circle which most closely corresponds to the abstract circle of the mathematician ; the ideal of a man is that man, existing or not existing, in whose composition and character are combined all the excellent qualities which most distinctly and most emphatically make up manhood. The ideal woman, in the same way, is the woman in whose presentation all that is most womanly stands forth most attractively, and takes captive most irresistibly. Now the natural result of a delight in Ideals is to create a certain noble discontent with what is common, accompanied by a fine relish for whatever approximates to the ideal. Hence the potency of Love in the world, "Love, unvanquished in fight," as Sophocles sings, whether against gods or men ; for, discounting the mere sexual appetency which moves brutes as well as men, the love of which poets sing, and philosophers discourse, is neither more nor less than a rapturous recognition of an Ideal, or, as we may vary the phrase, an impassioned admiration of Excellence. Every man, of course, is not gifted with this capacity for ideal rapture in the highest degree. When it asserts itself in a very high degree we are accustomed to call it genius ; but it is, nevertheless, a widely human capacity, and may be recognised not seldom in the humblest spheres, where it has received that fair amount of culture which all human excellence requires. In the back slums of our great manufacturing cities, where the human being grows up under the most adverse influences, you will find not seldom little patches of order and neatness amidst the general disarray, from which you might furnish a useful hint or two to my lady in the equipment of her boudoir ; and the crude rudiments of architecture in the wigwams of the Indian savage are not without touches of graceful ornamentation, which the most accomplished architect may not disdain to appropriate. In literature and the arts a high capacity for the ideal presents itself, either passively and receptively, in the production of what is called a fine taste and delicate sensibility for beauty, or energetically and constructively in the shape of the creations of literary and artistic genius. And here at last we have the image of God in man set forth in lines of most indubitable parallelism. The poet is a maker and a creator; so is the sculptor, the painter, the musician, the artist, each moulding the proper material at his disposal, and lording over it like a god.[1] The analytic investigations in which chemists, anatomists, physiologists, and other such scientists delight, justly excite our admiration; but the peculiar style of their researches, having to do rather with breaking up than with building up, prevents them from exhibiting that perfect analogy to the divine energising in the work of creation which we find in the constructive

[1] When Spinoza (*Ethics*, I. 17) asserts in the strongest terms that the human intellect and the divine have nothing in common but the name, he must be thinking either of the analytic action of the cognitive intellect, mentioned immediately in the text, or he must be contrasting the absolute dependence of the human soul with the absolute independence of the self-existent and self-causative Divine Nature; for as far as concerns the intellectual work of an ideal artist, we have only to conceive the soul of the sculptor shaping out his ideal in the inside of the clay, which serves him as a body, and we have a similitude of the action of the divine and human intellect, than which nothing could be more complete.

productions of the poet, the painter, and the architect. We justly attribute knowledge to the Supreme Being; but though the term scientific may well be applied to the divine workmanship, it is never applied to the divine function; whereas, if we choose to call the world the living Epos of the great cosmic poet, whose words are deeds, and whose deeds are miracles, we should be saying what no pious person would consider irreverent, and no thoughtful person impertinent.[1] Nor is it in the world of fair thoughts and grand imaginations only that the divine faculty of creative sovereignty displays itself in man. In the general who masses a confused host into calculated order and deft disposal; in the statesman who wisely uses the prejudices and the passions of a heterogeneous multitude, and bends them to his purpose as Neptune does the waves; in the apostle who sallies forth into waste fields of social decay and organises the crude hosts of human stragglers into well-ordered churches and communities;—in all such men the inspiration, the work, and the triumph of an ideal are even more clearly visible than in the less substantial creations of the poet and the painter. Napoleon, Bismarck, and Wesley are gods, each in his own world and after his proper fashion. Why then, we may now ask, have the lower animals no

---

[1] Almost the same as Plato's phrase in the closing sentence of the *Timæus*—ὁ κόσμος εἰκὼν τοῦ νοητοῦ Θεοῦ αἰσθητός—the sensible image of the intelligible God; for the work of an artist is in very deed the most express image of his thought.

poets, no painters, no prophets, no apostles, no literature, no churches, no worship? Simply because they are not created in the image of God in the special sense in which man is. No doubt they have their work to do, and they do it well; but it is marked out for them in definite and invariable lines, not projected with the freedom of a self-determining ideal. What they do, more correctly speaking, is done for them,—by them only as tools in the hands of a workman. They are machines; they are chronometers, which go without fail only because they cannot go otherwise. They cannot blunder because they cannot choose. They are the most perfect and accomplished of all slaves, but slaves nevertheless; and, therefore, not created in the image of God.

So much for language and the ideas and ideals which, as an essentially human endowment, it expresses. The other broadly human characteristic which presented itself for notice under this head—Laughter—may be discussed in a single sentence. The ridiculous is the reverse side of the reasonable; and as the obverse side deals with the congruous and the proper, so the reverse with the incongruous and the absurd. Of course the perception of both depends on comparison; and a laugh is a judgment, accompanied with an agreeable kind of nervous excitement, pronounced on the unsuitableness of the junction of two things which are in their nature apart. But brutes pronounce no judgments, therefore they cannot laugh. They may be astonished or scared by any odd appearance, as of a man standing with his head between his legs, which they say frightens bulls; they may even grin perhaps occasionally, in the lowest sense of that word; but they certainly never laugh.

VI. A sixth important principle contained in this pregnant scheme of the Creation is the doctrine of periodical seasons of Rest and cessation in the process of the creative energy, indicated by the constitution of the Sabbath (chap. ii. 2, 3). How this hangs together with the abolition of the Saturday's rest under the Christian dispensation, and the consecration of the first day of the week for religious purposes, will be discussed in detail afterwards in a separate discourse. For the present, it will be enough to say that what all history and all geology prove to have been a prominent fact in all stages of the world's development, is here set down in the narrative form as an institution, prophetic of the special Seventh Day's abstinence from labour, afterwards so prominent amid the peculiarities of the Hebrew polity. What we have to learn from it is simply this,—that as the alternation of rest and labour lies deeply seated in the constitution of things, being visible equally in the seasonal changes of the physical world, and in the periods of repose in which society seems to be gathering strength for the successive acts of its destined progress—taught by these broad facts of mundane life, and even more feelingly by our own personal experience, let us fix it in our minds that the only way to preserve a capacity for continued work is diligently to observe recurrent periods of rest, and that we shall in vain hope to reap the full fruits of our waking hours, so long as we persist in withholding its natural dues from Sleep.

VII. One only point remains in conclusion. At the end of each day's work, the seal of divine approbation is stamped on the result in the words, "AND GOD SAW THAT IT WAS GOOD,"—a feeling of satisfaction in the contemplation of the ever-fresh miracle of the creation, which sounds everywhere through the lyrical utterances of the Hebrew mind, in the psalms of David, and elsewhere. And this, no doubt, is the healthy and the happy and wise way of looking at the rich blossom of reality, of which we are a part, as the greatest of modern poet-philosophers has expressed it in the introductory hymn to his significant drama of human destiny :—

RAPHAEL.
" The Sun doth chime his ancient music
'Mid brothered spheres' contending song,
And on his fore-appointed journey
With pace of thunder rolls along.
Strength drink the angels from his glory,
Though none may throughly search his way :
God's works rehearse their wondrous story
As bright as on Creation's day.

GABRIEL.
And swift and swift beyond conceiving

The pomp of earth is wheeled around,
Alternating Elysian brightness
With awful gloom of night profound.
Up foams the sea, a surging river,
And smites the steep rock's echoing base,
And rock and sea, unwearied ever,
Spin their eternal circling race.

MICHAEL.

And storm meets storm with rival greeting,
From sea to land, from land to sea,
While from their war a virtue floweth,
That thrills with life all things that be.
The lightning darts his fury, blazing
Before the thunder's sounding way;
But still thy servants, Lord, are praising
The gentle going of thy day.

ALL THE THREE.

Strength drink the angels from thy glory,
Though none may search thy wondrous way:
Thy works repeat their radiant story
As bright as on Creation's day." [1]

But, as we all know, there is another side to the picture,—a side brought prominently forward by the Evil Spirit in the great German drama, and by certain negative and meagre, or it may be, to speak more charitably, morbidly sensitive and unreasonably impatient philosophers among ourselves. "*Ich bin der Geist der stets verneint,*" says Mephistopheles: "*I am the Spirit that always say* NO!" and there are persons

---

[1] Goethe's *Faust:* Prologue in Heaven.

at all times—not a few—without any pretensions to diabolic inspiration, who make a frequent use of this unfertile particle. There is, no doubt, such a thing as Evil; and whoso is forward to find faults right and left and all round in this world will have no difficulty in finding them; for even the pious Pindar complains that the gods to mortal men dispense two bad things for one good. Some likewise have gone forth in these latter times, and have asked plainly, "*Is life worth living?*" so that the question becomes a serious one, Whence this Evil in a world blazoned so full of goodness has its fount? and it is a question which may be asked and answered modestly, with a fair amount of satisfaction to reasonable persons. The old Persian solution of the difficulty, by assuming the existence of an Evil God, co-equal with the Good God, but eternally at war with Him, must be rejected, for the obvious reason that Good and Evil in the world do not appear arrayed in hostile and distinct ranks, but seem to grow out of the same root, and get entangled in a tissue which no mortal skill can disenravel. Besides, if it can be clearly proved that one great part of what we call Evil is clearly relative, and another great part is demonstrably necessary for the attainment of a higher good, the theory of a Supreme Evil Principle will be found to explain a great deal too much. Another theory that has been called in to explain the inequalities of fortune, and the unmerited sufferings of so many unfortunates wearing the front of the human form

CREATION OF THE WORLD.

divine, is the theory of guilt transmitted from a previous state of existence. "*Has this man sinned or his parents, that he was born blind?*" But this principle, however practically efficient in the faith of the Brahmanists and Buddhists, and however fairly enshrined by the prose of Plato and the verse of Virgil, may wisely be dismissed on what appears to have been the ground taken by our Saviour, that we know and can know nothing about it, and that religion has to do always with the question what we are and where we are, not whence we came or with what inheritance. A third method of dealing with the difficulty is that which has been generally received in the Christian Churches, and takes its start, like the Brahmanic and Buddhist theologies, from the principle of inherited guilt; but guilt in this case, not confined in its operation to the individual who committed the original sin, but spreading itself from the first created man, like a leprosy, over the countless millions of the unhappy human race. According to this theory, the world, as originally made, was perfect, and in every respect deserving of the blessing pronounced on it by the Great Artificer; but since the fatal disobedience of the first man, it was shaken out of joint, dislocated, and disrupted, so as to present the spectacle that the Roman Empire did in the days when such monsters as Heliogabalus and Commodus could wear the purple where the Scipios and the Catos had been citizens. This tremendous theory of a sweeping inherited curse seems originally to have been worked up from the narrative in the third chapter of Genesis of the primitive sinless state of our first parents in the garden of Eden, and their ejection in consequence of disobedience to the divine command. But it is more than doubtful whether the Christian Churches have not here committed a grave mistake, by their prosaic habit of interpreting as literal historical fact what was penned in the spirit of Oriental parable and allegory. In this sense Adam is merely a name for every man, or any man, who at any time or place plants his individual will in stout self-sufficiency against the divine ordinances by which the world is maintained in its propriety.[1] Every man who

---

[1] I am glad to see that I have here stumbled upon almost the very words of *Bunsen* with regard to the fall in his great *Bibelwerk*, Genesis ii. 5, whence I translate as follows :—" As to what concerns the FALL OF MAN, it belongs plainly not to the world of historical men, but to the general idea of man ; an idea, however, which becomes history in the case of every individual man. The fall of Adam is the personal deed of every individual human being from the beginning of history to the present day." And in this view I say with him, v. 16, "That the SERPENT is the selfish understanding asserting itself rebelliously against the moral nature and the divine command." Le Clerc's commentary on the nature and significance of the serpent, "*Nobis ut in re obscurâ, tutissima videtur ignorantiæ confessio*," would not have been necessary at the present day, when comparative philology and comparative theology have opened to us a wide field of induction in such matters, of which a hundred years ago scarcely one or two of the wisest could have dreamt. *Dillmann*, in his Commentary on Genesis (*Leipzig*, 1875), while dissenting from Bunsen, says in a general way what is really not generically different : "The serpent (iii. 1) is a real power, not a mere symbol of cunning thoughts cherished in the

sins yields to the seduction of the serpent—that is, the conceit of superior knowledge to be obtained by an act of disobedience to the Supreme Disposer; and the consequence is to every man to-day, and to the end of time, as long as sin shall be in the world, ejection from Paradise. And the Western Churches unfortunately were not the only persons who, by an overstrained consistency to a literal interpretation of an allegorical text, turned the broad fact of original sin, as we see it daily before our eyes, into a sternly compacted doctrine of inherited guilt. We see in the Evangelic history repeated instances of how the Apostles themselves required to be enlightened as to the real spiritual meaning of the allegorical garb in which our Saviour was wont to clothe his higher teaching; and even St. Paul, though no man tore himself more valiantly free from subjection to the ceremonial literalness of his countrymen, may have derived from the teaching of the Talmudic schools in which he was educated[1] certain notions about the significance of Old Testament figures foreign to the spirit of the essentially

heart of man against the divine law." Symbol or no symbol, it means the rebellion of unsanctified individual intellect against cosmic order and law; and this is all with which the intelligent and religious reader has at the present day to do.

[1] The doctrine of a historical fall is distinctly taught in the Apocryphal book, *Wisdom of Solomon*, ii. 23-4, a passage in this respect perfectly singular, I believe, in the whole breadth of the Old Testament writings. Here also the word διάβολος, *devil*, is used for the first time.

ethical gospel which he preached. Certain it is that in the Epistle to the Romans, though in nowise essential to his main argument, he seems to place an historical Adam in the same position that our federal theologians do, as the representative head of a race doomed to misery by the inheritance of a rebellious blood from his veins. Whether the Christian Churches are bound to consider themselves committed to the stern consistency of this doctrine (of which I find no trace in the Gospels), theologians may decide ; but it certainly does appear to me that such a fashion of explaining the origin of evil raises more difficulties than it removes, and is chargeable, no less than the other shifts of a metaphysical theology, with proving a great deal too much ; the fact being, as I shall now show, that the great majority of the evils which the doctrine of the fall of man lays at Adam's door are no evils at all, but only the unavoidable imperfections which cleave to all finite creations, or they form the necessary stage for the enactment of the great drama of human life. Take Death for instance. That it is an evil, and a great evil to the individual, who can doubt ? To be torn away roughly and darkly from the familiar vision of this glorious world, our home for so many pleasantly varied years, with all its fond looks of human love, and glimpses of supernatural grandeur ; to be severed from all this rudely by a sudden pitiless stroke, or a slow, cruel, unrelenting wrench, though it were only for a season, to return again like the fabled Pythagoras, with a more glorious body to revisit the shimmerings of the sun, with a new heaven and a new earth;—this indeed is a great evil, on which only a wise Socrates, once in a thousand years, or a triumphant martyr at the stake, can look with calmness. But is it an evil to the world? Think for a moment. If there were no deaths, in a very short time there could be no births? If the millions of Coptic race in the days of the Pharaohs had remained in a lusty longevity, from century to century peopling the green fringe of the fertile flowing Nile, where would have been room for the Greeks and the Arabs and the Turks that came in afterwards? The never-ceasing succession of fresh young lives, the eternal rejuvenescence of the race, always springing up most luxuriantly when most savagely trampled down, always leaping up from the womb of time with a joyful curiosity to greet the ever-new spectacle of the ever-old wonder of the universe—this constant outburst of fresh life from the inner fountains of the Divine creativeness could not possibly be without Death. Therefore, as Doctor Paley, the great genius of British common sense, said, *Immortality on this earth is out of the question.* In the great scheme of Providence, death, as Goethe somewhere has it, is only a trick of nature, to show the fertility of her resources, and to clear the course for the display of a more abundant life. But, if we must die, why in such a painful and disagreeable way? Well, that is like asking why a strong and well-compacted box cannot be broken up with a light puff, as you would blow out a candle. I cannot tell you why, except in a general way, that the laws of the world were not made, nor its solid consistency cared for, merely with a view to your convenience.[1] Do you demand that the law of gravitation shall cease to act, when on any occasion you may be passing under a cliff, whence a fragment of a rock may topple down and break your bones? God is omnipotent, you think, and might easily, in such cases, interpose to save the pain and increase the comfort of his creatures. Believe me, good friend, that such interposition, for the sake of your leg or your little finger, and the legs and little fingers of thousands and tens of thousands of persons coming into misfortuned collision with the great forces of the universe, would end in universal confusion and universal carelessness. Self-importance is the vice that lies at the root of all querulous complaints against the divine order of things; and so it is here. Imagine yourself, for a moment, not a man, but some other creature—say a salmon,—and consider how you would be affected in judging of some of the evils that this creature may have to encounter in its adventurous passage from a salt to a fresh water sojourn. You are a salmon; and just when you have commenced

---

[1] *Rerum perfectio ex solâ earum naturâ et potentiâ est æstimanda; nec ideo res magis aut minus perfectæ sunt propterea quod hominum sensum delectant vel offendunt, quod humanæ naturæ conducunt vel quod eidem repugnant.*"—SPINOZA, *Ethic* I., Appendix in FINE. And MARCUS ANTONINUS, πρόσεστι δὴ τὸ ἀναγκαῖον καὶ τὸ τῷ ὅλῳ κόσμῳ συμφέρον οὗ μέρος εἶ· παντὶ δε φύσεως μέρει ἀγαθὸν ὃ φέρει ἡ τοῦ ὅλου φύσις, καὶ ὃ ἐκείνης ἐστὶ σωστικόν.—*De rebus suis*, ii. 3.

to shake your scales clear from the brine, and are bracing yourself for your upward voyage, eager as a racer to run a race, you come right against a steep black wall of basaltic rock, down which the broad current comes with headlong fling, and sweeping scourge, and thundering lash, that debars all progress. What then? You, as a salmon, no doubt, think you are grievously wronged, and conclude somehow that the world is out of joint, and wonder why the Almighty does not interpose to smooth all river courses, or to give you the power of a miraculous leap wherever you may desire it. But what says the philosopher looking down from the top of the cataract, or the angler watching at the bottom of the swirling cauldron? Simply this, that the courses of rivers were never shaped, and in the nature of things could not possibly have been shaped, to serve the convenience of migratory fish; and that salmon have no right to complain when their progress up a stream is stopped by the impediment of a beautiful waterfall, or even if they should happen to be hooked by a false fly, or entangled in a treacherous net to furnish a lightly dispensable delicacy to the banquet of some dainty feeder. And so in similar cases of which the number is legion. The evil is always an evil to the man or to the salmon, as the chance may be (for evil is never by design, only accidental), but not to the universe.

Some people, in arguing these grave matters, are willing to concede the truth of the view just stated in reference to physical evil; but betwixt this and moral evil, they are accustomed to draw a broad line of distinction. But the more closely I scan this imagined demarcation, the less clearly do I discern it. In the main, I feel in every case compelled to "account for moral as for natural things," and to say with the poet—

> "If storms and tempests mar not Heaven's design,
> Why then a Borgia or a Catiline?"

All moral evils grow from two roots—from ignorance or from selfishness; from lack of knowledge, or from lack of love. Let us see how far in the general case these evils, no less than the physical evils at which we have glanced, are altogether relative, and absolutely necessary for the production of a higher good. Let us for a moment suppose all ignorance banished, and what would be the consequence? Most people have heard the famous saying attributed to Lessing, that if an angel from heaven were to offer him knowledge in the one hand, or the search after knowledge on the other, he would prefer the search. This answer, with a single stroke, clears away the mist from many a mystery. Ignorance in itself is not an evil; but the forbidding of ignorance to grow up into knowledge, when the divinely implanted germ thereto lies in every creature. Growth in knowledge and the search after truth are amongst the purest and most stimulating of human pleasures; yet both grow, and by the very terms of the case can grow, only out of the root of ignorance. Banish ignorance; and forthwith you banish not only the pleasure of seeking for knowledge, but the pleasant relation of teacher and taught, and the lively play of intellectual communication between the less informed and the better informed members of an intelligent society. A world in which everybody knew everything as well as any other body would be a world in which nobody could learn anything from anybody; as a garden in which no weeds grew would be a garden in which the gardener would have nothing to do. For let it be taken always as a necessary postulate in all moral questions, that excellence and happiness consist in the evoking of energy; and that energy can in no wise be evoked so well as by struggling with evils and overcoming difficulties. Let us therefore accept ignorance as the gardener accepts nettles, or the farmer field marigold, to be dealt with in the way of disappearance, but with a certain catholic recognition of their right to have been what and where they are, not with a curse. Nor is it otherwise with vice, which indeed bears exactly the same relation of finite imperfection to virtue that ignorance does to knowledge. This the Greeks saw clearly, and therefore marked all moral deflection by the same word that signifies an error in precision of vision— ἁμαρτάνω—*to miss the mark, to err, to sin.* And does not Solomon also say that every sinner is a fool, and every sin a folly? and does not Socrates, the great missionary of practical reason, bring the matter to a proved paradox, that to sin is merely not to know what you are and where you are, and to dash your head against a hard granite wall, imagining it to be a soft cushion? Yes, verily, to sin is always to blunder; and, as imperfect short-sighted creatures, we have no right to be surprised if it be our destiny to grow up in a school of blunders, that we may learn not to blunder, as children by falling frequently learn to stand, and by creeping to march. No doubt the mere knowing faculty, however acute, will never make a hero, or work out a noble life. In man, being man, and not tiger, the social instincts, which Socrates calls the τὰ φιλικὰ, must always be supposed; but granting that element to make a human society possible, immoral conduct must always be unreasonable conduct, and must lead to the ruin and wreckage of a human life, just as certainly as an error in one step of his calculation must vitiate the summation of an arithmetician. But if sin be only a mistake, what then is guilt?—guilt, the greatest of all human evils, according to Schiller—

"*Das* LEBEN *ist der Güter höchstes nicht:*
Der Ubel Grösstes aber ist die SCHULD."

Guilt certainly is fundamentally nothing more than a mistake; but it is a mistake, or rather a feeling that flows from a mistake of a very peculiar kind, a mistake very different from that of making a false move at chess, or giving a false ball at cricket. It is a mistake which involves the betrayal of the citadel of a man's own soul; it is a mistake which puts a man into startling antagonism, not only with the whole moral world, of which he is a part, but into woeful contradiction to himself; it is a mistake which implies the dethronement of the highest faculty in man, and the usurpation of the moral sovereignty by the lowest. Therefore it is justly held to be a much more serious thing than an error in any speculation, or in a curious analysis of things indifferent—things which are less connected with his real happiness, it may be, than the button upon his coat. Nevertheless, in its greatest potency it is only a mistake arising either from deficiency in the social instinct or a habitual neglect in the application of reason to social relations; but in any case, in its essential character not less of the nature of a blunder than any blunder that it is in the nature of a variously limited and curiously composite creature to make. The possibility, or rather the certainty, of moral blunders is given in the existence of such a creature as man. Sin, therefore, is not absolutely an evil, the existence of which mars the perfection of the divine creation: it is only an imperfection naturally cleaving to a finite creature so wonderfully constituted as man.[1]

[1] SPINOZA rather looks upon sin and all other defects as a proof of the perfection of the universe—perfect, that is to say, in such a fashion that, like a well-furnished museum, it contains specimens of all things from the lowest to the highest, from the worst to the best. "*Iis autem qui quærunt Cur Deus omnes homines non ita creavit ut solo rationis ductu gubernarentur, nihil aliud respondeo quam, quia ei non defuit materia, ad omnia ex summo nimirum ad infimum perfectionis*

Then "every sin deserveth *not* God's wrath and curse both in this world and that which is to come." Certainly NOT. Sin is bad enough without that. It has been the fashion of theological dogmatists in all ages to intensify and exaggerate moral instincts till they become immoral absurdities. In pulpit logic I have heard it stated, not once or twice, but many times, that a sin against the law of an Infinite Being deserves an infinite punishment. It is as true logically, and much more true morally, that a sin by a finite being deserves a finite punishment. Punishment, indeed, in the concatenation of things which belongs to the scheme of a perfectly wise and good Being can mean only a spur to produce amendment; without which issue in a well-ordered world it has no right to exist. The permanent existence of essential Evil in a world which exists for the manifestation of good is inconceivable; and an inexorable persistence in castigation, which would be savage and barbarous in an earthly father to his child, cannot be benevolent or beneficial in the attitude of the Father of all good things to his erring progeny.

One final difficulty remains. Though the sorrow which is the fruit of sin be a natural sequence, and a condition precedent of higher good, we cannot certainly

---

gradum creanda."—*Ethics* I., Appendix, *in fine*—that is to say, a world composed solely of creatures of the highest degree of perfection would be a world deficient in the variety of possible forms, and in this respect, as a whole, more meagre and less perfect.

pretend to say the same of the sufferings, which not only confound the innocent with the guilty,—as may lightly happen under the action of invariable physical laws,—but which seem to afflict the best men in the worst times with peculiar persecution, ignominy, and anguish. This is really the only chapter of Evil in the world that ever gave me any very serious consideration. Let any one ponder seriously the sufferings of the noble Italians who first stirred the insurrection against Austrian intrusion, before the recent liberation, the long-drawn sorrows of a Pellico in a Venetian, and of his fellow-patriots in a Moravian, dungeon; or look back to the twenty-seven years of butchery practised on the faithful Covenanters of Scotland some two hundred years ago by a perjured king and a brutal ministry; or indeed, any account—for their number is not few—of the cruelties and barbarities which have been systematically carried on by bad men armed with power, against good men mailed with honesty;—and he will then clearly enough perceive that in such cases honesty has not been, as the proverb has it, the best policy, but the direct road to misery, humiliation, and death. Of this sort of thing St. Paul and all his fellow-soldiers in the glorious work of redeeming the world from the intolerable yoke of Roman violence and Greek sensualism had large experience; and his view of the matter he expressed in a sentence which will leap spontaneously from the bosom of every sound-hearted man, when those pages of history, carved in suffering and blazoned in blood, are brought vividly before him. "IF IN THIS LIFE ONLY WE HAVE HOPE IN CHRIST, WE ARE OF ALL MEN MOST MISERABLE." And this is the feeling unquestionably, that has led noble spirits in all ages to plant the banner of hope on the grave, and to claim citizenship in a world beyond, where the oppressor comes not with his blind scourge, and righteousness never fails of its just reward,—an optimism this, the only one the human imagination can conceive, that shall completely wipe out this great evil from the chronicles of the divine administration. But even short of this optimism there are not wanting some considerations which go strongly to moderate, if not altogether to remove, the painful impressions made by these sanguine memorials of human folly, or human wrath. In the first place, they are altogether exceptional phenomena, occurring only at great intervals or periods of the remoulding and reconstitution of society; they are the throes that accompany a new social birth; and it may, in the nature of things, be impossible that any great social birth can take place without labour and sorrow; for the old and the new state of things, in such circumstances, will never adjust themselves without a struggle; and a struggle between such mighty forces means blood. In the general case, however, it is not Folly but Wisdom that governs the world; not wrong but righteousness that prevails. In the common law of things, the good man is the prosperous man; and piety combined with sense and energy will lead to no persecution but such as a proper man will bear lightly, and be all the better for bearing. This the brave old Hebrews knew well, and have bravely proclaimed in many golden sentences: " Happy is the man that findeth wisdom, and the man that getteth understanding : for the merchandise of it is better than the merchandise of silver, and the gain thereof than fine gold. She is more precious than rubies : and all the things thou canst desire are not to be compared unto her. Length of days is in her right hand ; and in her left hand riches and honour. Her ways are ways of pleasantness, and all her paths are peace. She is a tree of life to them that lay hold upon her ; and happy is every one that retaineth her."[1] Then consider this further. Martyrs and confessors are not the only class of persons who lay down their lives for the good of the human community to which they belong. Every man who, in critical circumstances, faithfully stands to the post of danger where he is placed, is giving up his life freely in order to save the lives of others. The conscript boy, torn from his father and all that he holds dear, to dice away his sweet young life in a cause with which he has no concern, and which may not even be for the honour of his people, is a martyr no less than Patrick Hamilton blazing in his coat of pitch in front of the Castle of St. Andrews, to gloat the sacerdotal insolence of Cardinal Beaton. The only difference is that the one is a martyr to the external force which makes absolute obedience in the last

[1] Proverbs iii. 13-18.

resort the cement of the social edifice, and the other to that inward force of moral conviction, from whose lordship the soul of man can no more withdraw itself than his bodily eye can refuse to rejoice in the brightness of the sun. And, sooth to say, there are many deaths of fools and sinners every day that have more pain, and less compensation for their anguish, than the philosophic protester with the cup of hemlock for his evening draught, or the martyr in the Roman Colosseum, with the grip of the tiger at his throat; and so we may take the breath from all large lamentation over the unmerited sufferings of humanity, by roughly saying: Death is the penalty, sharp but short, which all men must pay in some shape or other, for the glorious privilege of having been alive. This is the Stoical view of the matter. Christianity gives brighter hopes. The Stoic or the Academy may preach resignation; but consolation is to be found only at the foot of the Cross.[1]

[1] Viscount STRATFORD DE REDCLIFFE asked himself the question why there should be a future existence; and he answered: "Because on any other hypothesis the world would be a piece of magnificent nonsense."—From Dean Stanley's preface to the *Eastern Question*, by Viscount Stratford de Redcliffe. London, 1881.

I do not go so far as this; but it certainly seems to me, that without the complement of a future state, not a few things happen in the present state, which, to our moral nature, necessarily appear in a high degree imperfect and unsatisfactory. Goethe founded his faith in immortality (see Eckermann, and the second part of *Faust*) on what we may call the law of guaranteed progression; that is to say, a law in the moral world analogous to the law in the physical world, which makes the bud of the spring pledge the flower of the summer, and the flower of the summer a sure prophecy of the fruitage of the autumn.

II.

THE JEWISH SABBATH AND THE CHRISTIAN LORD'S DAY.

"Let no man therefore judge you in meat, or in drink, or in respect of an holyday, or of the new moon, or of the Sabbath days."—COL. ii. 16.

THERE is no institution open to general observation that so emphatically marks a Christian country as the observance of the first day of the week as a day of rest in some form or other. No doubt the difference in the details of observance, so far as they assume a positive shape, varies considerably; but in one negative point they all agree, the abstinence from week-day work or regular business. Diverse indeed is the form which the Christian Sabbath presents to the European traveller, in Paris say, and in Edinburgh, in a west Ross-shire glen, or in a Middlesex tea-garden. In Paris every foot is tripping, every causeway is rattling, and every face is gay; in Dingwall or in Stornoway there is a silence in the streets, a heaviness in the tread, and a gravity of aspect in the people, that to the superficial Continental observer might seem the result of a secret congruity between the souls of the inhabitants and the cloudy influences under which they behold the light of the sun. Many a west Ross-shire man would fear to look his clergyman in the face on Monday, if he were seen on Sunday carelessly and with an unscrewed face sauntering beyond the precincts of the farmyard; in any German town you will see the whole population, according to the picturesque description in Goethe's *Faust*, streaming out of the city gates on Sunday as thick as Londoners on Epsom Day. To a passing observer the Scottish Sunday might appear altogether religious, inspired both inside and outside the Church with a genuine piety of an unusually sombre aspect; the German or Parisian Sunday altogether secular. But the contrast is not so complete in detail as it appears in the gross. Let the critical Scottish Sabbatarian, who imagines himself more holy than his neighbours, only rise a little earlier in the morning, and take a turn into a Catholic Cathedral at Munster or Cologne, and he will find the floor of the building like a theatre on a benefit night, crowded with prostrate worshippers of all sexes and sizes. Neither is the evening altogether devoted to amusement, as any one may see in Holy Rome, where some of the most effective services with ceremonial and preaching are given in the afternoon. So much for the variety of presentation; but the principle everywhere remains the same, strictly in accordance with the negative character of the command, "On it thou shalt do no work." The command was Jewish originally, and continued distinctively so during the early centuries of the Church; at what time it was adopted as a distinctive badge or symbol in the Christian escutcheon I cannot exactly say: perhaps nobody knows. But the practice of affixing the ten commandments to the wall of our English churches very prominently behind the altar, gave an open public warrant for the transference of the fourth commandment, with its name and obligations, literally and distinctively to the Christian Lord's Day.

How far this was logically and consistently done it will be the object of the present discourse to inquire.

Of the beneficial nature of Sabbatical institutions generally, no sane man can have the slightest occasion to doubt. The alternation of labour and rest, exertion and repose, lies too deeply seated in the constitution of the universe to be ignored in the machinery of any well-constituted society. Accordingly, in all countries, whether the months are divided into heptads, as with modern Europeans, or into decads, as with the ancient Greeks, we find long lists of feast days and holidays spread largely through the year, which served practically the beneficial purpose of the Jewish Sabbath. No doubt the hebdomadal observance of a day of rest, like so many other enactments of the great Hebrew lawgiver, went far ahead of the general wisdom of the Greeks and Romans in this matter. The certainty and shortness of the recurrent day of total rest is a blessing to the modern man far above that which the holidays of the ancients could confer upon the Athenian man of business and his slaves, who might perhaps, under a hard taskmaster, be excluded from the general relaxation without any legal ground of complaint. Still the principle of the necessity of days of rest and recreation was fully admitted, and the combination of this rest with solemn religious services publicly acknowledged.

That there should be a Sabbath, therefore, in the shape of periodical cessation from hard work and professional business, I take for granted as an undisputed position in every sound system of Sociology. And each seventh day having been consecrated both by Church usage and public enactment for this purpose in all Christian countries, there can be no reason with practical men for interfering with so beneficial and authoritative an arrangement. It is only, therefore, with the manner in which the hebdomadal rest is to be observed that any difference of opinion can exist; and as this difference of opinion with regard to the use of the sacred day grows in certain classes of society out of the teachings of their recognised guides in spiritual matters, with regard to the nature of the Sabbatical obligation, we shall require to discuss both these matters in some detail. The grounds on which the obligation for Sabbath observance is placed are by no means a matter of indifference. In a large community there are always not a few people, especially if they are swayed by a strong bias in one direction, who will be ready, as soon as they find a flaw in the logic by which a good cause is supported, to rush to the conclusion that there is a rottenness in the cause. Against such in the present day there is special reason to provide.

We have chosen our text from St. Paul's Epistle to the Colossians, as being a very distinct and emphatic one; but, to show the full significance and bearing of that text, it will be better to take the matter historically, beginning with the Gospels, so that step by step we may feel our footing sure, and not be led, in a fashion too common with professional theologians, into a one-sided conclusion from an exaggerated importance attached to an isolated text.

Now, in the first place, whosoever is even superficially familiar with the character and tone of the Gospels, must have felt that their main characteristics are pure ethics and rational piety in their most human aspects and in their most catholic principles; and that there is extremely little either of institutional enactment or intellectual doctrine in their composition. A doctor of theology with Athanasian and other metaphysical dogmas in his head, to be believed implicitly on pain of damnation, our Saviour certainly was not; much less was he a lawgiver like Moses, with a book of Leviticus, full of ceremonial, judicial, sanatory, and political regulations affecting the external conduct of individuals and the material framework of society. The Captain of our salvation is a Man of the Spirit, who does not prescribe outward conduct, but breathes into us the breath of a new life, out of which, as from a vital seed, the firm root, the stout stem, the exuberant leafage, and the fruitful blossom, will be evolved by the necessary law of growth. This contrast between the legal character of the Mosaic dispensation and the ethical tone of the Gospel, was prominently put before his disciples by our Lord in the Sermon on the Mount,—a discourse in which to any man who has a moral sense, the peculiar character of Evangelic teaching stands as unmistakably out as the character of Scottish scenery amid the pine forests of Braemar or the birchen groves of Killiecrankie. Now the Sabbath is distinctly a matter not of ethical motive but of institutional law; and the presumption therefore is, that in such spiritual teaching as our Lord delights in no such enactment could appear. The Sabbath, although springing out of the universally human necessity for periodically recurrent times of rest, is, in its particular form of a special sanctity attached to every seventh day, and in the necessity which it involves of an understanding with the civil authorities to make it effectual, essentially the outcome of institutional law, and cannot find a place in a gospel of purely moral motives. No doubt Jesus did observe the Jewish Sabbath; but this he did simply because he was a Jew and had been circumcised as a Jew, and celebrated the passover after the fashion of the Jews to the very end of his life. His relation to Judaism was like that of Savonarola to Popery: he never protested against the seat of Moses as Luther protested against the Papal chair. The contrast between his own doctrine and that of the men of old time, so emphatically stated in the Sermon on the Mount, was not a contrast which necessarily implied war; it was a contrast between the severe schoolmaster of boys and the mild teacher of men ; a contrast destined to disappear by development, in virtue of which the great teacher could most truthfully say—"*I came not to destroy the law, but to fulfil it.*" That the founder of the Christian Church did not formally abolish the Jewish Sabbath proceeded from the same reason that he did not formally abolish circumcision or the passover. It was not these ceremonies and institutions to which he objected, but the placing of the power and virtue of religion in institutions, ceremonies, and sacerdotal traditions of any kind. Nevertheless, after his death, these things naturally, though gradually no doubt, and not without a struggle, fell off; simply, of course, in spite of St. Paul's frequent protest that he was a Jew, and in spirit a much better one than his accusers (Acts xxvi. 22, and xxviii. 17), because his unreformed brethren cast him out of their communion, as the Pope and his Cardinals cast out Martin Luther. The Christian Church thus became distinctly antagonistic to the Jewish ; and in the same way that our Protestant Reformation forced the Reformers to denounce openly certain prominent doctrines of the Roman Church, while they allowed or half allowed others, so the Christians had formed themselves into a separate and antagonistic society, when certain of the Pharisees, who, like St. Paul, had become Christians, and, like him, did not cease in one sense to remain Jews, declared their notions of the essential Judaism inherent in Christianity by insisting that "it was necessary for all converts to be circumcised and to keep the law of Moses" (Acts xv. 5). Now in this law of Moses the Sabbath as a peculiar institution (Neh. x. 31, and Ezek. xx. 12) was included; and the venerable assembly of Apostles and Presbyters in Jerusalem had the whole question formally brought before them as to how far, and in what special points, the Jewish law was obligatory on the early converts from Heathenism. Their answer, therefore, was as comprehensive as it was public and authoritative; and what did they say? That the Gentile converts were bound to "abstain from things polluted by being offered to idols, and from fornication, and from things strangled, and from blood." Now the Gentiles of Antioch, to whom this apostolic rescript was sent, must have been destitute of common sense, if after this they could have imagined that either circumcision, or the seventh day abstinence from work, or any other characteristically Jewish observance, was obligatory on Gentile Christians. And if any more authoritative testimony on this point could be required, the witness of the great apostle of the Gentiles, who was himself by descent and connection a Pharisee, and who was literally face to face with Judaising Christians in all parts of the known world, will supply the additional weight. In the text which heads these remarks he flings overboard with a lofty evangelic disdain those very sabbaths and new moons, and certain notions of abstinence from meats and drinks, which assume so formidable a place in the solemn league and covenant, to which, under the guidance of Nehemiah, the assembled princes and Levites, and priests of the people, set their seal. That St. Paul, in his position as apostle of the Gentiles and founder of the Christian Church in Asia Minor and in Greece, could have used such language to the Colossians, if he believed the observance of the Sabbath obligatory on Christians, is not credible. The great apostle, whatever things have been said of him by persons who have a trick of pitting him against his Master, was at least a man of sense and a gentleman, which is more, I fear, than can be said of not a few of his expositors.

The above two passages contain all that is distinctly laid down in the New Testament with regard to the observance of the Jewish Sabbath. Its express disownment in these passages by apostolic authority is not in the slightest degree affected by the fact mentioned (Acts xiii. 42-44), that the Gentile Christians, in the early ages of the Church at Antioch, were wont to come together and hear the Christian doctrine expounded to them on the Sabbath day; for the synagogue was the necessary cradle of the Church; and it was only as strangers intermingling with a Jewish congregation, in a Jewish place of worship, that the first converts had any opportunity of hearing the gospel preached. Their observance of the Sabbath in these cases, or rather the use they made of the Sabbath, was a matter of necessity, or convenience, certainly not of obligation.

In the argument for the Jewish Sabbath, as stated by Scottish theologians, great use is frequently made of the Old Testament and of the Ten Commandments; as indeed it was a common habit of Divines and Lawgivers of the fifteenth and sixteenth centuries to quote from the Bible as one book, and not a collection of books belonging to different times and places, and to interpret it accordingly. But this is a method utterly destitute of any critical basis, and leading to not a few most unwarrantable conclusions and arbitrary restrictions.

Foremost amongst the arguments from the Old Testament, of course, stands the Statute of the Ten Commandments, which not only, as already remarked, asserted a special place on the walls of our churches before the Reformation, but is put forward with equal prominence in the popular catechisms of the most extreme of our Protestant places of worship. Nevertheless, I think it is plain, both on the face of history, and from the nature of the case, that these Ten Commandments are a part of the Jewish Law, were promulgated in a legal form to the Jews, and were never re-promulgated in the same form to the Christian Church. That they bear in the main a legal type, savouring nothing of the spirit of the gospel, opposed as it is to mere legality, is quite plain from the negative terms in which most of the enactments are couched. Thou shalt *not* steal, thou shalt *not* commit adultery, and so forth, are commandments which are given to prevent crime, not motives supplied to create virtue. No doubt the keystone of all Jewish law, the grand central truth of the Divine Unity, as opposed to the general polytheistic tendencies of the ancient world, is given in a positive form ; so also is the grand social bond of reverence to parents : but this is by no means sufficient to give to the body of these Ten Commandments the spiritual character belonging to gospel precepts. The prominence given to the fourth commandment in the Decalogue — a commandment of a distinctly institutional and arbitrary character, and recognised by the Jews as peculiarly national (Ezek. xx. 12) — ought to be sufficient with unprejudiced minds to show that the Decalogue was not promulgated, and was never intended to be accepted, as a universally binding human charter of social morals. Our Lord we read recognised these commandments, just as He recognised the Sabbath, circumcision, and the passover, because they happened to be there, and were there also in their right place, and with all due sanction, so long as Judaism existed as the larva out of which the chrysalis Christianity was to be evolved. But this is a very different thing from formally re-enacting an institutional statute in the body of a new economy. We must rather say that our Saviour looked on the negative enactments of the Decalogue as schoolboy elements, to serve the purpose of juvenile drill, till the teaching of ripe manhood should be in season. And the commandments which He enunciated, and which should have been taken as their watchword by the Christian Churches, and blazoned in gold letters on their walls, were the well-known two of a positive and penetrative quality and with an essentially generative potency—*Thou shalt love the Lord thy God with all thy heart, and thy neighbour as thyself.* And in this view it is significant enough, that when He addressed the well-known words to the young man, *Keep the commandments,* the Sabbath day is not mentioned,—an omission which admits of only two explanations: either our Lord did omit the commandment, as the writer of the Gospel leads us to believe (and in this case the natural reason of the omission is to be found in the arbitrary and institutional nature of the injunction, which is altogether foreign from a religion of spiritual motives); or, if the narrator and not the speaker is to be credited with the omission, in this case the presumption is, that the narrator and the documents which he used, made the report on the supposition that our Lord could not have given his sanction to the keeping of a commandment which was at the time one of the most distinctive badges of Judaism, as opposed to the practice of the Christian Church. A similar remark applies to St. Paul. In a familiar passage of the Corinthians (1 Cor. xvi. 2), he certainly does not mention the fourth commandment; and it is inconsistent not only with the passage in the Colossians, but with the spirit and scope of his teaching, that he should have intended, in a general incidental remark of this kind, to have given any formal sanction to a notion which he had in other places formally disclaimed.

But what does the Mosaic record itself say? The 20th chapter of Exodus distinctly enough, I imagine, puts the Decalogue as a compend of the main points of social law, given specially as an introduction to the general body of Jewish social and ceremonial law : so that the only ground on which the general human obligation of the Sabbath can be placed must be outside of the Mosaic ceremonial altogether, and coeval with the existence of the human race, as may appear at first blush from the general impression made on modern readers by the well-known passage (Gen. ii. 3). But modern readers, in interpreting ancient books, and especially Oriental books, are continually falling into blunders. It is well known to all Biblical students that the book called the first book of Moses is no more entitled to be looked on as a homogeneous composition of the man Moses, than the book of Psalms is to be looked on as the homogeneous composition of the man David. Instead, therefore, of looking on the 1st chapter of Genesis (and the three first verses of chapter ii., which belong to it) as the first chapter of an old historical record, let us understand that it is no history at all, but rather a philosophico-theological account of the creation of the world, in a narrative form, like the parables of the New Testament, and as such complete in itself; and in this light let us attend to the real philosophical truths which it announces, not to the social institutions which it is imagined to inaugurate. Not to mention the other great cosmic principles which it embodies, it is plain that the principle of periods of rest closing in epochs of formative energy is set forth in the institution of the Sabbath, which, as it appears in Genesis, may be looked on as supplying to the Jews the philosophical principle on which their peculiar institution depended, not as issuing a formal command to all the sons of men, from the rising to the setting sun. But even supposing that the vulgar notion of a primeval cosmic command did belong to this narrative cosmogony, and that the observance of one day in seven was a duty divinely imposed on the whole human race from the birth of man downwards, it is plain to me, from the language of the Apostle Paul, as also from the whole tone and temper of the New Testament, that this institutional ordinance and restrictive statute—for such, in lawyer's language, it is—not having been formally sanctioned at the launching of a new and spiritual economy, must be considered as having been formally abolished, or tolerated only out of kindly considerations in those assemblies of the early Christian Church which could not tear themselves free from the restrictions of the Jewish law under which they had been brought up. In addition to all this it ought to be considered that for the assertion that the Sabbath was originally proclaimed as an obligatory enactment on the whole human race, there is not the slightest vestige of a proof, either inside the Mosaic history of the patriarchs or outside of it ; for the hebdomadal division of time alluded to in Genesis was a matter that arose out of the natural presidency of the moon with its four phases over the twelve months of the year ; and even this hebdomadal division of time, though known to the Egyptians, who were great astronomers, was not acknowledged by the Greeks and Romans till the age of the Empire when the foundations of all old usages were loosened, and all novelties were lightly engrafted. This is carefully stated by Dion Cassius, the Roman historian, who flourished about 200 A.D., in an interesting passage about the Jews in the last part of his account of Pompey and the subjugation of Palestine.

If to all this mass of Scriptural evidence we add the admitted fact that for three whole centuries up to the time of the Council of Nice and the Emperor Constantine, there is a continuous chain of evidence to the effect that Sabbatarian observances were regarded as a feature of the Jewish as opposed to the Christian Church, we may, with all the cogency of a strictly logical argument, lay down the proposition :—*That the Sabbath is not a divine institution now, by direct sanction of God's law, obligatory on any Christian. It is obligatory only on Jews.*

The special dicta of the Fathers and Church Councils on this subject, which, as we have said, so firmly nail down the conclusion, will be given forthwith; but as their testimonies are closely interwoven with the observance of the Christian Lord's Day, as contrasted with the Jewish Sabbath, it will be convenient, in the first place, to state the Scriptural argument, with regard to the Lord's Day also, before we wander into a region where certain classes of extreme Protestants, however unreasonably, are less careful to be at home. And here let me make one general observation. The incidental manner in which these external observances, whether relating to holydays or to the form of polity, are mentioned, taken together with the spiritual character of the Christian religion, ought to be sufficient to show to any reasonable person that it was not in the view of our Lord and his apostles to deal with the details of what may be called the working machinery of the Church; they were anxious only to supply the steam and the plastic forces. Beyond this they left things to take their form as circumstances might allow, common sense dictate, or expediency tolerate, with the general overriding proviso, of course, "that all things be done decently and in order." Christianity is not a religion of ordinances; so, when we turn up that most valuable record of the earliest doings of the Church, the Acts of the Apostles, we find that when St. Paul, in the course of his frequent missionary voyages, was at Troas, he found the disciples on the first day of the week assembled there to break bread, and took advantage of the occasion to deliver them an expository discourse. Now, standing alone, this single text would warrant no conclusion; but when we find the same apostle making a collection for the poor Christians in Jerusalem, and telling the Corinthians to lay by something for them on the first day of the week, we cannot avoid the conclusion that the Church in the earliest times had a habit of coming together as a Church, and for some religious purpose, on the first day of the week, to which practice it is plain that the apostle alludes in his admonition to the Hebrews (x. 25), that "they should not forsake the assembling of themselves together, as the manner of some is." These passages, interpreted by the nature of the circumstances, and by universal practice through long centuries, simply prove that the day of the week called by the Romans Sunday (*solis dies*), and by the Jews the first day of the week, was afterwards called by the Christians the Lord's Day, the *dies Dominica* of the Western Calendar, and if not by direct apostolic institution, certainly with apostolic approval and sanction, fixed by them for their weekly meetings as a Church, for the sake of religious worship and mutual exhortation. This is all we know or can know from Scripture of the great Christian festival of the Lord's Day, as distinct from the Jewish Sabbath, with which some Judaising Christians in the early centuries, and some rigid Calvinistic Protestants in the north part of these islands, have been so forward to confound it.

The doctrine and practice of the early Apostolic Church in this matter, which we have now shortly to indicate, is precisely what might have been expected,—

H

flows, indeed, as naturally from the teaching and language of the Apostle Paul as a corollary in Euclid follows from the primal proposition. Nothing, in fact, but a violent invasion of some foreign force into the infant Church, could have introduced an element which apostolic authority had so emphatically thrust out.

The following extracts from two of the most notable of the patristic authorities, in a matter so universally acknowledged, may serve for a whole chain. In the *Apology* of Justin Martyr (i. 67), who flourished in the second century, we read as follows :—

"We Christians always keep together, and those among us who are rich help those who are poor. And for everything that we eat we offer up thanks to the Maker of All, through Jesus Christ and the Holy Spirit. *And on the day of the Sun* all who live whether in the town or in the country have a meeting ; and when they are come together the memoirs of the apostles are read, and the writings of the prophets, as far as time allows. After the reading, the president of the meeting gives an address, exhorting to the imitation of the excellent things that have been read. Then we all rise and pray. And when the prayer is finished, bread and wine and water are brought round, and the president prays and gives thanks according to his power, and the distribution is then made, and the participation in the elements which have been blessed, which also are sent round by the deacons to those who may be absent. Then the wealthy among us, every one according to his good pleasure, gives a contribution, and the sum, when collected, is deposited with the president ; and he out of these contributions gives help to *orphans* and *widows*, to sick persons, or those who are in prison, to strangers, and equally to all who are in want. And the reason why we come together on the day of the sun is because it is the first day of the week, the day in which God, scattering the darkness, brought a world out of chaos, and the day also in which Christ our Saviour rose from the dead; for on the day before the day of Saturn he was crucified, and on the day after Saturn (which is the day of the sun) he appeared unto his disciples, and taught them those things which we have delivered unto you."

The same author, in his *Dialogue with Trypho the Jew* (8), introduces his adversary, saying—

"If therefore you will hear me, first be circumcised, then keep according to our custom the Sabbath day, and the feasts and the new moons, and generally do all that is written in the law: then haply God will have mercy on you."

This is distinct enough; and his own, the Christian point of view, is no less sharply outlined (12, 18, 43)—

"You pride yourselves on circumcision in the flesh, but what you require is a new circumcision in the heart; and the new law enjoins on all men a *perpetual Sabbath*. But you for one day of the week keep yourselves idle, and think this is piety, not understanding for what purpose the Sabbath was prescribed to you; abstaining in the same way from unleavened bread, you imagine that you are fulfilling the will of God. But in all these things the Lord God whom we worship hath no pleasure. But if any one amongst you is a perjured person or a purloiner, let him cease from his evil ways: if a fornicator, let him repent; this *cessation from evil works* is the Sabbath and true Sabbath of God."

"We also, O Jew, would have observed unconditionally this fleshly circumcision of yours, and these Sabbaths and these feasts, if we had not known on what account they were imposed upon you, viz. on account of your iniquities, and on account of the hardness of your hearts."

"As therefore with Abraham commenced circumcision, and

with Moses Sabbaths and offerings and feast days, and you on account of the hardness of your hearts were enjoined to observe these things, so, according to the counsel of the Fathers, all these things were ordained to cease by the advent of his Son, of the stock of Abraham, of the tribe of Judah, born of a virgin, even Christ the Son of God, who, as the eternal law and the New Covenant, was proclaimed to all men in your own prophetic books."

Our next witness is Eusebius, the well-known Church historian, contemporary and biographer of Constantine, whose name, as connected with the first formal public disownment of Greek and Roman idolatry, indicates a new starting-point in the moral history of the human race. In his *Ecclesiastical History* (i. 4) this writer has the following characteristic and highly interesting passage :—

"Whosoever will say that all the righteous men that lived from Abraham backwards to the first man, were, if not in name, yet in deed Christians, will not be far from the truth : for the name of Christian signifies nothing more than a person who through the knowledge and teaching of Christ is distinguished for sober-mindedness and righteousness and order and moral courage and piety, and the confession of one true God who is above all : and all these virtues the earliest patriarchs practised no less than we. But of the circumcision of the body they knew nothing : as neither do we : of *Sabbath observance* also they were ignorant, even as we ; nor had they any care of meats, clean and unclean, or any such things : all which were introduced afterwards by Moses, and ordered to be observed as typical of something better ; whence it comes to pass that among us Christians no such observances are at all known."

It remains now only to state as a historical fact in

what manner and to what extent the Roman Emperors gave a civil sanction to the celebration of the Christian Lord's Day. An institution like the Jewish Sabbath among all classes of society implying an abstinence from business at certain recurrent periods plainly could not exist without a common religious conviction possessing the whole community, and asserting itself by penalties when the common regulation was countervened. In other words, a regularly and strictly kept Sabbath or day of rest is impossible, except as a State ordinance. It not only, therefore, did not exist in the Christian Church before the conversion of Constantine, but could not exist. Nine-tenths of the early Christian congregations, as the social machine was then regulated, were engaged in some sort of obligatory work both on the Saturday and the Sunday; and therefore their Lord's Day observance could not consist in a Judaical abstinence from business on that day, but simply in using the leisure hours of the day for a congregational meeting, in the same way as prayer meetings and charity sermons and missionary meetings are often held among ourselves on the evenings of week days when the shops and counting-houses are shut. The Lord's Day to the Christians of the first three centuries was in no sense a day of rest, or a Sabbatising, but only a day of worship and fraternal recognition. This, however, was manifestly far from a satisfactory state of things; and one of the first favours, therefore, that acknowledged Christianity had to ask from the civil ruler was that such an interruption of public business might take place on the Sunday, that devoutly disposed Christian persons might have an opportunity of assembling together for religious purposes without the distraction and the weariness which the occupations of everyday life too frequently bring along with them. A representation of this kind was no doubt the motive power which called forth the enactment of the imperial convert so lauded by his ecclesiastical biographer. Here it is :—

IMPERATOR CONSTANTINUS AUG. HELPIDIO.
Omnes judices, urbanæque plebes et cunctarum artium officia venerabili die solis quiescant. Ruri tamen positi agrorum culturæ libere licenterque inserviant, quoniam frequenter evenit ut non aptius alio die frumenta sulcis aut vineæ scrobibus mandentur, ne occasione momenti pereat commoditas cœlesti provisione concessa. Dat. Non. Mar. Crispo II. et Constantino II. Coss.—COD. JUST. iii. 12, 3.

The exception here made by the Roman Emperor in favour of agricultural work might well be made occasionally by the authorities, civil and ecclesiastical, of the more humid and inclement part of the world which we inhabit; for here, as in all other matters connected with Sabbatical observances, the grand human maxim which cuts at the root of all superstitious rigours and artificial orthodoxies is regulative, " *The Sabbath was made for man, not man for the Sabbath.*"

The only other imperial edict with which we need trouble ourselves is that of Theodosius, who was a much more thorough-going religious reformer than Constantine; for two statutes exist in his code, one in which he declares it sacrilege for any person to carry on lawsuits or business of any kind on Sunday, or the Lord's Day, and another specially in favour of the Jews, to the effect that no revenue officer or tax-gatherer should sue them for money on Saturday, or any other of their sacred days; the terms of the two distinct enactments plainly showing that there was no confusion in the imperial mind between the Jewish Sabbath and the Christian Lord's Day.[1] The fiction of some Scottish theologians that the law of the Jewish Sabbath was transferred by divine command into the Christian Lord's Day finds no support from these enactments. So far as rest from general business was concerned, both were co-existing distinct festivals, or sacred days, the one kept sacred by Christians, the other by Jews; and both from their very nature incapable of receiving social recognition except from the order of the civil magistrate. The abstinence from business on the Lord's Day is in all Christian countries a matter of civil statute, not of divine law.

---

[1] VIII. 8, 3.—*Solis die quam dominicam rite dixere majores, omnium omnino litium negotiorum, conventionum quiescat intentio. Debitum publicum privatumque nullus efflagitet ne apud ipsos quidem arbitros vel in judiciis flagitatos vel sponte delectos ulla sit agnitio jurgiorum. Et non modo notabilis verum etiam sacrilegus judicetur qui a sanctæ religionis instituto rituve deflexerit.*

VIII. 8, 8.—*Die Sabbati ac reliquis sub tempore quo Judæi cultus sui reverentiam servant neminem aut facere aliquid ulla ex parte conveniri decere precipimus, cum fiscalibus commodis et litigiis privatorum constet reliquos dies posse sufficere.*

How then is the Christian Lord's Day to be observed by all good Christians and wise citizens of Christendom in this nineteenth century? Nothing can be more plain. In the first place, the distinctive character of the Christian institution as contrasted with the Jewish one must in no wise be forgotten; abstinence from labour is the one and sole obligation laid on the Jews by the Mosaic code; congregational assembly for the purpose of religious worship is the one and sole obligation laid on Christians by the immemorial practice of the Church, not certainly without apostolic sanction, and, what is not of less consequence, by the essential naturalness, reasonableness, and profitableness of the observance. The observance of the whole or some part of the first day of the week for religious exercises is a part of the consuetudinary law of the Church, with which no man but a whimsical crotchet-monger would quarrel, and which every sound thinker on social science, even though himself not a Christian or a religious man, must approve. The objections which we not unfrequently hear against Sabbath observance in this country, so far as they proceed from sober thinkers, are aimed not against the rational observance of a day of rest, or a day of worship at certain recurrent times, but only against those exaggerations and caricatures of the observance, which some formalists among the ancient Jews, or Judaising Christians in the early centuries, and some grim rigorists in this Scottish corner of the world, have pushed into public prominence. Among the ancient Jews, one section contenting themselves with the most easy literal observance of the fourth commandment, seem to have satisfied their consciences with the merely negative abstinence from work, and allowing every seventh day either to rot in swinish indolence, or to fume itself off in dainty luxury. Against these St. Augustine, in a well-known commentary on the 91st Psalm, uttered a weighty word, contrasting in sharp terms the Sabbath which Christians keep, a spiritual Sabbath of the soul, consisting in the serenity and peace of mind which can be obtained only by a rest from sin and every evil work.[1] Another section of the Jews, connected probably with the ascetic sect of the Essenes, a sort of Quaker and Total Abstinence fraternity, carried their rigorous superstition about Sabbath observance to such a ridiculous extreme, that, as Origen tells us, emulating the self-emaciating absurdities of the Hindoo Yogees, one of their most notable heads, a Samaritan, by name Dositheus, actually made it a point of holy duty, in whatever attitude the first moment of the day had found him, in that position to remain till the lapse of the fully reckoned time: if sitting, then to Sabbatise in the sitting attitude; if standing, then to continue standing; and if recumbent, then in recumbency to remain![2] These absurdities have not been equalled even by the sober genius of the most grim of Scottish Calvinists, who seem, by screwing their countenances on Sunday

---

[1] Augustini *Opera Col. Agripp.*, 1616, viii. 366.
[2] ORIGEN, *De Principiis*, iv. 17.

to a minute exactness of enforced gravity, to wish to make amends for the singular disrespect with which they treat all the most hallowed and most typical festivals of the early Christian Church. But apart from these ridiculous oddities of grim Calvinistic Modernism, the recurrent season of rest, which convenience and propriety have brought in as a statutory adjunct of the religious services of the Lord's Day, is in every view so natural, so salutary, so civilising, and so elevating, that the observance of a Sabbath, in fact, from the very constitution of human nature, becomes a duty imperative on every man who will live reasonably in this reasonable world. About the details of the observance there is little need to enlarge; the main point is that people should set distinctly before them the grand problem of life, to make each man of himself as complete a human being as possible, and to know assuredly that no practice tends so much to the development of a complete, well-harmonised, and well-rounded human character, as the wise keeping of one day of rest in seven. The two things to avoid, and for the avoidance of which Sabbatarianism is a sovereign remedy, are, first, the weakening of the functions by the unremitted strain, which in these fast times is a great mischief worker, even with the help of the Sabbath; and again, the narrowing and cramping influence which mere professional occupation never fails to exert on the persons who suffer themselves to be engrossed thereby. About the first nothing need be said; the maxim

Est modus in rebus; sunt certi denique fines,
Quos ultra citraque nequit consistere rectum,

has been sounded in the popular ear by every wise man from Homer to Horace, and from Horace to Wordsworth, and needs only to be enounced, to be attended to; and whoso attends not to it will certainly pay for his neglect not seldom the severest penalty of the inexorable divine law, however sweet may have been the seductions by which he was led into the path of the grave transgression. But the other evil influence which Sabbatarianism was instituted to check, is not so generally acknowledged, and therefore less frequently guarded against. If it be true, as the poet has it, that a man grows larger with his larger sphere, it is no less true conversely, that a narrower sphere makes the man narrower; and of all narrowing influences known, the most persistent and the most unavoidable is what is vulgarly called "the shop." No matter how intellectual, or how morally elevating the habitual occupation of a man may be, still the day after day exercise of the same function, within a certain prescribed circle, as in a treadmill, tends, while producing a preternatural dexterity in one direction, to wither, and at last altogether to stupefy and deaden the sensibilities of the soul. The "shop," by its demands and continuous action, really forms a sort of prison, from which a man should set himself free on every convenient occasion; and for this necessary act of self-liberation the Sabbath is for all men the wisely instituted opportunity. Show me a man who habitually carries on, so far as the law of the country allows him, his weekly occupation without intermission on Sunday, and I will show you a man narrow in his sympathies, awkward in his adaptation to circumstances, and the slave of some artificial machinery of which he ought to be the master.

Supposing then the Sunday free from the trammels of business, and the tyranny of a professional train of ideas, how shall a man employ himself? A Christian of course will go to church, at least for one diet of the day; and he who is not a Christian will do so wisely also; for two reasons, first, because Christianity is essentially an ethical religion, by the teachings of which every moral being may profit, and then because it is an unhappy thing for a man, a member of a social organism, to withdraw himself from all part in that which, according to Socrates, is the most distinctive act of a reasoning animal—the acknowledgment of the great common source of all existence, of all reason, and of all excellence. The necessity of the religious nature being gratified, a reasonable man is free to spend the remainder of the Lord's Day in the manner most beneficial to his own special well-being. If he is what is called a working man,—that is, a man who, by the hard labour of bone and muscle, feels himself much in want of a periodical cessation from all exertion,—he may spend much part of the Sabbath most profitably by lying at length on a sofa, on a primrose bank, or a thymy hillside, as his circumstances may allow. Those who are less exhausted by their week-day work will of course use the day of rest not so much for absolute repose as for various kinds of mental exertion, such as may interfere as little as possible with the serene temper that belongs to the day, and at the same time may in no wise invade the rest to man and beast provided with such benevolent foresight by the great Jewish legislator. Music and sketching in the country, easy social gatherings among friends, and healthy games, such as croquet, lawn-tennis, golf, boating, though scarcely permitted by British usage, are contrary neither to the letter nor to the spirit of the Mosaic command, which, though not enjoined on Christians, has, from the wisest motives, been adopted into our code of social ethics. The same remark applies to the visitation of Botanic Gardens and Public Museums of Art and Science, which not only afford an agreeable recreation to the most intelligent part of the working classes, but may help to withdraw a section of them from places of low and even vicious resort. The only thing to be seriously attended to here is, that no Sabbath sports shall be allowed to commence before two o'clock in the afternoon; otherwise, recreation might run away with religion; and one day in seven spent in a round of frivolous dissipation would tend to intensify instead of allaying the evils arising from the strain of unremitted business. For persons of extraordinary energy, that portion of the day of rest which is not employed in the exercises of religious worship will usually be devoted to whatever kind of exercise is least provided for by the habits of their profession. Sedentary persons should walk as much as possible; persons whose time is consumed in a mechanical routine of unintellectual business should devote some part of the Sunday to the cultivation of some favourite science, in the prosecution of which intensity of zeal might compensate for scant leisure; while scholars and professional teachers would find it for their advantage to open no professional book on the Lord's Day; but, if they will read, to take a long swim in the broad sea of general human sympathy. But before all things, on Sunday a man should take care to give special attention to his moral and spiritual nature, a culture only too apt to be neglected in the engrossing pursuit of gain or power, or honour or reputation, or whatever other bubble the foolish world may be hunting after, instead of the jewel wisdom. This special culture may best be found in the study of the Scriptures, and in the lives of great reformers, such as Buddha, Confucius, Martin Luther, Dr. Chalmers, Oberlin, Dr. Channing, and generally of great and good men and women who have done something noteworthy for the elevation of their species, whether under the Christian or the heathen dispensation. There are no more profitable "Sunday books," using that phrase in the moral and not the religious sense of the phrase, than the works of such good, pure, and noble heathens as Socrates, Plato, Epictetus, Marcus Antoninus, Cicero, and Seneca. The study of such authors,—pursued not in a philological spirit, but for the sake of their human contents only,—brings with it the double benefit of presenting to us immutable morality free from the technical slang and sectarian shibboleths with which it is so apt to be intertwined, and at the same time stimulating our moral energies by the example of men who stood on a platform of equal moral altitude with our own, but with much more difficulty in the assertion of it. Minute and copious rules with regard to Sabbath-keeping no wise man will lay down; but he who knows not how to use this blessed opportunity for cherishing that purity and nobility of purpose in life, which business may strangle, and professions can but feebly cultivate, does not treat himself as a good rider treats his horse, and will come out, whenever the balance of life requires to be struck, in some important respects as a deficient man. The Scottish people have exposed themselves to no little just ridicule by their strict views on Sabbath observance; but it has not always been considered that strict Sabbatising, with its natural accompaniment, Bible-reading, has acted for three centuries as the principal agent in the formation of the serious, solid, substantial, and thoroughly reliable character so typical of our people. It is better, as human beings are constituted, to be a trifle too serious, than to float through life in an element of levity and frivolity,—better, since the golden mean of virtue can scarcely be obtained, to hold the rein too tight than to have no reins to hold; for out of a certain ethical severity, as from a root, the greatest national virtue has been found to grow; while from looseness of ethical ideas and levity of practice the greatest nations have been ruined. If the Scottish people are destined to such great overthrow as overtook Tyre and Sidon, Rome and Constantinople, it will not be the severity of Sabbatical observance that will prove the occasion of their fall, but their inability to reconcile their theology with the science of the age, and the spiritual creed which they profess with the pomp of seductive materialism with which they are surrounded.

III.

FAITH.

"Now faith is the substance of things hoped for, the evidence of things not seen."—HEB. xi. 1.

I HAVE often wondered, having been a church-goer in churchly Scotland for half a century and more, how amid the prominence justly given by all thoughtful men of all parties to the great Pauline and Protestant doctrine of salvation by faith, those who enlarge on this theme have so often, or I may say, in Scotland, almost universally, taken the key-note of their discourse rather from the Epistle to the Romans than from that notable chapter in the Hebrews to which the prefixed verse belongs. For without entering into the disputed question of the authorship of this Epistle, which cannot in the slightest degree affect its place in the canon, it must strike any person who applies even a superficial amount of thinking to the study of the New Testament that this chapter is the only one in which a formal definition of faith in a purely scientific shape is given; and not this only, but given with a long sequence of striking illustrations, which must render the practical significance of the abstract definition patent to all understandings: whereas, in the Epistle to the Romans, through the whole sweep of the argument, down to the end of the eleventh chapter, where the practical part commences, the writer has certain sacerdotal pretensions, Pharisaic conceits, presumptuous imaginations, and vainglorious notions, mainly in his eyes, with reference to which the doctrine of salvation by faith is stated in a peculiar contrast to works, which does not, and, indeed, could not, occur in the more wide and general view of the great moral principle given after the philosophical definition in the Hebrews.

Let any man, therefore, who wishes to know philosophically and practically the length and the breadth of this glorious principle of Christian faith — the great root of all moral soundness in society — breaking loose bravely from the crust of local prejudice and the pressure of an inherited terminology, look this chapter of the Hebrews freely and fully in the face, and see what it means as the great authorised interpreter of the moral history of the world, not only in the case of Abraham, Isaac, and Jacob, Moses and Daniel, and Samuel and all the prophets, but also in all the leading assertions of human worth and social dignity in later times, whether against sacerdotal intolerance in Constantinople and Rome, or political atrocity in Naples and Milan.

On the technical words used in the definition — for they are in a manner technical, having been appropriated both in metaphysical theology and in logic—it is not necessary to make any detailed remarks. The English word *substance* is merely the curtailed form of the Latin *substantia;* and this, again, is merely the Latin transference of the Greek ὑπόστασις, meaning *that which stands under or underlies, substratum.* That, therefore, which distinguishes a reasonable faith, conviction, or belief from a vain wish is simply the amount of solid substantial element which it contains. In other words, faith is a reasonable and a substantial hope, and it is at the same time a proof (ἔλεγχος, *elenchus*) ; for, as neither the future nor the invisible can be seen,—the future because it is not arrived, and the invisible because it is incognisable by sense,—the one proof or evidence that belongs to both is the reasonable substratal element which they imply.

Of faith, conviction, or belief, there are three kinds, not to be confounded, all of which, to a certain extent, seem to have been within the view of the writer of this chapter. *First,* There is historical belief, or faith in the reality of some fact not known directly to the believer. *Second,* Metaphysical or theological faith, faith in an inward invisible power, not distinctly apprehended, but necessarily inferred from its significant manifestation. *Third,* Moral or practical faith, an abiding conviction of some truth, which necessarily leads to action tending to a realisation of that truth. This last is peculiarly the living faith of Christians, which has produced all the victorious apostleship, fruitful martyrdom, and triumphal progress of the moral world: and it is this, of course, which the writer of our chapter mainly insists on and largely illustrates. Nevertheless, a word or two, by way of contrast and qualification, may be profitable on the other two kinds, which, like the axioms and postulates in Euclid, however relatively small in bulk, are necessarily implied as the starting-point or root of the rich ramifications of the third. As for the first, the historical faith, or the belief in credibly attested facts, there are religions, such as the ancient Greek, in which the historical element is so small and so accidental to the system, that it need not be practically taken into account. Greek religious mythology, or mythological religion, was so purely the growth of a reverential imagination, acting on the powerful forces of the physical and the powerful passions of the moral world, that a devout Pindar, Æschylus, Socrates, or Xenophon, might feel his faith firmly rooted in it, without having been called on to append his credence to a single seriously attested fact; but it is otherwise with our Christianity, a religion so deeply grounded not only in the personal character and lives of its founders, but in the accredited history of continuous centuries, that for this very reason the writer of our Epistle rather assumes the historical materials of his faith as an admitted postulate, than sets himself, like a professor in a University, to prove the necessity of a firm foundation of historical belief to every man calling himself a Christian. The early Christian Churches, indeed, stood where they stood, and professed what they professed, on the basis of certain generally accredited historical facts; and a mason could no more pile a pyramid or a palace without bricks or square stones, than the writer of the Epistle to the Hebrews could argue as he does, without the postulate of a strong substratum of received facts. As for St. Paul himself, it is quite certain, not only from several notable places in his Epistles, but also from his missionary discourses in the Acts, that he considered the literal reality of the resurrection of our Saviour as the keystone of his whole preaching. Nevertheless this historical faith, being rather a necessary reasonable postulate of Christianity, than Christian faith as a vital principle of action, is not specially alluded to in our chapter, unless indeed we assert that the creation of the world mentioned in the third verse, as apprehended by an act of faith, must be understood to mean a belief in that grand manifestation of Divine wisdom, on the authority of the author of the Book of Genesis. We prefer, however, to regard the faith spoken of in the third verse, by which we know God as the Creator of the world, and the act of faith likewise mentioned in the sixth verse, without which it is impossible to please God, as falling under our second category of metaphysical, philosophical, or theological faith,—that is, the belief in an ultimate unseen cause or principle, of which all outward, visible, and sensual things are the manifestation and the effect; and what the apostle in the Romans states as the ground of this faith, that every reasonable manifestation of effects necessarily implies a reasonable cause of that manifestation, is precisely the same as the argument of Socrates, that I have as much cause for believing in God by his manifestation in the world, as I have for believing in myself or any of my friends, by the expression of their character in their features and in the dramatic process of their life. This is the language at once of all profound thinking, all sound theology, all high poetry, and all healthy instinct; and if there be any that think otherwise, as in this age of feverous transition there haply may be, who boast themselves of the hollow vacuities and negative absurdities of *Atheism* or *Nihilism*, we must just let them lie like drunk men in the ditch till the fit is over.

The second great fundamental article of the Christian's creed, as stated by the apostle, is, as we have stated, the moral government of the world. This, though no doubt, as much as the first, a metaphysical proposition, to which a merely intellectual assent may be conceded, is nevertheless very different from it; for it concerns not the world of thoughtful speculation, but the world of moral energy, and cannot, without a manifest force on nature, be believed seriously without leading to a deliberate and determinate course of action. A man may believe that two and two make four without counting his pennies; but he cannot believe that decapitation is the penalty of high treason, and at the same time indulge lightly in familiar confabulation with conspirators. As to the ground of the moral law, and the reality of the Divine government from which it derives its sanction, we come to acknowledge it by an infallible manifestation of its power, exactly as in the case of physical law, only in a different region, and under more various and complex conditions. Society is an organism as much as a plant or an animal, and as such exists only by the cohesive power of certain moral laws, the cessation of whose action would instantly be followed by its resolution into an aggregate of hostile, confounding, and mutually exterminating elements. One does not require to travel to Bulgaria, or to be familiar with Turkish misgovernment, or no government, in any part of the world, to be made startlingly alive to the fact that the normal state of human gregariousness, which we call society, may at any moment cease when the cement of society, which we call sympathy, ceases to act, and the controlling power of justice or practical reason is disowned. Man is man essentially and characteristically by his consistent, reasonable action in relation to his fellows; in other words, by acknowledging the moral law. The moment he throws this law aside he becomes a beast, a tiger or a fox, or a combination of the two, with the addition of intellectual ingenuity to make the ferocity of the tiger more systematic, and the cunning of the fox more treacherous. And thus, as Mephistopheles says in *Faust*, he becomes "more brutish than any brute can be"—becomes transformed, in fact, into a fiend, a demon or a devil, in the fashion of which the records of our criminal courts, and the lives of unbridled men, drunk with power and pleasure in high places, furnish only too numerous examples. There can be no doubt, therefore, that man is by the constitution of his nature essentially a moral animal; and as the constitution of human nature, as of all nature, is Divine, and comes directly from God, the belief in the obligation of the law finds its root instinctively in the acknowledgment of the lawgiver. It is possible, no doubt, for a moral man to be an atheist, but it is not natural. The natural keystone of all moral ideas is God. "He that cometh to GOD must believe that he IS, and that he is the rewarder of them that diligently seek him;" in which verse seeking God and coming to God can only mean seeking to know and to conform to the divine law of which God is at once the author and the administrator. And this order of things is not arbitrary, but inwrought into the very conception of a social organism. It is, in fact, as absurd to suppose that the driving in of a nail or a screw should not tend to the binding together of two planks, as that the observance of the moral law should not tend to the well-being of society; for if, without law, society, as we have seen, cannot exist at all, much less can it exist comfortably or enjoyably. What we call a disorderly life and an ill-governed country is simply a person in whom, or a country in which, the action of moral law is feeble or irregular; and in all such cases it follows, as surely as ashes from flames, that the vitality of the person will be lowered, and the power of the State decline. God cannot deny his own nature; and the laws of nature, both physical and moral, which are the marshalled display of the divine wisdom, power, and goodness, cannot in any one case be contravened without a certain departure from the source of all divine reality ; and this, if repeated and continued in the same negative direction, must end in that separation and divorce from all essentially vitalising influences, which we call death—physical or moral, as the case may be. Look round about you, not far but very near, and see how the sorrowful records of broken fortunes, shattered health, and degraded character, in which novels and newspaper columns abound, give constant confirmation of the truth of this text. The persons who afford these sad illustrations of shipwrecked faith and ruined lives, did simply, in foolish thoughtlessness, insolent presumption, or unbridled wantonness, tear themselves away from the divine law, which, as in the person of our Saviour specially, so everywhere, is the stem of the vine, giving support and sap to all the branches ; and the branch now lies soulless and sapless, of all green beauty and purple glory divested, fit only to be cast into the fire. No doubt the extreme penalty which human authorities, as ministers of the divine law, impose on social offenders, may sometimes be escaped ; but the inward rottenness remains, eating surely and silently through the heart of a life at whose outward flourishes and painted prosperity the envious gaze of a thousand fools may be directed ; and no one can tell what amount of misery, degradation, and corruption may, in the natural process of the generations, evolve itself from the taint of one ancestral crime. The Greeks, as may be seen in their tragedies, had a strong feeling of this law of moral retribution; and we Christians should be quick at once to see its operation more largely, and to feel its terrors more effectively.

We now leave the ground of abstract principle, to consider how faith in God and in his moral government displays itself in the formation of character on the stage of history, and in the great drama of human life; and we shall start here with two familiar illustrations—one of a young person learning to swim, and the other of Christopher Columbus crossing the Atlantic Ocean, and discovering the New World. No fact is more commonly known than that the human body is lighter than its bulk of water, and therefore that it cannot sink unless pushed down. Why, then, do most persons find it so difficult to learn to swim? Simply because they have little faith in what they are told, that they will not sink, if they spread themselves fairly out on the wave, and use their palms steadily for oars, striking backwards as ducks do with their web feet. The want of faith implies the presence of fear; and so, being apprehensive of sinking, in the flutter of their spirits, instead of striking back with their palms quietly, they begin to beat the wave with a succession of violent plashes, which of course drives them down, the body not being light enough to stand any pressure in addition to its natural weight;

and thus, from lack of cool conviction and firm faith in the witness of experienced persons, months and years are often spent in futile attempts at achieving a dexterity which is one of the easiest that human beings can exercise—much easier certainly than leaping a wire fence, or riding a horse in Numidian wise at full speed without stirrups. Now, to pass from one of the cheapest exercises of faith to one of the most sublime, let us take the case of Columbus, on whose great achievement in navigation Schiller has written the beautiful lines—

> " Steer, doughty sailor, though the witling sneer,
> And faithless pilots droop with craven fear ;
> Still westward, westward, there the land must lie ;
> Even now thou seest it, there in thy mind's eye.
> Trust in thy God ; the land is there, or would
> Rise from the wave to make thy venture good ;
> Nature is leagued with genius to fulfil
> Her prophet's thought, and serve his venturous will."

And to the same purpose the following lines, entitled

" WISDOM AND PRUDENCE.

> " Whoso to wisdom's top would rise must know
> To bear a sneer from prudent wits below,
> Who see his starting-point with blinking eyes,
> But not his goal far 'mid the starry skies."

Now, what this means in plain prose most people know. Columbus was a poor boy, son of a Genoese woolcomber, who had gone to sea in his youth, and also, by study at the University of Pavia, had acquired such knowledge of geometry, geography, astronomy, and navigation, as was to be had at the time. His adventurous genius was fired by the accounts which he read of far distant parts of the world, whether in the books of the ancient geographers, or in the travels of the famous Venetian, Marco Polo. These accounts, taken together with the sphericity of the globe, in which he believed, warranted the firm faith that, if he only sailed far enough westward, he would certainly arrive, by a course the reverse of that generally practised, at the extreme east parts of Asia, China, Japan, and some vague extent of country beyond, known to poets down to the present hour under the name of Cathay. This conviction, as every one sees now, was in the highest degree reasonable, it being quite certain that if he could have held out long enough, and had the West Indies and America not stood directly in his way, he must have arrived at the far east land by steering ever more and more to the west. But the inspirations of genius and the prophetic indications of science were disowned alike by the prudence, the fear, the laziness, the indifference, or, in a single word, by the lack of faith in those to whom he made his appeal for the means to make this voyage of discovery; and even when fairly embarked, it was with the utmost difficulty, and with the help of a pious lie occasionally, that he could induce his doubting and despairing crew to obey his command, and follow out the adventurous quest. This example brings out most emphatically one essential quality of Christian faith, as displayed in most of the illustrations given by the author of the Epistle to the Hebrews, viz. courage, resolution, determination, and persistency; courage, be it observed, not only of the common military kind, which a man, like a dog, naturally has, being a fighting animal, but moral courage, to face without flinching whole batteries of ridicule and sneers, and words of grave authority and prudent warning from those who are wise in the wisdom that lies behind and around us, but who lack the vision and the prophetic faculty to see beforehand the reasonable possibilities of the future. This vision belongs to faith; *faith removes mountains.* The man of faith must succeed: because, to have a reasonable object, and to follow after that object with a wise persistency, are the two conditions out of which all high achievement grows. Nature, as Schiller says, is in league with genius; or, to use the language of religion, God, the author of external nature, being also the author of the inward reasonable convictions which are summed up in faith, cannot fail to make the external and the internal factors of human action meet in a common result. As the eye seeks the light, and the light finds the eye, so every grand inspiration, whether of prophet or poet, political or ecclesiastical reformer, geographical explorer or cunning engineer, finds the materials and the tools which it requires abundantly provided for the need. But the man who will succeed must seek, and he must see, and he must strike, and, above all things, he must believe. Nature does nothing for doubters.

Let us now take an example of living, active faith in the field of devout patriotic achievement, which the apostle, in this chapter, had more directly in view; and we cannot do better here than take the example whose features himself touches most in detail, viz. Moses. The position of the Israelites in Egypt was that of a band of foreign settlers, favoured originally, no doubt, by the patronage of the native monarch, but falling soon into the neglect and contempt which is the natural lot of an alien minority, and, in an absolute monarchy such as prevailed in Egypt, liable always to be reserved for doing the lowest kind of forced labour, under the most galling penalties, whenever an inconsiderate or ambitious ruler chose to strain his privilege to the utmost. Add to this, that besides being politically in Egypt, as prostrate before the native authorities as the Helots in Greece were before the Spartans, the Hebrews under the Pharaohs were living in a state of open and declared antagonism to the established religion of the land,—a state which, in a sacerdotal country like Egypt, necessarily added the bitterness of sacred bigotry to the insolence of despotic authority. Well, under these circumstances, Moses, a comely son of a stout Hebrew mother, providentially rescued from an early death in the swelling waters of the Nile, grew up under the notice and favour of a princess of the royal house, and, in this position, had prospects of worldly honour and advancement opened up, to which no limits might be set; for in all absolute monarchies, where there is practically no aristocracy, any man of talent, as we may see in Turkey and in modern Egypt at the present hour, may lightly leap to the right hand of the throne. A worldly man,—that is to say a selfish man, who lived merely to wield a selfish power, and to gratify his vanity by the adjuncts of a brilliant social position,—would never have allowed the advantages of such a situation to slip through his fingers. He would have served the Egyptians faithfully, as certain notorious Italians served the Austrians in Milan, that he might rise and rule; but he would have done so, as worldly men always do, only by sacrificing his best affections as a Hebrew, his moral dignity as a man, and the human ties by which he was naturally bound to his race, for a position of eminence, which, however worthy in itself, he could not honourably hold. But Moses was a man of honour, or let us rather say a man of faith; for he not only scorned to abandon his poor oppressed countrymen that he might become a court-favourite, but, as his future career showed, he had that in him which marked him out for being the deliverer of his enslaved kinship, and the creator of a mighty people; and the sacred narrative makes it abundantly plain that no man can do these things without faith in God, who is ever ready to help those who are willing to help themselves. The liberation of an enslaved people is indeed at all times an achievement which requires the highest exercise of faith of which a moral being is capable. For the difficulties in the way of such a systematic reversal of social position are immense, and the dangers of failure great; so that whosoever undertakes such a work, whether an ancient Hebrew lawgiver, or a modern revolutionary captain of volunteers like Garibaldi, must do so under the assured conviction that God is with him, and that he is fighting, and willing to give his life for the constitution of things which from the beginning God ordained for all times and all places. This is the foundation of what Dr. Paley, I think, calls "the sacred right of insurrection,"— insurrection, indeed, never lightly to be advised, or hastily to be undertaken; but there are unquestionably extreme cases, in which a man who firmly believes in a divine government of the world dare not allow himself to live under conditions which lend a continual sanction to the most shameless rapacity and the most systematic atrocity. When those who wield the sword wield it in the service, not of God, but of the devil; when the fundamental maxim of those who sit in the seat of authority is to promote all baseness and to crush all nobleness; when, in fact, civilised man becomes more ignoble under a civilised magistracy, in many respects, than the uncivilised savage and the vague wandering nomad;—then the man of faith stands up and says: "I will tolerate this no longer. God will help the man who helps the creatures of God to the free use of their natural faculties, and the free exercise of their natural rights." And whatever the advocates of peace at any price may say, this abnormal state of legalised lawlessness and authorised oppression is the real justification and the sacred necessity of war. " I came not to send peace but a sword!" as the Evangelic text has it; or, as it stands on the pedestal of the statue of stout old Maurice Arndt, on the esplanade above the Rhine at Bonn, " Der Gott der Eisen wachsen liess, der wollte keine Knechten." " *The God that caused the iron to grow wished not that slaves should exist.*"

We shall now take a hero from the modern world, in one of its most recent and notable achievements, VICTOR EMMANUEL, the late King of Italy, and understand how the same principle operates under circumstances considerably different. Here, however, to avoid misapprehension, let us distinctly premise that we hold up this monarch as an example only in his public capacity as a king of men. His faults and offences in one private direction may have been as great as they are commonly accredited, or may have been much more venial; anyhow, the examples of Solomon and King David in sacred Scripture, and of not a few others well known in secular story, seem to carry with them a special lesson of charity. With this proviso, let us endeavour to cast a sympathetic glance into the notable public career of Victor Emmanuel.

The Congress of Vienna, in the first quarter of the present century, which wound up the long series of political throes and convulsions that arose out of the great French Revolution, issuing its ordinances after a military triumph over the great Continental despot and usurper, General Napoleon Buonaparte, naturally placed

K

its results on the page of history as a *Restoration* of the previous state of things, which that transcendental fulminator had overthrown; but though naturally, by no means wisely; for Napoleon, however selfish in his nature and despotic in his proceedings, struck into the neighbouring European nations not in the vulgar style of an Asiatic conqueror, but rather, to adopt one of Hazlitt's well-known phrases, as the armed apostle of democracy, and, as such, along with his imperialism and Gallicism, had brought both into Germany and Italy a democratic element, which, when contrasted with the feudalism and petty princedom it overthrew, was of decidedly beneficent operation. But this the men of the Restoration, with Metternich, the great Austrian diplomatist at their head, could not or would not understand; they restored wholesale the bad along with the good that had been overthrown; and a war which had been undertaken in the name of liberty, to free Europe from the intolerable yoke of one great French tyranny, ended in re-establishing a number of petty tyrannies in the countries which had been made links by compulsion of the great French Empire; and poor Italy, the garden of Europe, whose beauty had long made her a marked prey for lustful neighbours, was not only parcelled out among the troop of petty absolutists under whom it had suffered such degradations, but was handed over without limitation to the disposal of Austria, the most blind, bigoted, persistently and ruthlessly conservative of all the great European powers. Only a nation sunk in the lowest depths of social degradation could tolerate this; so, in the year 1821, the great secret conspiracy of the Carbonari arose in Naples, and planted there the small seed of the glorious tree of Italian unity and independence with which good men in these later days have refreshed their eyes. The first outbreak of this noble conspiracy to make one free Italy, and shake the Austrian out of the saddle, as generally happens in such cases, failed. It was not till the year 1848, under the influence of the famous Liberal manifestoes put forth to the electric joy of Italy by the late Pope on his accession, that Charles Albert, the King of Sardinia, who had succeeded to the throne in 1831, came boldly forward and asserted from Turin the principles of constitutional freedom in the face of the foreign government by soldiers, priests, and policemen, which had its dark fortress, and enacted its grim tragedies, at Milan. Of this Charles Albert Victor Emmanuel was the son; and when the father, after the unfortunate issue of the campaign of 1848, resigned the throne, for the wise reason that he did not feel he could do any more good in that position, his son Victor took his place, and had to transact the humiliating conditions of peace that followed the defeat of the Italian cause at Novara. Now this was the moment in which the faith of the king was tried as the faith of Moses was tried in Pharaoh's court, and in the modern as in the ancient case came out triumphant. The Austrian general, Marshal Radetzky, at a meeting with the young king, when he naturally hoped to find the petty sovereign of Turin as meek and yielding as a small pigeon between the claws of a great hawk, proposed as the prime postulate of the most favourable conditions of peace, that the Italian sovereign should abolish the constitutional statute, or charter, granted to his people by his father, and adopt the policy of repression and obscuration followed by Austria as the great representative of absolutism in Italy. But Victor Emmanuel, though in a position as riskful and as apparently hopeless as that of Moses beneath the shadow of the Memphian pyramids, would not betray his people. He was a man of faith; and his faith taught him to believe that the government of Italy by German foreigners, with the conditions and qualities which are inherent in such a government, was contrary to the will of God and the right moral order of nations and peoples; that, as a king, the trustee of the liberties of his people, it would be high treason in him to sell those liberties to Austria or any other power for a mess of pottage or a bag of gold; that in obedience to the will of God he must absolutely reject all conditions, however favourable, that would stamp his name with dishonour and brand his people with slavery; and that, hopeless as it at first appeared to dislodge the great enemy of Italy from the seat of power, changes in the political world were sure to occur, perhaps at no distant date, which, if wisely taken advantage of, would result in the long-desired ejection of the Germans and the gathering of all Italians under a native Government.

The following, accordingly, are the recorded words with which—his first public act—the young king replied to the proposals of the Austrian marshal.

"Marshal, I reject your proposals; and sooner than subscribe to such degrading conditions, I am ready to renounce, not one crown only, but a thousand. The charter which my father granted to his people, his son will maintain. Is it a war to the knife which you desire? Be it so; you shall have it. I will make an appeal to my people; and, severe as is the blow with which you seem to have crushed us, you may yet find to your cost what a general rising of the Piedmontese people can do; or, if we must succumb, we will succumb without shame. The House of Savoy knows the path of exile, but not the path of dishonour." On hearing this declaration, the marshal, though he was obliged to withdraw his conditions of a more favourable peace, yet had the generosity to make his noble adversary certain concessions, which, in default of that nobility, would have been withheld; and history narrates that, after the conclusion of the peace, on parting, he made the observation to his generals: "*Dieser Mann ist ein edler Mann; er wird uns viel zu thun geben.*" "*This man is a noble man; he will give us much to do!*"[1] And so verily he did. Victor Emmanuel, through his whole life, remained true to his principles, and had not, as all the world knows, to wait long years before favour-

---

[1] See *Vittorio Emanuelle II., Re d' Italia*, by Felice Venosta. Milan, 1878.

able events in France and Germany, wisely taken advantage of, enabled the king of little Sardinia to become the monarch of big Italy, bravely redeemed at last from the iron hoof of a foreign despotism, and from the nightmare of a secular priestcraft.

From these and such-like examples, those who are accustomed to interpret with humility and reverence the lessons of Divine Providence in that concatenation and sequence of things which we call history, will understand that all heroism, of whatever kind, whether in the political or the religious world, or the world of individual achievement, is the result of some sort of faith,—a faith if not always in God and the divine government of the world, which is the culminating form of all faith, at least in a fixed order of things and the progress and happiness of human beings, as dependent on an unconditional and self-sacrificing recognition of that order.

It remains now that we indicate with a single word the relation of the general doctrine of faith as expounded in our chapter to the special teaching of St. Paul in the Epistle to the Romans. The relation of these two epistles in the matter of faith is exactly that which we have just expressed by the words *general* and *special*. The author of the Epistle to the Hebrews teaches positively, and in its widest range, the doctrine of faith. The direct object of St. Paul was not to expound faith in a positive and comprehensive form, but to expose the vanity of a certain kind of works, and of works generally in a certain aspect, put forward as a substitute for faith. The works against which the epistle is directly written are the ceremonial and legal works, mainly of an external character, on which the Jews plumed themselves, and in virtue of which they conceited themselves to be something inherently better than their neighbours, and possessing a certain special recommendation to the favour of the Almighty. These conceits were pretty much like those which some of our modern oligarchs or pseudo-aristocrats entertain in this country; who, because they happen to have been born of famous ancestors, or of fathers and grandfathers in a certain honourable position in society, think themselves entitled to assume an air of superiority, and to look down on what they call their inferiors with contempt. All such claims of imaginary excellence before God and in the face of men St. Paul puts down, in the first place, as showing a total misapprehension of the nature of the moral law, and the true dignity of man founded thereon; for he is not a Jew who is one outwardly and in external observance, but inwardly and in the spirit; just as we might, in reference to the aristocratic snobbery just alluded to, say that he is not a duke who is greeted in the court and in the market-place as your Grace this and your Grace that, but who is a leader of the people in spirit and in fact, according to the proper signification of the word *dux*. And, in the second place, the great apostle uses what the logicians call an *à fortiori* argument, to the effect that, as the moral law is an ideal of perfection to which imperfect and finite creatures can never altogether attain, it is a law confronted with which all men, even the best, must confess themselves sinners; much less can the most strict observance of the merely external and ceremonial part of such law entitle any sinful creature to put forth proofs of merit and claims of reward before an all-holy God. It was not, therefore, at all against works absolutely viewed, but against works put forth as a meritorious claim, or against the vain conceit of self-righteousness, that the Epistle to the Romans was written; and we see plainly that, whereas faith, the mother, as we have seen, of all heroism, and the general inspiring soul of all noble acts, implies a belief in an ideal state of the moral world which is not, but ought by all means to be,—self-righteousness, as a substitute for this moral steam, so to speak, implies a low and generally also an artificial ideal of the law of duty with which persons of feeble moral pulse and low social aspirations are only too apt to remain content. And herein we have the true key not only to St. Paul's glorification of faith in the Romans, but also to the emphasis given to that doctrine by Martin Luther, Calvin, and other most prominent fathers of the Protestant Churches. As the Jews with the ceremonial law in St. Paul's time, so Christians generally, at the age of the Reformers, were, by the teaching of the priesthood, seduced into the belief that works principally of an external and ceremonial kind, performed in obedience to Church authority, might be substituted for the length and the breadth of the moral law applied to all the relations of life as the alone adequate measure of all social duty and all saintly attainment. Thus individual acts of real or imaginary virtue were divorced from the soul that ought to inspire them, and religion was made to consist in observances which had no vital connection with a noble life or a manly character.

As for St. James, whose denunciation of faith has been a stumbling-block occasionally to a certain class of extreme Pauline Christians, it is scarcely necessary to remark that he only says prominently and categorically what St. Paul says incidentally or by implication, viz. that Christian faith has no meaning at all, and does not in fact exist, unless as manifested in Christian works. The contradiction between the two writers, as in not a few vexed moral questions, is only verbal. Works as a claim are one thing; works as an evidence another thing.

IV.

THE UTILISATION OF EVIL.

"Did this man sin or his parents, that he was born blind?"
JOHN ix. 2.

THE question proposed here is a distinctly metaphysical one; and as such the Great Teacher of the faith which worketh by love might well have waived it as idle and profitless; which, indeed, He did on a similar occasion, when He was asked by certain inquisitive and captious persons, whether they on whom the tower of Siloam fell were sinners above the rest of their brethren; to which question the answer then was : *I tell you, Nay; but except ye repent, ye shall all likewise perish ;*—words plainly intended to direct the speculative faculty of men away from the fruitless inquiry of why evil has happened to others, in order that it may settle fruitfully on the great interest of preventing evil that may happen to themselves. Here we see, in an eminently striking light, the practical character of Christianity set forth in opposition to that seductive itch for expending intellectual strength on insoluble problems, for which the ancient Greeks and the modern Germans have been so distinguished. The persons who put the deepest questions are not always the deepest thinkers; because, if they would only think a little deeper, they might find that the question is one which cannot be answered, and therefore should not be proposed; or, even if it can be answered, the answer is one which could do the questioner in his present position no good, or might even do him harm by distracting his attention from the duty that lies directly before him. Nevertheless, the imaginative tendency in the human mind was not created in vain; men are entitled to ask questions on the most difficult subjects, and to expect an answer to them, so far as the limit of the human faculties allows of the answer being understood. Children are constantly putting questions, to which they will often receive from an intelligent parent a perfectly satisfactory answer; but sometimes the father or the mother will say wisely— *That is a question which I cannot answer just now; the materials which supply the answer are not yet within the scope of your vision or the grasp of your hands; when you are ten years older I will tell you; or perhaps you will have found out the answer for yourself.* Just so with grown persons—who are all children in respect of the Infinite Father—in the domain of religion. God may answer our thoughtful questions about the method of His government of the world, or He may not; but He never does forbid us absolutely to put questions, provided always they are proposed not in a pert and petulant spirit, but with an earnest love of truth, a humble sense of our limited capacities, a loving sympathy with what is beyond, and a sacred reverence for what is above ourselves. It is the spirit that makes the question good or bad, pleasing or displeasing to God; the answer is given according to the capacity, temper, and position of the questioner at the time when the question is put; or it may not be given at all. We are not entitled to have all questions answered, any more than we have a right to fly like eagles, to run like hounds, or to be all eyes like the cherubim.

The questions which an inquiring mind is led to make in reference to the many and complex phenomena of the material and moral world that compose our environment are, when analysed, found to be of three kinds:—First, the question *how*, or through what instrumentality, any phenomenon is produced? Second, By *what* agency, by what force, or power? Third, For what purpose, and with what result or, as we shortly say, *Why?* The two first of these questions, belonging partly to physical science as the science of external phenomena, partly to metaphysical science as the science of unseen, primary, and originating forces, are questions which concern methods of operation, or the doctrine of operating forces generally; the third question is a question of aim, object, and result, or, as Aristotle loved to call it, τέλος, the end or consummation of a thing. This last question is in its very nature always practical, while the other two may be put and answered for the mere gratification of a speculative curiosity. No doubt the knowledge that thunder is caused by the discharge of a subtle and fervid fluid dispersed through the world, of the same nature as that which any man may produce by the friction of certain dry bodies in connection with a certain simple machinery,—this knowledge, I say, may lead to important practical results, as we see in the manufacture of thunder rods, and other wisely calculated safeguards against the action of the electric matter. But this practical application of the knowledge obtained by the answer of the question *How?* is not necessarily connected therewith; stands, in fact, so widely apart from it that the discovery of a method of operation among natural phenomena is often made by one person, and the practical application by another. But the question *For what purpose?* leads directly into the field of action, and comprises accordingly the whole important domain of personal and social morals, of politics, and that most important field of theology, always to be approached with reverence and sacred caution, which is called the theory of the Divine Government. What is the chief end of man? For what purpose do you and I walk the earth? For what purpose did God create the world? Why, above all things, proceeding as it does from so powerful and perfect an intelligence, is it so compassed about with misery everywhere, so blotted with vice, so marred with every sort of irregularity? These, it will be observed, are among the most serious, the most important, and also the most difficult questions that the human mind can propose; and questions which evidently go so deep into the whole scheme of the Divine Government, that if, in reference to some points, an answer were altogether withheld, we should wisely consider it as the most natural thing in the world. What we are entitled to know certainly, created as we are with reasonable faculties, is the object or purpose for which we ourselves exist, the good to which we must direct our steps, the model from which we must take our design. If we have no means of knowing this, we are indeed the most miserable of creatures; and a pig which asks no questions, or a worm which looks up to no stars, will be a much more happy, and in its way a more perfect creature than man. But beyond this sphere of our plain and well-marked life-work, if, in reference to the great complex whole of things, we ask the old question, What is the origin of evil? or, For what purpose does evil exist in the world? we have no right to expect a complete answer —which, indeed, from our point of view, may most probably be impossible; we have no right to expect any answer at all. And yet God, who is always more lavish of His gifts than we are wise to use them, has given an answer to at least one of these questions. In the case of the man born blind the question is answered, not from what cause or by what agency, but for what object and with what result. "Neither hath this man sinned, nor his parents; but *that the works of God might be made manifest in him;*" in other words, that Christ might be glorified before men by removing the blindness; or more generally, *Evil exists that there may be a field for the manifestation of goodness.*" Let us endeavour to throw light on this great principle by showing its application in the wide field of cosmical phenomena and human life; and let us look upon it altogether practically, as the Great Teacher did. Men are the grand instruments whom God uses in the perpetual world-work of transmuting evil into good. This is our highest honour and privilege here,—always to be "fellow-workers with God." Work we must most certainly, in some fashion or other, so long as we live; and working with God as willing tools in His hands is our only guarantee, whether for comfort in our work or for permanency in its issues. To work in any other way is to dash our head against a granite wall, or to spill precious ointment on the ground, of which no man shall be able to give any account.

Let us look, first, at some obvious phenomena of evil in the physical world. What is more common in this land of flood and mountain than a storm? What is more terrible than the sudden black squall coming down from the top of a Highland gully, spreading a frown of savage iron-blue over the shimmering face of the loch, and lashing into a wild race of angry billows its lately placid breast? Contrast with this exhibition of the fierce and savage element in nature the serene beauty with which the purple shoulders of our Highland Bens are often clad for bright weeks together in the month of August or September, and the balmy breath which easy mortals inhale for eight months in the year on the fertile banks of the Nile, or beneath the pillared shadows of the Athenian Acropolis; and you wish that this golden peace of physical nature were eternal, and that no such things as storms and squalls, and whirlwinds and waterspouts, thunder and lightning, and terrible fits of subterranean fever, were known in the world. This is natural. But let us suppose your wish granted, and all the stormy evil which you lament in the outward world instantly and for ever abolished. You will have made a great gain, no doubt. But have you lost nothing by this banishing of the stormy form of evil from the physical world? One thing you certainly have lost—the variety which you at present enjoy in the change of the seasons, the wonderful charm of ever-recurring novelty amid deathless rejuvenescence. Is it possible that unvarying monotony of any kind, even of perfect peace, should be productive of as much happiness as the change of rest and commotion in nature which we now enjoy? Again, let us consider that, though light be the great good of the outer world—pre-eminently, indeed, the good—yet that mere light, without a certain admixture of darkness, could not be productive of those striking effects of variously distributed light in which a great part of the beauty of the world consists. Let us remember that a picture is not possible by mere light. So far, therefore, as the luxury of the eye and the feast of the pictorial imagination are concerned, we may see certainly how that darkness, which is an evil, and one of the greatest, exists with this effect, that the works of light are thereby more effectively manifested. But to recur to the storm :—If there were no storms at sea, there would, of course, be no shipwrecks, but most certainly also there would be no seamanship. Remove storms and currents and sunk reefs—which are the evils which beset the path of the sailor through the briny depths—then skill is no more necessary to navigate the sea; then that grand admixture of adventure and caution and presence of mind which makes the naval hero, would no more be required; and any child who launches a paper boat might do the work of a Cook, a Franklin, and a M'Clintock. If there were not a constant expectation of sudden danger, it seems impossible that the watchfulness, the circumspection, and the promptitude of character necessary for the avoidance of danger should exist. The forms of danger, therefore, that constantly meet us in the external world, whether in the shape of storm or any other unexpected difficulty, though comprising some of the worst forms of evil, plainly exist to render a greater good possible; that is, to form the strength of character which grapples with and overcomes them; and in this way the works of God are made manifest amid the tumult of the tempest and the roar of wild winds, after a fashion which, in the cradled bosom of peace, were utterly impossible.

Let us now cast a glance on the intellectual world. The two great forms of evil here are ignorance and stupidity. How many enlightened statesmen in every part of Europe at the present moment are daily and hourly grappling valiantly with the first of these evils; how many laborious schoolmasters and schoolmistresses and learned professors are lamenting vainly over the second! And not only teachers of youth, and ministers of education and sharp-eyed inspectors, and writers of leading articles and publishers of encyclopædias, but lawyers and doctors and engineers, and all sorts of persons, are engaged in a life-long battle with various forms of ignorance and stupidity. How many law-pleas arise, not from mere selfishness and a desire to overreach, but from the want of clear-headedness and distinct definite ideas about what the parties concerned really meant—from some misty understanding out of which a misunderstanding is sure, on the first convenient opportunity, to emerge, and out of this misuderstanding again, a lawsuit? How much work of all kinds in the world is constantly going on merely to remedy the evils which a want of calculation and foresight in the original designers had caused? A lamentable fact, you will say. Well, I allow it has a lamentable aspect; but if you were to have your pious wish, and to abolish ignorance and stupidity altogether, I rather think it easy to show that you would produce a state of things much more lamentable. Only suppose a world from which ignorance was altogether banished—that is, a world in which everybody knew everything from the moment they were born. In such a world there would be neither teachers nor taught : no teachers where there were none that wanted teaching; no taught where all was already learned. Now only consider what this implies. The pursuit of truth is by universal admission one of the greatest pleasures of which a reasonable soul is capable. The commonest facts in education show this. In school and college it is by no means the mere outward attractiveness of the subject that fixes the fluttering attention of the young student—not the piercing blaze from the oxy-hydrogen blowpipe, or the gay coat of the humming-bird, or the various play of colour in the symmetrical crystal, but it is the pleasure which he feels in hunting out a principle, and ascending from the subject position of the scattered individual fact to the lordship of a general idea; that is to say, that which gives zest to his acquisition of knowledge is the fact that he is working his way out of ignorance. Knowledge, it has been said, is power—that is, when acquired and in the production of a result; but the sense of power is even greater in the acquisition of knowledge than in its application when acquired. James Watt, we may be sure, had more pleasure in inventing the first steam engine than Watt and Bolton had in making the hundreds and thousands of them that came afterwards. Here, therefore, we have the key to the existence of this particular form of evil in the world. Ignorance exists that the works of God may be manifested in the search after truth and the creation of knowledge.

Let us now notice the operation of the same great principle in the moral world—that stage on which all of us must act our parts in that fashion which makes our mortal lives either a harmony or a discord. For assuredly it is not intellect or reason merely in its purely cognitive and speculative form, which makes a man a man and not a monkey—a creature with a certain power of shaping his own destinies and realising his own self-projected ideal. Man is essentially a practical animal; he grows naturally up into a state and a church, and every variety of organised action; and to be practical he must be moral, for practice without morality is only another name for confusion, anarchy, and self-destruction. In this view the German poet sings well—

"*Das Leben ist der Güter höchstes nicht;
Der Ubel grösstes aber ist die Schuld.*"

" The greatest earthly blessing is not LIFE;
But of all human ills the worst is GUILT."

This fearful nature of guilt, its mysterious power of rending, shattering, and ruining the soul, renders us much more prone to be startled and shocked by the existence of moral evil in the world than by the contemplation of those physical and intellectual disturbances which we have just been considering. Nevertheless, it may be shown, as certainly as any demonstration in Euclid, that this most terrible of all evils is not permitted to exist in the world without a distinct view to a higher good. "God hath made all things for himself, even the wicked for the day of his power." So spoke the great Old Testament preacher; and we shall not require to go beyond the most obvious experience of common life to have the observation forced upon us, that not a few of the highest forms of virtue in a world without evil would be simply impossible. Take temperance, for instance. There are persons in the present day who are accustomed to speak as if the only proper way to deal with all sins of excess were to make them impossible, by removing to an impracticable distance, or by altogether annihilating, the stimulants to indulgence. I do not dispute the wisdom of this policy in a special class of cases, where the object proposed is to save weak characters from ruin. But if the object be to form strong characters, it is manifest that to remove the temptation is to destroy the virtue, to make this world no longer a school of noble self-training and manly self-control. If such virtues as moderation and temperance are to exist at all, they can only be found in a world where stimulus is strong and appetite unruly. In such a world God has placed us; and if we would act in happy accordance with that constitution of things which is His will, instead of yielding weakly to every flattering seduction that may approach us, we should rejoice in the offered opportunity of proving that we are men and not beasts, and that, if in other respects certainly inferior, in the habit of resisting strong temptations we are to all appearance superior even to the angels. At least so Seneca, the wisest of Roman moralists, thought, when he uttered his often-quoted sentence, that the successful struggles of a truly virtuous man in this world are often such as the blessed gods, in their shining Olympian seats, must look upon with envy.

Again, let us look for a moment at the highest of all human virtues—*moral courage*, a virtue which is possible only when a sacred passion, a firm will, and a strong reason, combine to give the world assurance of perfect manhood. In what atmosphere, I pray you consider, does this virtue flourish? The very idea of it certainly implies this, that at the time and place when its exercise is called for, the majority of men are wrong: οἱ πολλοὶ κακοί, according to the adage of the old Greek sage—" The majority are bad, or at least weak and cowardly." Plato, in his famous argument about the nature of justice in the Republic, fancies a case in which his pattern just man shall stand alone amid a world of slanderers and persecutors—a world in which he shall not even have the consolation of a single faithful bosom into which to pour the bitter stream of his sorrow for the degradation of the humanity to which he belongs. And he asks, as a testing question, whether justice, in such a world as this, will still be preferable to injustice, and holiness to sin. Such a case, so absolutely shorn of all elements of moral alleviation, has probably never occurred; for a Socrates, when he drinks the hemlock, has generally not only the good witness of his own soul, but the believing tears of a select band of disciples to fling a glory round the darkness of his last hour. But this unquestionably is a fact, that when the first great step is taken in any age of transition, when the whole mechanism of corrupt Church and State requires to be remodelled, the man who takes it must generally do so alone; and those who march to victory on the path which his finger foreshows must often do so over his grave. There are various epochs, not unfrequently repeated in the history of the world, when, if you believe very strongly in God, you are sure, like that very Socrates, to be accused of atheism. There are unhappy epochs when fools and brute beasts and diabolical monsters, or—what for purposes of government is little better—mere lay-figures and inarticulate wooden forms of humanity, are perched with the ensigns of authority upon thrones, while the wise and the good, and the noble and the brave—like the gallant Scottish Covenanters—are hunted over the moors by bloodhounds, and trampled under foot by savage dragoons. In such times whoever dares to be a man is sure to be called a traitor; and, while stars and honours and places of power are lavished on the worthless and unprincipled, the prison and the scaffold and the bare sea rock are the appointed wages of the virtuous. No doubt, when circumstances are favourable, you may come out of such a perilous struggle, like Knox, stamping a whole people with the mould of Christian manliness, or, like Luther, with the cheers of a regenerated world in your ears; but the chances are as great that whosoever meddles boldly with the perilous business of putting new life into the ossified framework of some crazy but long-venerated social organism, will be cut off, like Huss, violently, in the vigour of manly years, with a shirt of flaming pitch about his breast, while his ashes shall be cast into the rolling river to find their way down to the billows of the restless ocean. Here, therefore, in the most distinct language, we read that the greatest virtue in the world is possible only when the world is possessed by a half-stupid, half-diabolical determination to have nothing to do with virtue. The most confounding spectacle in the world—the conspiracy of all the Mights to crush the single little innocent Right—takes place, that the works of God may be manifested in that strength of soul which can defy a world in the single consciousness of rectitude. Never, indeed, does innocence appear more innocent, never does strength appear more strong, than on such occasions. The flames that envelope, but consume not, preserve the manifest witness of the God-protected child; and the little seed which is watered by the martyr's blood grows up into rich luxuriance in places where the common dews of heaven would have been ineffective. Such is the mystery of evil, by divine predestination constantly transmuted into good.

The practical conclusion to be drawn from the consideration of this subject is sufficiently obvious. All speculations about the origin of evil, which end in mere speculation, are idle, and receive no encouragement from the teaching of Christ as it is exhibited in the interesting history from which our text is taken. But the practical purpose which evil serves in this world under Divine superintendence, we are not only permitted, but invited to consider, viz. that the works of God may be manifested in and through men, by every variety of human agency exercised upon every variety of human condition. This, therefore, is our business. If we meet with obstructions in our path—as who does not?—we are not to inquire whence they come, unless that question, when answered, may help us to the practical solution of the only question which properly belongs to us: How may they be removed? We are to rejoice in all difficulties as the grand training-school of a hardy and vigorous manhood. We have to deal with moral impediments when they meet us in the course of life, just as engineers do when they are making a road and find a huge mountain in their way—either tunnel through it or wind round it. If we meet with opposition in our attempts to preach truth, or to do good in our particular sphere, we are not to let our hearts sink forthwith and our hands drop, saying, Nothing can be done; but we must say bravely, as the ancient Romans did, *What are our enemies but fuel to feed the flame of our victories?* If we fall heir to a field which is so thickly beset with thistles and stones that we with difficulty find a free spot for the dropping in of good seed, let us not sit down whimpering for some fat shining paradise in Buckinghamshire or Haddington, but let us rather, in the spirit of our text, remember that, if evil in the shape of thistles and stones were not permitted, the works of God could not be manifested in the farmer's clod-subduing skill, and in the continuous inroads which the cultured land in all well-conditioned countries is taught to make on the waste. Are there many weeds in your garden? This text teaches that weeds are only a luxuriant device of nature to make a good gardener possible. A gardener who should puzzle his brain about the origin of weeds, instead of taxing his muscle to pull them out, would justly be laughed at; but we are all gardeners, each in his several corner of the Lord's vineyard, and we have no right to indulge in fruitless speculation about the origin of what is bad, so long as a single turn of a hoe or a spade can make it in any degree better.

To conclude: I am not averse that young gentlemen at college, and others at their time of life, should try their intellectual strength occasionally by attempting the solution of a metaphysical problem. But the experience of more than fifty years' continuous thinking on the different questions of human origin and destiny has taught me that the principal use of such excercitations is to teach us the very moderate limits within which they can be healthily and innocently indulged. If we do not fall in love with some pretty crotchet of our own, and attribute to it imaginary virtues—as all fathers are fond to do with their own children—we shall not be long of coming to the conviction that action, not

THE UTILISATION OF EVIL.

speculation, is the proper business of men on this earth, and that a man can no more gratify certain longings of the soul with regard to metaphysical truth than he can learn to leap out of his own skin, or drop a candle into the deep dark well whence his brightest thoughts often spring up. Puzzled and perplexed by the baffled attempt at the solution of what, to us, under our present limitations, must ever remain insoluble, we shall be driven into action, as to the only field where intellectual energy, if combined with moral dignity, is sure, under the divine blessing, to produce a double fruitage—the fruit of prosperous growth without and the fruit of pure satisfaction within. Regard this life as a brave soldier does a great campaign, determined to "do or die," and you have the only sure guarantee at once for happiness and victory. And remember that it is not in your power, any more than it is in that of a soldier on the eve of a battle, to alter the conditions under which you act. To run away you will find practically impossible, and to fight feebly is always more dangerous than to close hand-to-hand with the enemy. Life is a serious business, and you must learn to treat it seriously. "Μέγας ὁ ἀγών," says Plato, in an often-quoted and noble sentence of old Greek wisdom, "μέγας ὁ ἀγών ἢ χρηστὸν ἢ κακὸν γενέσθαι." "Noble is the struggle of which the issue is whether a man, in the life which he leads here below, is to be bad or good;" but it would not be noble, if it were not a struggle; and it could not be a struggle, did not such a power as evil exist against which good had to fight a battle and to achieve a victory. This is a great mystery ; but it is also a great fact. Be it our business to deal with this fact wisely ; for upon this depends the great issue whether our human life, under its present conditions, shall be a shameful blunder or a glorious success.

V.

LANDLORDS AND LAND LAWS.

"Woe unto them that join house to house, that lay field to field, till there be no place, that they may be placed alone in the midst of the earth."—Isaiah v. 8.

THERE is no ingredient in what may be called the raw material of society more important than landed property; and no fact connected with this ingredient more important than its well-proportioned and well-balanced distribution through all the classes of which the State, as an organised society of human beings, is composed. How this arises we may readily see; because, before the growth and expansion of manufactures, which are always secondary in the development of the social forces, and in their full blossom deal in much that is superfluous, in all countries the land was the quarry out of which the possibility of existence was evolved; the foundation on which depended both the number and the character of the men that formed the nucleus, and were to remain the bones and sinews, of the body social. The land was the scene on which the great drama of social life was enacted; the root out of which the most necessary element of popular well-being firmly grew; that part of the social organism which was at once most permanent in its character, most firm in its hold, and most vivifying in its associations. If *Pro aris et focis* be the great and most potent battle-cry of all nations, who by virtue of this cry achieved for themselves a place amongst noble and independent peoples, *pro agris* might have been present by implication to complete the triad; for the patriotic passion is robbed of its most powerful feeder when the *family* and the *fireside* are left without their natural adjunct in the *field*. A man with gold in his pocket may prosper anywhere; and a lucrative trade in articles for which there is a large demand may be carried on by the sagacious capitalist in any part of the world; but the possession of landed property makes a man naturally belong to a definite spot; and the facts, and the forces, and the associations of that spot make him feel a home there, and there only, as a bird feels in its nest. It must, therefore, be the aim of every wise State to have as many persons as possible brought up under the influence of this firmest of social bonds, and this most potent of patriotic inspirations; in other words, a well-calculated distribution of landed property among the citizens is, and always must be, one of the principal objects of a wise Government.

This being the case, we shall not be surprised to find that this matter of the wide distribution of landed property among the citizens was one of the principal points on which the legislation of the most notable free peoples of antiquity turned; and the great point kept in view by these legislators seems to have been equality; at least, such a distribution of the landed property—the qualification for citizenship—as would prevent its becoming a monopoly, and, as such, an instrument of oppression, in the hands of a few. Citizens were not to be beggars; and in order to prevent them being such, arrangements must be made to hinder the common soil of the fatherland from being usurped and used for purposes of private aggrandisement by the few. In his account of the foundation of Rome an ancient writer tells us that two jugers of land were allotted to each citizen. Now, though no man who has any critical knowledge of history would accept this statement with regard to these early times as a literal historical fact, it may certainly be taken as representing an almost universal notion entertained by the ancients that, if not an absolute equality, certainly a very free distribution of landed property among the citizens, was an essential condition-precedent of a Constitutional State. Aristotle, accordingly, in his *Politics*[1] (a book which ought to be the *vade mecum* of every practical politician), while he disapproves of certain laws proposed by theoretical speculators in order to create and perpetuate a race of absolutely equal proprietors, has no hesitation in condemning emphatically the later development of the Spartan Constitution, according to which the land had become concentrated in the hands of a few, and the

[1] ii. 9.

many left in landless misery; for this monopoly of the land in the natural course of things led to the depopulation of the country, and the diminution of the number of free and independent Spartans; whereas the State requires not only a large population for public service, but a population as much as possible founded on the distribution of landed property among the citizens. And, besides this, as he states again and again, great inequality in this important adjunct, or rather foundation, of citizenship, is apt to cause discontent, and to set class against class in a constant fret of jealousy, hatred, and strife. Indeed, his opinion on this subject is only the unavoidable application of the great cosmical principle which he was the first to set forth categorically and to illustrate in detail, that *all extremes are wrong*, a principle in every respect well worthy to be sealed for ever with the name of an intellect at once the most comprehensive, the most commanding, and the most practical, that the world has ever known. In obedience to this maxim we may certainly start with the postulate that in all agrarian questions very small properties, and very large properties, as a rule, are equally wrong; and as for equality, we may say yet further, that, at least as conceived by doctrinaire theorists and communists, it is neither desirable nor possible. Not desirable, because monotony and an absolute level of any kind is tiresome and stupid; not possible, because the all-wise and all-wealthy Creator has made luxuriant variety, and not bald uniformity, the key-note, so to speak, of the sublime hymn of his creative energy which we call the world. Plant two seedlings from the same nursery, upon the same hillside, on the same soil, and under influences apparently identical, yet they will not grow up exactly alike; and, if this be the case with two trees, it will be the case much more with two hundred or two thousand trees; with the number planted and the space of ground covered, the chances of variety in size and solidity, in leafy luxuriance and in graceful symmetry, continually increase. Absolute equality among men, as among trees, is a dream. Let us suppose that a new colony is founded by a company of exiles from their native country altogether destitute of capital, having only brain and muscle to subdue to the use of man the rich extent of the uncultivated wilderness. Let it be taken as a just arrangement (though for many reasons it might be both unjust and inexpedient) that the occupied land shall be divided among a hundred colonists equally,—in lots, say, of twelve acres,—it is manifest that if, in order to realise the speculative Paradise of a certain class of doctrinaire thinkers, this arrangement were made by law perpetual, so that none of the original colonists or their descendants could, by any possibility, be left landless in the midst of their landed brethren, the effect of this would be to stifle altogether the impulse to exertion in the hands of the more industrious, and, what is worse, to maintain the idle and worthless upon the soil which they had neither the capacity nor the desire to cultivate. Not that any of the colonists should set his heart absolutely on the acquisition of more territory at the expense of his neighbour, but simply that when his neighbour fails to do his duty to the soil, it is for the public weal that no hindrance should be set in the way of its falling into the hands of the man who knows how to use it. If a man will not work, neither shall he eat. The State can have no interest in keeping a man upon the land with the nominal dignity of a citizen proprietor who lets his lot lie fallow, cherishing a grand growth of rushes, dock, and ragweed, rather than salubrious corn and barley and rye. It is far better that his prudent and industrious neighbour should grow big at his expense than that he should be protected in his indolence, as a cumberer of the ground, and the breeder, belike, of a spawn of children more worthless and more profitless than himself. Let accumulation, therefore, as in other cases, have its natural scope in land. The survival of the stronger in its own province is a very proper law. A wise forester increases the value of his forest by seasonably thinning the trees : no wise statesman will endeavour artificially to prevent the natural thinning process of Nature in society, which she achieves in favour of those who have insight to discern, enterprise to start, and resolution to follow forth, any fruitful scheme that advances by grades of steady growth to the natural climax of a well-merited accumulation.

But accumulation how far? Ay, there's the rub;

for, if accumulation is to go on beyond a certain point, more and ever more, we have Aristotle pulling the rein immediately,—Aristotle, who never errs, and Nature at his back, and the evangelical prophet Isaiah, too, as our text seems most distinctly to assert. We must, therefore, set ourselves to inquire where and how, in the wonderful remedial processes which, through much tribulation occasionally, she is always instituting, Nature has provided some self-acting machinery by which the great evil of land-monopoly in the social state may be prevented. And here, happily, we have not far to seek. When a man dies, his property, by the law of Nature, is either divided among his children, or, as belonging to nobody, it falls to the State; or it may be disposed of in any way that the laws of the State have chosen to mark out. In other words, family claims and laws of succession are the machinery provided by Nature for the redistribution of lawfully accumulated property. But this matter requires to be looked into more narrowly. In the first place, it may be asked, *Is a man, by the law of Nature, entitled to make a testament, so as to have it respected after his death?* Certainly not. The claims of the family to the land of the deceased father no doubt are natural; and a father may, if he please, as in the evangelical parable, give to each of his sons, during his lifetime, the portion that falls to him; but when he is once gone, the stage is clear, and, whatever his wish and preference while alive may have been, the survivors have rights to assert above which the desire of a departed person can have no call to despotise. On the demise of a landowner there may be very valid reasons, both economical and political, why the sons should take the property rather than the daughters, or the eldest son rather than the other sons, or the elder brother rather than any of the sons; in short, in many ways the succession to a landed estate may be so doubtful, and leave room for so many disputes, that it will require an express enactment of the State to vest firmly any property in the act of passing from the dead to the living. Here, therefore, the wisdom or the folly of legislators comes in; and here is the well-head of all the blessing or bane that has followed to society from the legal right of making a testament, and the laws of heritable succession which rule the cases where a testament may not have been made. Nature evidently, by the claims of the children, which arise out of the natural social monad,—the family,—as we have already said,—means distribution; but how that distribution shall be managed she leaves to man, as the natural agency by which she carries out her purposes. Well, it is manifest, as Aristotle also remarks, that the equal distribution of the land, after the death of the owner, if the property be small, tends to beggary; of which examples are easily found beneath our eyes here, in the subdivision of small farms in Ireland and in the Highlands, which has turned certain districts of our country for a season, to use MacCulloch's favourite phrase, into a "rabbit warren." Nature does not desire this; aiming, as she always does, at the best; therefore the State, and the landlords, as her servants, are bound to see to it that the subdivision of very small properties, or small tenancies, shall in no case be allowed; that the eldest son, or some efficient member of the family, according to a regulated scale, shall succeed to the property, and that, as a compensation to the other members of the family who have no share in the land, a proportionate share of its fruits shall be allotted to them as their legitimate portion. Of course this is a matter in which consuetudinary law, parental prudence, and good feeling among the claimants, may, under favourable circumstances, often be much more efficient than any formal legal prescription; but anyhow, the evil of excessive subdivision must be provided against, before the process of Nature for a wise redistribution of large properties, by the death of the proprietor, can be carried out. But, sure provision being made against this perilous relapse into lots too small for the maintenance of a substantial class of small proprietors, the direct object of all wise legislation must be to prevent, not to further, the massing of many properties into one. That the adventurous cultivator should have free scope, during his lifetime, to add field to field in the way of legitimate growth, and also by special grace of the State enjoy the privilege of leaving his accumulations safe in the hands of his family when he dies, is all that a sound policy demands, with the view of giving free sweep to the natural instinct of acquisition. Beyond this, much accumulation tends to evil, and ought to be watched with a jealous eye by the law, whose business it is not to pamper the few but to protect the many. In the general case, therefore, we must say, if we are to carry out the process of redistribution after death, which seems both natural and politic, such a law as the English law of primogeniture is to be condemned. Leaving it perfectly free to any large proprietor to leave his whole landed property to his eldest son by testament,—not, of course, because it is wise in every case, but because testamentary freedom is desirable,—there is no reason why, if he happen to die intestate, the property should not be redistributed fairly among his sons and daughters, for whom any special provision may not have been made. To interfere here were directly to thwart Nature in her beneficial tendencies towards restoring that equipoise of social forces which is constantly being disturbed by the existence of properties spreading beyond the proportions of a manageable magnitude. Much less should any considerations of family pride or aristocratic importance be allowed to forge fetters for the land beyond the term of its natural usage by the proprietor. As free as the original holder received the land to dress it and to improve it, so free ought every successive holder to receive and to use it. Nature, in wishing redistribution, wishes that the partition should be made for the sake of use, not for the sake of possession; and that the use may be fruitful, it must be free. All entails and settlements of land, beyond the actual living progeny of the person who disposes of it, are to be looked upon as invasions of the rights of posterity, and monstrous usurpations by the fancies of the dead over the faculties of the living. To perpetuate a property by entails and settlements in favour of unborn parties is, by a stroke of most unwarrantable intervention, at once to hinder those who possess the land from making a free use of it, and to prevent those from possessing it who could make a wise use of it. Such selfish and unfruitful exclusiveness is directly in the teeth of the grand liberality of competing forces which is everywhere manifest in the constitution of the universe.

But it will be said, no doubt, Why all this zeal against large properties and old families? If it can be shown in fact that large properties, large farms, and old families are the very staple of which English grandeur and prosperity is made up, it will be vain to preach against these things from a mere abstract text, even with Aristotle's great maxim to back it—that *all extremes are wrong*. We have discovered many things since Aristotle's days; and modern States are managed on principles of which the Stagirite, from the narrow range of his old Greek experience, could form no conception. Well, let us examine the action of large properties in detail. I am not a Radical, and can have, assuredly, no prejudice against them, because they are, in this country, a notable adjunct of an aristocracy whom I have every reason personally to love and publicly to respect. It is plain, for one thing, that a large proprietor is possessed of a leverage which can belong to no small one, in the free range of action which is open to him in any course of improvement which may seem expedient. He is an absolute monarch in his own domain; and, if his resources are only equal to his power, he can drain more bogs and plough more waste land in a year, sometimes, than a colony of half-starved dwarf proprietors could do in a century. Of this we have a notable example in the improvements made in the Sutherland property at the commencement of the present century, of which an account was placed before the world by Mr. Commissioner Loch,[1] and in the yet more gigantic operations of the present Duke with the steam plough on his land, whose praise is in all the churches. A similar halo of economic glory enriches the name of the noble family of Bedford, connected as it is with the famous works in the Fen District of East England for redeeming vast tracts of morass from water, and vast tracts of land from the incursions of the sea. The princely house of Torlonia stands wedded in the same way to the drainage of the Lago di Lucino on the Abruzzi side of the Apennines. But it is the special boast of England that, more than any other country with a powerful aristocracy, she can connect the most illustrious names in the blazoned roll of her nobility with the peaceful exploits of agricultural improvement, and the kindly

---

[1] *An Account of the Improvements of the Estates of the Marquis of Stafford in England and Ireland.* By James Loch, Esq. London, 1820.

amenities of the ancestral manor-house and the resident squire.[1] But the large landlord is not only, in his best Avatar, the most liberal in expenditure for agricultural improvement, and the most rapid in the march of economic progress ; he may also, if he chooses, and in this country he generally does, add the charm of luxuriant decoration to the profit of a bald utility with which the small proprietor must perforce have stood contented. It is only the large proprietor who can conceive the idea of what is technically called landscape gardening : even our biggest farmers are mostly Utilitarians ; and a country cut out into thousands of five or ten acred separate allotments, whatever riches it may possess, when well managed in respect of productiveness, certainly never can compete with the large property system in the matter of beauty. And, when we consider with what a large-hearted generosity so many of our great British proprietors open their beautiful grounds, not only to the neighbouring residents, but to the general company of tourists, who are not always innocuous in their traces or gentlemanly in their freedoms, we shall not be disposed to grumble very grimly at the tradition which has kept Dunolly Castle in the hand of the M'Dougalls, or Taymouth in the hand of the Campbells. The remarks here made on the benefits resulting from large properties, with the exception of the æsthetical adjuncts, apply naturally to large farmers, as opposed to

---

[1] See the account of Lord Dufferin's improvements on his Irish estates in Godkin's *Land War in Ireland*, p. 182. London, 1870.

small farmers. The large farmer is a man of some capital; and capital means power; he lives not, like the small farmer, for a subsistence on the soil, or a mere trifle more; but he boasts a liberal profession, to the practice of which he brings all the concentrated action of well-directed labour, and all the subtle appliances of science, and is thus in a condition to draw the greatest material product from the soil with the least proportionate outlay. This process, in which his transforming energy triumphs gloriously over the inform domain of the unfruitful clod, is called "high farming,"—a process, of course, in which the Highland crofter will find it impossible, and the Westphalian peasant proprietor extremely difficult, to be his competitor.

So much for what may be said in favour of what may be called the greatest possible accumulation principle in the matter of landed property,—a principle which, of all countries in Europe, has found its greatest exemplification in Britain, and particularly in Scotland. Nevertheless, Aristotle is not wrong. For, in the first place, we must remark that in all questions of magnitude there are degrees: and what is true and beneficially true of large properties,—that is, properties of a size considerably above the largest of the small,—may not be true of very large properties. There are diseases produced by high feeding similar in type and identical in results with those produced by low feeding; and so it may be, if Aristotle's doctrine of the mean is universally valid, in rural economy. As to the æsthetic part of the business, to take this first, any person who travels the country with his eyes open may observe that men of moderate property,—say with a rental of from £2000 to £4000 a year, or even less,—have done as much to improve the look of the country as mightiest millionaires and thanes with some £20,000 or £50,000. Of this there are various causes. Your very big proprietor, whose domain may stretch from twenty to thirty miles across the country, cannot be everywhere present; he can use personally only a small part of what he possesses; and he may content himself with environing with a special girth of beauty the favoured spot of his own residence, while all the rest of his domain, especially the more remote districts, lie in comparative neglect or rot in utter squalor. Let this not be thought strange. Your lord with £50,000 a year can afford to lose, or not to gain, a thousand or two annually, without notice; but the small proprietor must turn every clod : hence his industry and thrift, and fruitful triumph over adverse circumstances, as in France and Flanders, and many parts of Germany, are not less notable in their way than the steam-plough achievements of his Grace of Sutherland, or the well-registered profits of Mechi and the high farmers. Nay, it is certain that the small peasant proprietors of the Continent, and even the much-abused and often most inhumanly treated Highland crofter, under wise superintendence, will by perseverance and diligence turn a waste into a garden where neither mighty lord nor rich high farmer would condescend to turn a sod. High farmers are like high-bred race-horses; they will not be found dragging dray-carts. To æsthetical decoration of course your peasant proprietor can pay little attention; but even in point of neatness, and a look of substantial comfort, he will often be found outshining the large proprietor in those parts of his domain which do not lie immediately beneath the master's eye. But this is not all, nor the worst. Your large proprietor, even when a good man, and with social sympathies, is by the necessity of his position an enemy to the growth of a numerous and influential local gentry; he needs but one manor-house; and, whatever amenities and utilities are wont to grow out of the manor-house, as a centre of local culture and a nucleus of local prosperity, are found at only one point,—it may be a remote corner of a widely extended district. In the economic distribution of the soil, the families of the gentry scattered through a county are, like the ganglions in the nervous system of the human body, centres of potential local action—little subordinate brains, so to speak—whence the motive and sensitive apparatus of the different organs is supplied. In all such cases, of course, distance from the centre implies feebleness of the conveyed force. As in a large hall, the light of a candle in one corner radiates feebly and more feebly, till in the most distant parts of the room utter darkness prevails, to be prevented only by the introduction of other lights, with establishment of new centres of radiation, so a number of comparatively small proprietors, in respect of what we may call social radiation, act more beneficially than one large proprietor. Take an actual case. The Island of Mull, west of Oban, with which I happen to be intimately acquainted, is possessed at present by some sixteen or seventeen proprietors of considerable importance. Now imagine the whole of this beautiful island to be bought up, or to fall by succession into the hands of any of our great territorial nobility, or any of those cotton, iron, or coal lords who have made their phylacteries so broad in these last days of John Bull's transcendental prosperity,—does any person imagine that the Island of Mull would, in any respect, be the better for this consolidation of many small into one large property? Certainly, in respect of population and society it would be a great deal worse; in respect of produce it would, in all likelihood, not be better; nay, it is quite possible that the big man who bought it might buy it for the express purpose of turning it into a deer-forest; and a very nice deer forest it would no doubt make, thirty-eight miles long by twenty broad, and with the sea all round it, to save the expense of a fence. Nor would this be all. Without exactly turning the whole island into a deer forest, he might do on a large scale, what I much fear has already been done by selfish proprietors on a small scale,—turn all the peasantry out of their rural holdings, that they may settle in the neighbouring boroughs, and save the landlord, by one bold stroke, at once from poachers and poor-rates. All this, according to British notions, British law, and British practice, might be quite correct, and would find advocates, no doubt, in quarterly reviews and daily leaders, sufficiently eloquent, with a whole storehouse of phrases from authoritative books on political economy, to prove that it was all quite right; that every Englishman is entitled to do what he likes with his own; and that Mull,

> " The fairest isle that spreads
> Its bright green mantle to the Celtic Seas,"

has every reason to be congratulated on the change. But social instincts, I imagine, in this instance, and that rude confronter of inexorable logic called common sense, might prevail at once over political economy and the deer-stalking proclivities of our sporting aristocracy. People might begin to say that property in the soil of a country is a somewhat different thing from property at a fireside in a cosy chair, or in a well-buttoned pocket; that in a civilised state of society absolute property, even in movables, may not exist, inasmuch as by taxation, laws of succession, and otherwise, even movables may be forced to pay their tribute to the common good; but that the owners of land are in a peculiar sense the holders of property, not for their own pleasure or profit only, but for the general protection, cherishing, and furtherance of the local population. Landed proprietors in fact, are, in some sense, trustees for the public good; and, as a matter of history, the great lords of the soil received their privileges from the Crown on the condition of certain prestations for the public service; and, though it is quite true that these special services, from changes in the social machinery, are no longer required to be performed, the absolute disposal of large tracts of national property is of a kind which involves too many grave social issues to be tolerated by any wise Government; and the principle remains that a man, for instance, cannot be allowed to fence round Ben Muicduibh exactly as he fences his private garden; or to obstruct the passage from the sources of the Dee in Braemar to the floods of the Spey, as he might close a lane leading from one field of his ancestral manor to another. Landed property, as has been well said, has its duties as well as its rights; but the duties, however obvious, have not seldom been neglected without social discredit; while the rights, however impolitic, have been enforced by legal authority, and sanctioned by that usage of centuries which passes for right with the unthinking.

But I have yet a worse charge to bring against large properties: they necessitate vicarious administration, and readily become the fertile mother of one of the worst of all social sins which a landed proprietor can commit, habitual ABSENTEEISM. If a landlord be, as it appears, a proprietor of a peculiar kind, entrusted with a special sort of property, on which the local prosperity of the country in a great measure depends, it is plain that, as in other cases, the duty of overseership will be best performed by persons who do not live at the end of the world, but rather at home with their eye directly over the district of which they are the guardians. Now, the greater the district, of course, the more difficult, even in this age of ready locomotion, the duty of personal presence and personal inspection, and the stronger will be the temptation—or, may we not rather say, the necessity?—to the proprietor to hand over his overseership wholesale to a resident factor or factors. In this case, while the maxim *Qui facit per alium facit per se* will satisfy all legal claims on the lord of the soil, the conscience of the community may justly think itself entitled to pronounce a verdict not in anywise so favourable to this practical assignation of proprietary duties into the hands of a third party. Government by commissioners and factors is not, and never can be, so considerate, so equitable, and so kindly, as the direct administration of the proprietor. A factor on a large property is, in fact, very often in the position of a trustee on a bankrupt estate; his principal, though not formally bankrupt, wants money, and it is his duty to get it as quickly as possible, no matter how harshly and how unceremoniously. This is the secret of what has taken place to our knowledge not unfrequently in the Highlands; the factor has been guilty of acts of social severity, which were forthwith disallowed by the great proprietor as soon as they came to his knowledge. A good factor,—that is, a kindly and humane-hearted factor,—once said to me that half the bad things that had been done in the Highlands were done by the factors. It can scarcely be otherwise. The factor has not the parental feeling towards the people that belongs to a good resident proprietor; moreover, he has often a great deal more to do than a man can manage conscientiously in detail; so he applies an unbending general law to all cases; and then, like other mortals, anxious to save himself trouble, he is no friend of a numerous population, and prefers, from reasons of personal convenience rather than of public utility, getting £1000 yearly from one big absentee owner, resident perhaps a thousand miles away, to the same sum paid in parts by ten small resident farmers. And thus large estates, large farms, and factorial management have formed together an unholy alliance, by which the absentee lord of the soil has been acquitted of all social duty, and the people who lived under his protection sacrificed, in a manner equally impolitic and inhuman, to the convenience of a practically irresponsible mandatory, the crotchet of a doctrinaire economist, or the greed of an intrusive speculator.

Among the many acts of baseness branding the English character in their blundering pretence of governing Ireland, not the least was the practice of confiscating the land, which, by Brehon law, belonged to the people, and giving it not to honest resident cultivators (which might have been a politic sort of theft), but to cliques of greedy and grasping oligarchs, who did nothing for the country which they had appropriated but suck its blood in the name of rent, and squander its resources, under the name of pleasure, and fashion, and courtliness, in London. Now, this takes place in Scotland also, though not to the same extent. Some of our biggest landholders, thank heaven, are our best landlords, and never more pleased than when they are amongst their own people ; but generally we must say that small proprietors are more likely to be resident proprietors, because they cannot afford to spend eight months of the year in London or Paris ; and it would be in vain to deny that there are large landed proprietors who are seldom seen on their properties except in the shooting season, and who, from their general style of administration, are suspected of being much more anxious to preserve the game than the human population on their estate. These are bad landlords and worthless citizens, and only a shade better sometimes than the unconscientious nobles and the grasping graziers who have, at different epochs and under different circumstances, juggled the Irish people out of their natural inheritance in the soil.

There remains one other count in the indictment, which, in Great Britain particularly, demands to be brought into special prominence : I mean the social, political, and juridical power, which our law, consuetudinary and statutory, has vested in the owners of the soil. In Scotland, not only are the large proprietors, and those who hang by their skirts, absolute lords of districts much larger than many a German principality sometimes, but they are the actual makers of the laws which regulate the relations of the great lords to the small people on the soil ; and the makers of these laws would have been miracles of human virtue indeed, if, under such influences, they had made them otherwise than with a special kindly regard to the interest of their own class. No man, speaking from the platform of common worldly morality, can blame them for this; they are men; they have been entrusted with absolute authority over the lives and properties of thousands of their fellow-men; and being so entrusted, they will surely use it as the instinct of their class directs, and abuse it too; and unless the old Greek adage—οἱ πολλοὶ κακοί—be altogether false, the majority will always be found to have been in favour of the abuse. Nay; has it not been well said that power, pleasure, and pence, are the three baits of the devil? and the greatest of these three is power. Now, I believe, no person, not living in the country and in a dependent position, has the slightest idea of the tyrannical character, and essentially oppressive, or if not positively oppressive, certainly repressive operation of the existing landlord-made laws, under the shield of which our large proprietors of this country legally override the natural rights and equitable social claims of the people under their jurisdiction. Our laws of tenant-right, or rather of no-right, were evidently devised for the express purpose of keeping the class of people who cultivate the soil as much as possible under the thumb and at the mercy of the great man of the district; and the well-known servility with which it is expected that agricultural tenants shall vote with their local lord on political matters—and sometimes on ecclesiastical matters too—is of itself a public proclamation of the great economic truth, that large landed properties, when combined with land laws made by the landlords of these properties, have a direct tendency to crush personal liberty, and to prevent the growth of any sturdy manhood that may come under the upas influence of their monopoly. If the greatest manhood of the greatest possible number be the highest ideal which a wise polity can strive to attain, very large properties and very oligarchic laws are certainly not the best machinery for attaining that object.

Let me now sum up what has just been said in a single proposition. While large properties, under wise administration, certainly possess their own peculiar vantage-ground, which renders them tolerable, enjoyable, and even profitable as a variety, their general influence on the social state of a country is not such that any wise Government should feel justified in giving them encouragement, much less in upholding special laws tending to prevent them breaking down into smaller properties, when, in the course of nature, such a redistribution of property in the soil may normally take place; and, as in other matters, with regard to the distribution of land, all one-sidedness is to be avoided, and that state of possession is to be regarded as normally the best where large, small, and medium properties are found through the country, with a wise regard to the circumstances of the district and the capacities of the cultivator. On this basis I shall now proceed to state, shortly, the duties of landed properties, so far as the size of estates is concerned; and what changes in our British land laws ought to be made, in order to give effect to the principles of natural equity and social position in this matter. Let us suppose—a very common case in this country—one who, by diligent attention to a profitable business, combined with some lucky chances, has some fifty or sixty thousand pounds at his credit in the bank more than he knows what to do with. Being of a cautious temperament, and not liking to cast his anchor in distant waters—eschewing foreign bonds and foreign mines—he buys an estate of a moderate magnitude, yielding a rental of say about £2000 a year. Though, as is well known, landed property yields only a small return for the purchase-money, no person will consider this an unwise investment, being, in the first place, more surely rooted and more permanent than any other, and conveying with it not only certain graceful amenities of rural life, but a social position, a dignity, and an influence which, to most men, is more valuable than any percentage, however high, obtained from floating capital. Well, the man who buys land, buys it, not merely to possess, but to use and to improve it; at least, this is the only natural and legitimate motive for the purchase of land; just as a scholar buys books, not to fill his benches, but to read and to consult. We shall suppose, therefore, that our prosperous trader has retired from business, or holds to it only as a sleeping partner, with the view of possessing land for the purpose of improving it, and of causing blades of grass to grow and blossom of trees to flourish where only waste and barrenness had been before. We shall suppose, further, that the superintendence of this portion of the soil, and his sphere of action as a land improver and the bishop of his people in secular matters, give him full, healthy, and pleasant employment, and then ask what motive may he legitimately have for further acquisition of territory? Not the mere boast of possession, certainly, or the vainglory of being called the lord of many leagues; for this is an illegitimate motive as much in the court of social utility as on the platform of pure reason. But if, on the other hand, the property of an idle or worthless neighbour comes naturally into the market, he is quite entitled to buy that, if he thinks he can superintend it to good purpose, and perhaps, at the same time, round off the corners of his estate, and make a scientific frontier to his domain. To prevent an enlargement of this kind would be to declare war against the instinct of acquisition, which God, for the wisest purposes, has implanted in every human heart, and which cannot be barred off without cramping the energy and limiting the productive powers of the community. A man also may legitimately enlarge his property in order to make a provision for his family—that is to say, he may purchase as much property as, when divided, will suffice for a portion to his sons and daughters; but he is not entitled to add acre to acre and field to field for the purpose of building up his eldest son into the dimensions of a county magnate, and founding, as the phrase goes, a family. This is a vanity, and a peculiarly British one : a vanity not merely empty in its conception, but unjust in its principle and pernicious in its operation ; pernicious in many ways, but specially, so far as concerns our present purpose, in this—that it encourages the growth of enormous properties, and prevents the action of that redistributive process which, as we have seen, Nature wishes for the proper balance and equipoise of landed property in the community. No doubt there may be cases in which it is right and proper that a man's landed property should be left to his eldest son after his death ; the liberty of testing, therefore, in this respect, should remain free. But what we say is,—and the moral law, whether proclaimed by the wise Greek, or the most Evangelical of the inspired Hebrews, imperatively commands us to say it,—that the founding of a family, and the locking up of the land for a succession of generations, is an excess and an abuse, which, like the Scottish thirst for much whisky, or the Turkish lust for many women, does not tend either to the real profit of the individual or the general good of the community. For, to omit all other considerations, it is manifest that a law or practice which at once hampers the worthy possessor of land in the use of it, and props up the unworthy users in the possession of it, claims no countenance and deserves no encouragement on the ground either of public policy or of personal virtue. The two great duties which a landed proprietor has to perform to society are to improve the ground and to cherish the population. If it can be proved that the so-called founding of families, and creation of very large properties in an uninterrupted succession of eldest sons, is favourable to the exercise of those two main functions of a landed aristocracy, let this practice be favoured; if, as I believe, no such proof can be adduced, but rather some pretty strong indications to the contrary, let it be discouraged, and all laws which give artificial support to such unreasonable and unprofitable practices be swept from the Statute Book, without mercy.

From the tenor of the above remarks it will be sufficiently obvious what changes in our land laws are necessary, in order, with the least possible disturbance of existing interests, to restore the lost balance of property in the soil, so necessary to a well-constituted civil polity. In the first place, all laws of entail, and practices of settlement going beyond the life of the direct inheritor, must be disallowed. In the second place, all feudal formulas, or other cumbrous machinery of legal verbalism, making the transfer of landed property difficult, slippery, and expensive, must be abolished, and a public compulsory register established, by means of which it may be possible in England, as in the Colonies, to transfer a lot of land, by a single registered writ of assignation, as easily as a ship. In the third place, while the freedom of testing, which we derive from the law of the Twelve Tables, shall not be interfered with, so as to prevent any proprietor, if he pleases, from bequeathing all his land to an eldest son, at the same time, when a man dies intestate, the presumption of law shall be that he meant his property to be divided equally among his heirs, and such division accordingly shall be made. In the fourth place, a law might be made, that when a landed proprietor marries an heiress, the property that she brings into the connubial estate shall in nowise, after death, go to the same son of the marriage who succeeds to the paternal property, but shall always devolve either to the second son or daughter, or to some other issue of the marriage, as the heiress by testament may direct. In the fifth place, the whole law of landlord and tenant ought to be so revised as to give to the tenant a position as independent as possible in his social relation to the proprietor, and, as far as law can do it, prevent the proprietor from the exercise of the unconditional supremacy which at present may often make him the absolute monarch rather than the limited sovereign of his domain. Of course, before all these changes can be effected, there will be hard work to be gone through, and loud outcry among large classes of people whose ideal of life is sitting on easy chairs and doing as their fathers did before them. But the difficulties, as in many matters of social reform, will consist rather in the want of will to do than in the toughness of the work to be done. Such changes will be opposed, first of all, by the landed proprietors who have been bred on false principles of artificial privilege, selfish monopoly, family vanity, and monstrous accumulation. Fed upon bad food for many generations, the blood of any animal will be poisoned and the race degenerated; and so, from hugging narrow and exclusive notions century after century, with mutual admiration, and no strong signs of public disapprobation, it is no wonder that a class of people should have grown up who believe that the prosperity of the commonwealth depends upon the wideness of the gap which shows itself between themselves and the mass of the community. Closely allied with the landed proprietors are the lawyers, not a few of whom, whether as conveyancers or as factors, contrive to exercise more real power over the estate than the actual owners. In no country are the abuses of the law, specially the laws relating to land, more monstrous and more clamant than in England; and the statesman has yet to make his epiphany who shall gain a more unsullied and more durable reputation by the codification and simplification of the English laws, than can be achieved by a long procession of democratic Reform Bills, or pandering to the sectarian lust of pulling down Established Churches. But neither lawyers nor landlords would have any power to keep entire the vexed tissue of perversities and monstrosities which we call our land laws, were it not for the third great difficulty of the case—viz. the indifference of the great mass of the people. Occupied as they are with fruitful industries in the great towns, and having their whole social energy exhausted in the accumulation of cent per cent returns on mercantile speculations stretching from the rising to the setting sun, they allow the lawyers and the landlords to take their own way in country matters, and play the local despot, or the local fool, as the case may be, with impunity. Besides, the very rich among our urban middle classes not unfrequently become infected with the virus of oligarchic exclusiveness, eager to imagine themselves somebody by walking over some thousands of acres they can call their own ; and this mercantile plutocracy and the aristocracy of birth combine in an unholy alliance to fence off the land in huge untenanted solitudes from distribution amongst the people who could occupy and improve it ; while the poorer class of shopkeepers, artisans, and professional men of various kinds, looking on the land as a thing altogether out of their reach, leave the plutocracy, and the aristocracy, with only an occasional growl, to manage or mismanage it at their pleasure. This I confess to be the great difficulty that besets the path both of land and of law reform in this country. If the great mass of the urban population were as intelligently interested in the reform of the land laws, and of the law, as they are feverishly excited in the political contentions of the hour, there would be a clean sweep of entail laws and long settlements by the first strong ministry that might get into power; and even the encouragement of the growth of a race of peasant proprietors—the favourite butt of contempt in the vulgar English mind—might be looked upon as a most safe and conservative measure of social policy by the wisest men of all parties. For the real fact unquestionably is, that measures tending to a large redistribution of the landed property of this country, now locked up in the hands of a few, though generally looked on as Radical, and somewhat of a Red hue, are in their nature essentially Conservative, and are conceived by all sober thinkers in this country not more in the interest of the landless many than of the landed few. If it be a good thing for the now excluded many to have some real stake, however small, in the soil of the fatherland, and if it be a good and a wise thing for persons of moderate fortune in this country to have the opportunity of investing their savings rather in the safe ground of home soil than in the slippery quicksands of Egyptian bonds and Peruvian mines, it is no less a good and a wise thing that the living aristocracy of this country should not be hampered in the management of their property, by enthralment to the capricious restrictions of the dead, and that the influence of substantial noble families should be increased by two centres of social influence instead of one in the vast district over which their present lordship extends. The wisest thing that many a wide-acred duke or earl in this country could do in the way of increasing his family influence would be to divide his immense property into two halves, keeping the one half to himself as sufficient for all practical purposes, and dividing the other half, as independent properties, among his sons and daughters. The present lack of popularity in some local magnates, of whose excellent character no man doubts, is caused partly by the fact that the magnate is so very mighty, and by virtue of this very mightiness contributes nothing to the social life of the district of which he ought to be the soul. Let our great local thanes rather extend themselves amongst the people as strawberries do along the ground, by throwing out rootlets forthwith to establish themselves as separate plants, and their popularity will become as wide as the wise multiplication of their roots. In this natural system of expansion, I believe, lay the wonderful strength of the Highland chieftains before the commercial system made its cold invasion, substituting money for men in all the glens. The tacksmen in those days were the near kinsmen of the great lord, stout social centres of a numerous lusty population, where an absentee Dumfries farmer now hires a solitary shepherd to watch the browsing of a few melancholy sheep on the braes. And if at any time to take their stand on a monstrous extension of exclusive domain, a legal claim of absolute lordship, and a bristling fence of class privileges, is a most impolitic procedure for a landed aristocracy, it is specially so in this democratic age, and in this country of decidedly popular institutions. In such an age and in such a country, the social isolation of the aristocracy, whether by virtue of land laws, or by any other cause, fraught as it is with frequent occasions of recurrent irritation, has a tendency to alienate the hearts of the people from their natural social lords, and to generate hatred, as Aristotle remarked long ago, betwixt class and class, instead of the mutual love, confidence, and respect, which is the only sure cement of society. Let them, therefore, bethink themselves in time, and concede to the people spontaneously what they may not be able to maintain against them in the long run. But even if they should ultimately succeed in that unhappy policy, by which they have already contrived, in some districts, to rob the British army of its best soldiers, our soil of its most effective labourers, and our country of its most trustworthy citizens, it will be a poor tribute to their memory if a future historian shall sum up their exploits in a curt repetition of the sad sentence of Pliny, LATIFUNDIA PERDIDERE ITALIAM,[1]—Large properties have ruined Britain!

[1] "Modum agri in primis servandum antiqui putavere; verumque confitentibus, latifundia perdidere Italiam, jam vero et provincias."—*Nat. Hist.* xviii. 6.

VI.

THE POLITICS OF CHRISTIANITY.

"Dreamers who despise dominion and speak evil of dignities."
JUDE 8.

THE Reverend Samuel Wehrenfels, Doctor and Professor of Theology in the University of Basle some century and a half ago, and who, in addition to profound theological learning, possessed the happy knack of inditing pleasant and significant epigrams, among others interesting to readers of the Christian Scriptures has this on the Bible—

> *Hic liber est in quo sua quærit dogmata quisque,*
> *Invenit et pariter dogmata quisque sua.*[1]
>
> "The Bible is a wondrous book;
> For men of every kind
> Seek there, and, seeking, find with ease
> The dogma to their mind."

A sentence of most excellent significance, whether taken in the sense meant by the writer, as a reproof to men of his craft who quote the Scriptures with a ready sophistry only to confirm them in their party prejudices,

---
[1] Werenfelsii *Opera:* Lausanne, 1739, vol. ii. p. 509.

or as a compliment to the sacred book, which, like the book of Nature, from its infinite wealth and variety, may seem to favour either party who subjects it to a partial interrogation, because it favours both. How true the couplet of the learned doctor is it requires no very profound knowledge of ecclesiastical and political history to perceive. In affairs of State absolutists like the Anglican doctors of the Restoration, and revolutionary Radicals like Mazzini, have been equally forward to quote the Bible as their warrant, and have both done so with a certain measure of truth, though not without a large qualification of error. In the Christian Churches, as at present constituted, I cannot be very far from the truth when I say that the teaching of the theological professors consists mainly in a systematic course of unconscious sophistry, by which the students are trained to use the Scriptures as a repository of fencing tools to ward away any attacks that may be made on the traditional dogma, popularly accepted as infallible,—a process by which the Catechism unobservedly creeps into the place of the Bible, and the symbolical books of the Church, even in Protestant countries, quietly usurp the throne of the doctrine of which they profess themselves the interpreters. In the present discourse, leaving the theologians to explain away, as they so often do, the obvious meaning of Scripture, that it may subserve the glorification of their creed, I shall confine myself to the use and abuse of the Bible as an inspirer of political motives and a director of political conduct. For either in political, as in all social matters, the divine law of a reasonable and immutable morality must inspire all the impulses and govern all the proceedings of political agents; or in politics man must be considered as descending into an arena of intellectual tigerhood and foxhood, and presenting himself, denuded of all moral motives, as a monster in creation. This theory, no doubt, has been carried out with sanguinary consistency in the practice of not a few politicians, whose names note far-sounded periods of history—as by the Turks in Greece, by the English in Ireland, and by the Episcopising Stuarts in Scotland; but only a few brazen-fronted sophists,—represented by Thrasymachus in Plato's polity, or hard and harsh thinkers, as Hobbes amongst ourselves,—have ventured to present civil polity to the world in a garb of such unveiled and unlovely selfishness. We shall therefore not concern ourselves, as indeed the Bible cannot concern itself, with such ethical monstrosities, and proceed on the postulate that government is only morality applied to great masses of men, and that morality is divine reason and divine love panoplied in action.

More in detail, the postulate of our inquiry runs thus:—Government is the art of regulating and controlling the energies of an aggregate of human beings according to a law of harmony and unity, *i.e.* of making any number of human beings act harmoniously together under a common influence and for a common end, in such fashion that the multiplicity, of which the aggregate is composed, under the abiding action of that influence, and with the constant tendency towards that end, becomes a unity : in other words, it is the business of government, with the view of evoking and regulating the social instincts and tendencies, in the culture of which the chief end of a social being consists, to prevent, by a strong unifying force, that process of severance and disintegration to which the unfettered individualism of the units of an independent aggregate naturally tends. And in order to achieve this unity—by no means an easy affair, as many pages of sweatful and blood-bedraggled history amply show—three things are necessary : common interests to move, common ideas to inspire, and a common authority to control. What, then, is *good* government? Good government is when the individuals composing the social aggregate are so stimulated and so directed and controlled in their action, that each individual puts forth his energies under such conditions that by the natural laws of action and counteraction he achieves both for himself as an individual, and for the community of which he is a member, the most perfect life of which the individual and the community is capable.

Now, observe, this implies that the individual shall be free to put forth his personal energies in such fashion and to such an extent as to make the whole consist of the greatest possible number of healthy, vigorous, and effective units; in other words, good government implies LIBERTY. A government without liberty is not a government of reasonable beings, but, even in its most perfect form,—as in the intellectual absolutism of Plato's polity, or the sacerdotal absolutism of the Papal Church,—a government of a reasonable machine; for it can exist only by annihilating the very moral character of the units which it is instituted to evoke. On the other hand, the idea of good government involves no less essentially that this freedom shall be exercised always under such direction, control, limitation, and restriction, *i.e.* LAW, as the existence of a social organism necessarily implies,—that is to say, the liberty which good government secures implies the sacrifice of that absolute independence which is inconsistent with common action, and the submission to that authority which is necessary to enforce all laws of common action. A good government, therefore, must be a firm government and a strong government; the man who sits in the coach-box must have full command of the whip and the rein as occasion may require; and whosoever would not be the trembling slave of usurping violence, must hire himself as the willing servant of legitimate authority. This is the most important and the most difficult of all practical problems to learn in the social life; for liberty is like wine and like fire; it tends constantly to an excess; it is a word the very sound of which intoxicates the soul of many a hearer,— justly enough, perhaps, if the hearer has lived for long years like a caged bird within the iron restraints of some cruel masterdom. But after all liberty is only the starting-point, not the goal, of a great career of civilisation ; not the enjoyment of an unshackled liberty, but the recognition of a reasonable limitation, makes a man characteristically a man, as the singer sings—

> "The beasts of the forest are free ;
> The wild tornadoes that sweep the sky,
> The tempests that harrow the sea ;
> But man is a thing more divine ;
> With reasoned subjection
> He makes his election,
> And bends with awe
> To sovereign LAW
> And limits that wisely confine."

Let us therefore here, as in all other matters, beware of the extreme of excess on the right hand, as much as of the extreme of defect on the left. All health, all strength, all excellence, all most effective energy, lies in the mean ; and GOOD GOVERNMENT may thus safely be defined as the just balance of natural liberty and reasonable authority in a social organism.

Would we set before our eyes a perfect type of that wonderful action and counteraction of opposite forces to a common end, in which a well-ordered society exists, we shall seek in vain perhaps among constitutions and politics, the works of men ; but in the field of divine workmanship St. Paul has placed vividly before us an ideal, in that which of all things in the world is dearest to each man's self. Hear how he speaks with regard to the unity of the Church, of which each member is subject to the head, and yet rejoices in the liberty wherewith Christ hath set us free :—

" For as the body is one, and hath many members, and all the members of that one body, being many, are one body : so also is Christ. For by one Spirit are we all baptized into one body, whether we be Jews or Gentiles, whether we be bond or free ; and have been all made to drink into one Spirit. For the body is not one member, but many. If the foot shall say, Because I am not the hand, I am not of the body; is it therefore not of the body? And if the ear shall say, Because I am not the eye, I am not of the body; is it therefore not of the body ? If the whole body were an eye, where were the hearing ? If the whole were hearing, where were the smelling ? But now hath God set the members every one of them in the body, as it hath pleased him. And if they were all one member, where were the body ? But now are they many members, yet but one body. And the eye cannot say unto the hand, I have no need of thee : nor again the head to the feet, I have no need of you. Nay, much more those members of the body, which seem to be more feeble, are necessary : and those members of the body, which we think to be less honourable, upon these we bestow more abundant honour ; and our uncomely parts have more abundant comeliness. For our comely parts have no need : but God hath tempered the body together, having given more abundant honour to that part which lacked : that there should be no schism in the body; but that the members should have the same care one for another. And whether one member suffer, all the members suffer with it ; or one member be honoured, all the members rejoice with it."—1 Cor. xii. 12-26.

Here we see plainly that, while each limb of the wonderful organism called the human body must have its proper place and its free action, it claims that place and asserts that freedom always so that no member shall seek to be independent of the other, and that all the members shall constantly perform their part, not for themselves, but as members of the body to which they belong. In other words, the parts exist, as Aristotle teaches, for the sake of the whole, not the whole for the sake of the parts;[1] while the unifying power which controls the whole must so control it as to respect the free untrammelled function of each of the parts.

One observation more and we shall proceed directly to the examination of the Scripture texts and Christian tendencies which bear upon this important subject. As nothing human is perfect, and as a just balance of two antagonistic principles is of all things the most difficult, we must expect to find in history a constant swaying between the two contrary tendencies of which good government is made up. And, in fact, whether we con the pages of old Roman, or of modern British history, whether in the graceful concinnity of Livy, or in the brilliant luxuriance of Macaulay, we find the most interesting and at once the most significant part of the picture made up of the struggles, and more or less successfully achieved balance, of two antagonistic parties. The names by which these parties are known are as various as the diversities of circumstance or the accidents of language may dictate; but the struggle is ever the same.

---

[1] *Politics*, I. 2, πρότερον δὲ τῇ φύσει (*i.e.* in the scheme of Nature, in the divine purpose) πόλις ἢ οἰκία καὶ ἕκαστος ἡμῶν ἐστίν.

Call it a struggle between Power and Subjection, between Absolutism and Liberalism, between the party conservative of the past, and the party prophetic of the future, between patrician and plebeian, between Tory and Whig, between Church and Dissent, between Popery and Protestantism,—under various masks you easily discover the same contrast in the body social, which in the physical body is represented by the bones and the blood, implying the one the other as necessarily as, in St. Paul's illustration, the head requires the hand to carry out its conceptions, and the hand requires the head to have any conception to carry out. If blood be necessary to give the fervour of vitality to the body, bones are no less necessary to impart to it that firmness without which concentrated force and well-impacted blows are impossible. Give the blood unreined swing, and the excited vital force will swell into fever and flame into dissolution; let the bones appropriate more than their share, and a creeping ossification will stiffen the joints and block the valves of that most wonderful of all machines which we call the human body. So in the social world the two parties must exist—the party of motion and the party of stability; ever antagonising each other, and yet never extinguishing. It is not given to either party in the State,—whatever the hot conceit of faction may dream,—like Moses's rod, to eat up the other party. Conservatives and Progressives must tilt against one another with opposing lances, ever resuming the fight with various fortune, but never achieving an absolute victory; for the moment that one dies, the other dies with it; the liberty which both enjoyed lies bleeding on the ground, and despotism walks into the chair.

We are now ready for the great question, What part does Christianity play in this grave drama? How has the bright angel and the messenger of goodwill to men succeeded in controlling forces naturally so wild, and in reconciling contraries naturally so extreme? Or say, rather, How does she plant herself to succeed? What is her attitude, her method, her discipline, her medicaments? For though she has now reigned nearly two thousand years supreme over all peoples and potentates, the number of those who profess her allegiance is no true index to the strength of those who wear the badges of the cause, with a loyal acceptance of what the badge means. Let us see. It is plain, in the first place, that, if Christianity were a vulgar superstition, as some religions are, or are conceived to be, it could have nothing whatever to do with good government, because foolish opinions about the gods, and silly methods of conciliating their favour, have nothing in common with wise administration; but Christianity means morality, and morality growing out of the strongest cement of the social architecture, viz. brotherly LOVE; and this morality, applied to the guidance of life, means wisdom; wisdom being, in fact, truth and love applied to practice. So constituted, the function of Christianity in the political world must simply be to inculcate such truths and to inspire such emotions as in the intercourse of man with man tend to produce that proper balance of liberty and authority in which good government consists. But how?

At the first blush, and in the main, it seems quite certain that the religion of Christ pronounces itself strongly on the side of authority, order, subordination, and obedience to existing law; and this not only relatively in reference to the time and place when it appeared, but absolutely and on grounds springing out of its essential character and predominant tendency, for, to cite the most familiar passages, the Apostles (Rom. xiii. 1-7; 1 Pet. ii. 13-19) give express injunctions with regard to the duty of obedience to the powers that be, without any qualification, and that at a time when some of the laws were unquestionably bad, and some of the Emperors not only bad, but sensual, beastly, devilish, and in every way abominable. To set against this there is not the slightest tincture of sympathy with the language of murmuring, fret, discontent, bitterness, violence, revolt, and insurrection, which is characteristic of our extreme prophets of liberty,—Radicals, Socialists, Nihilists, and such like,—a class of men, accordingly, who show for the most part not only no sympathy with Christianity, but pronounce themselves emphatically against religion in every shape. Of course, no person will suppose that I mean here to identify the so-called Liberal party in our modern political movements with the wild men who think it a virtue to shoot the King of Prussia, blow up the palace of the Czar, or who not very long ago let the fire of Gehenna loose on the magnificent metropolis of France. But what I say is, that the colour and tendency of the New Testament teaching in its main lines is such that the advocates of divine right of kings and absolute obedience of subjects, according to the doctrine of King James VI. in his book on Free Monarchies, would find it much more easy to lay a finger on a score of texts that might seem to favour their doctrine than the apostles of the sacred right of insurrection could find it to produce one. Certainly, from the point of view of order and recognition of existing authority generally, nothing could be stronger than the terms in which St. Jude, in the chapter from which our text is taken, denounces the apostles of extreme and unchastened individualism. They are dreamers, slanderers, murmurers, discontented persons, walking after their own lusts, and with a mouth speaking mighty things, wandering stars, clouds without water, trees without fruit, wild waves of the sea foaming out their own shame. But further,—

The Author of Christianity, when, on several occasions, tempted and provoked to take the part of those who were inclined to rise against the established authorities in Palestine, answered most distinctly and most emphatically,—MY KINGDOM IS NOT OF THIS WORLD, and RENDER UNTO CÆSAR THE THINGS THAT ARE CÆSAR'S, AND UNTO GOD THE THINGS THAT ARE GOD'S. These words point to Christianity as occupying an altogether different field from civil government—a field which makes collision impossible, so long as the religious teacher and the civil magistrate keep each to his own business. Religion furnishes the sources of action : government directs the details. Religion supplies the steam : government manages the engine. Religion embraces the whole range of social action, because no action of moral beings can be made independent of moral motives : government covers only that narrow field of social action which admits of being regulated by prescribed rule and enforced by compulsory penalties. But more than this, it is specially notable that even in so far as Christianity, in certain circumstances, might not be willing to hold itself altogether aloof from political struggles, the virtues which it delights to put forward in the van of its moral scheme,— viz. meekness, gentleness, moderation, humility, and such like,—are not the qualities that go to breed a class of people forward to defy authority, and eager to stir up opposition. Let any man seriously consider the Nine Beatitudes in the Sermon on the Mount, which seem to me to stand significantly in the front of the Gospels, as the ten commandments do on the threshold of the Mosaic legislation, and he will not be able to imagine that any one of them supplies the least possible hint of a stimulant to that spirit of impatience, fretfulness, restlessness, wilfulness, and overbearing individualism of all kinds, which furnishes the natural fuel to Liberalism, and the spur to resistance in any country where an opposition party has been able to establish itself. Rather, taken in their literal sense, and in their main scope, the despised virtues of the Beatitudes, instead of a race of sturdy protestors against existing authorities, would tend to create a nation of Quakers,—a class of most excellent people, gifted with a surplusage of the most sweet-blooded philanthropy, but considerably deficient in the natural instinct of self-assertion, and altogether unfitted for the government of a world which they have, nevertheless, done not a little to improve.

Yet again : Even supposing that Christianity, when largely imbibed, had a tendency to infuse a spirit of opposition to constituted authority, common prudence and a fair amount of sagacity would deter its missionaries from mixing themselves up with what we may call the advanced or opposition or Liberal side of politics, or entering on any course of conduct that would lead it to plant itself in an attitude of direct hostility to the powers that be.

The apostles of a new and a high-toned religion have always enough to do to maintain their ground against natural and unavoidable enemies, without going out of their way to make them. To have intermeddled with revolutionary or democratic politics of any kind, in the state of the world when the Gospel was first promulgated, would have proved to the infant religion absolutely suicidal. And God did not choose fools but men of extraordinary sagacity and common sense to preach his gospel of moral regeneration to a corrupt world. But this is not all. As a political postulate, it is quite certain that authority, stability, and order are more essential to the existence of society than liberty, self-assertion, and individual independence. It is better for men to walk about and transact their business on a sure platform, though not without chinks and crazy planks here and there, than to be tossed about on waves of continual commotion and incalculable change. Christianity declares itself in favour of the more indispensable and the more comfortable alternative.

Lastly, the religion of the Cross, by placing our present earthly life in the position of a preparatory school to a higher state of existence (Philip. iii. 20 ; Col. iii. 1), teaches its disciples at once to bear the actual evils of a bad form of government with greater patience, and to look on the possible blessings supposed to proceed from any other form of government with comparative indifference. The Christian, like the philosopher and the poet, knows better than other men that the best blessings which human association confers can neither be given nor taken away by any form of government that human ingenuity can devise.

So much for the conservative aspect of Christian political ethics. But this is only the obverse of the coin : there is a reverse of course ; and the other face in so significant a coin of the currency of the moral world is not likely to be a blank. In entering upon this part of our inquiry, we must, before all things, beware of confounding — what has been frequently done—the historical accidents of the natural attitude, and, in some points, the necessary position of the Christian Church at its first start, with what we may call its seminal principles and its innate tendencies. In not a few fertile fields of theological discussion, the honest student of Scripture will observe a certain incapacity or unwillingness to discriminate between what is incidentally mentioned as existing in the primitive Church, under the then exceptive circumstances, and what must exist as an element of a Christian Church under all circumstances. The Sandemanians, for instance, who take no hare soup, and the Presbyterians of the Covenanting times, who drew their swords conscientiously on the faith that the constitution of the Genevan Churches was of divine institution, laboured under this error. It was expedient to abstain from blood at a period when the Christian Church was more than half composed of Jews, whose conscientious scruples on indifferent points demanded a kindly consideration from those who, like St. Paul, could assert the full range of evangelic liberty without fear. It was necessary that the early polity of the Church should be democratic, presbyterian, or, in not a few cases entirely what we now call independent, because churches so widely scattered could not, in the nature of things, be subject to any system of organised episcopal supervision. In the same way, it may have been expedient,—nay, rather, as we have just stated, it was absolutely necessary,—that the early Christian Church should, with the most scrupulous care, and a certain holy anxiety, avoid mixing itself up with any social movements that might be interpreted as rebellion, or what our Scottish lawyers in the days of the Stuarts used to call constructive treason, against the authority of the Roman Emperors. But we are not, therefore, to conclude with King James and the Royalist theologians of the Jacobite times, that the Christian Church hurls its ban of excommunication against all and sundry who at any time may have occasion to assert the natural rights of oppressed subjects against the violence of a usurping government, or the corrupting influence of immoral laws. This were to assert that if the Evil One once got himself firmly seated on the throne of the civil magistrate, and used his authority systematically for the propagation of all evil and the uprooting of all good, in this case there is no remedy for poor mortals—at least not from Christians —who are meekly to submit to slavery as to an absolute duty, and rejoice in oppression as a blessed pledge of the restitution of all things some day in heaven. Under the inspiration of a Christian Church holding such principles, no Robert Bruce could have drawn his sword for political freedom at Bannockburn, no Gustavus Adolphus could have worked out the principle of religious toleration by a thirty years' struggle in Germany. But Christianity was not a religion to plant itself in antagonism to the great instincts of natural justice and the dictates of common sense. It was neither Buddhism nor Quakerism, but with all its peaceful tendencies could assert itself, sword in hand, when the sword was, in the circumstances, the one effective instrument to establish a reign of justice upon the earth. Let us see how this appears.

In its method of attacking the human soul, the most characteristic trait in the religion of Christ is its powerful rousing of the personal conscience, and its direct appeal to the moral dignity of the individual,—a feeling which, when once evoked from the lethargic torpor in which it had long lain, acts in its own sphere,—that is, not only in the Church, but in society,—as an active ferment of liberty, within the safe bounds of secular authority and order; and may, so limited, in strong contrast to the one-sided intellectual absolutism of Plato, and the secular absolutism of the ancient Asiatic and African monarchies, justly be regarded as the nurse, in a certain sense, of democratic feeling, the bosom friend of political justice, and the declared enemy of all civil wrong and governmental oppression. In this view the Christian Church must historically be looked on as the cradle of political liberty, a virtue which belongs to it by direct descent from the Hebrew prophets, who were all fervid patriots, staunch assertors of all civil rights, liberties, and obligations, and specially on all occasions the advocates of the poor and oppressed against the rich and the lawless.[1] The contradiction between this aspect of the gospel and the submissive attitude above presented is only apparent. Christianity accepted the absolute government of the Roman

---

[1] See the Old Testament *passim;* and Stanley's *Jewish Church,* vol. i. p. 396.

imperialism just as it accepted slavery; the then basis of society was accepted as the necessary condition of social action, not approved of as an immutable arrangement. Christianity, as a religion not of social regulations, but of moral motives, could lay down no rule about forms of civil government any more than about forms of Church government. As little could it say anything about the social rights of different parties within any established order of civil or ecclesiastical polity. It only said generally, *Let all things be done decently and in order;* and, as a general maxim in ordinary circumstances, Obey the authorities, to whom the maintenance of order belongs. It said, *Honour the king;* but it said also, *Honour all men;* and the king or the magistrate was as much bound to respect the rights of the people as the people were bound to respect the rights of the king. In the same manner, therefore, that slavery was abolished gradually in Christendom, by the good seed of responsible personality bearing its natural fruit in the development of Christian society, so the imperial absolutism of Rome, however unconditionally submitted to by the early Christian Church, might be thrown aside as an effete form of polity, wherever the personal liberty which belonged to each member of a Christian Church had spread its noble contagion so widely through society as to render the continuance of an absolute and irresponsible monarchy inexpedient and impracticable. There was nothing in the essential nature of Christianity, however mild

P

and meek-faced at its start, to prevent its professors from standing up, in times of transition, as the champions of political change, and the ringleaders of an organised opposition to the so-called stationary or conservative politics. Nay more; if we suppose any form of government, say Democracy, or government by mere numerical majorities, to be theoretically the best, —which it can actually be, of course, when in any society the majority is wiser in the art of government than any minority that can be found,—in this case Christianity can not only not object, but it must work strongly towards such a consummation, inasmuch as its own principles in its own sphere are essentially democratic, every member of a Christian Church being equal before God ; and not only so, but because, whether divinely enjoined or not, the constitution of the early Christian Church as a moral association was, in its main features, essentially democratic ; the aristocracy of the Bishops and the monarchy of the Pope, whether expedient or inexpedient in the then social state of Europe, being, in the order of historical fact, unquestionably a posterior development. Nay more; Christianity is not merely democratic in its form and in its action within its own range, but it clothes all and each of its members with such a high moral dignity that the tendency of human nature to bow down before powerful and imposing oligarchies is met by a strongly antagonistic instinct of moral self-assertion ; while at the same time the feeling of equality and the sense of justice which belongs to an ethical brotherhood leads directly to an emphatic protest against those artificial and conventional claims of superiority, on the basis of which certain favoured minorities in the social body delighted to lord it over, and sometimes harshly to oppress, the less favoured majority. Generally, we may say that, as an essentially ethical religion, inspired by LOVE, Christianity must strive after the realisation of a reign of justice upon the earth ; and as such must warmly sympathise, and as occasion offers, energetically co-operate, with all political measures tending to restrain the natural selfishness of parties in the possession of power, and to protect—which, indeed, is a special function of all good government—the weak against the strong. And forasmuch as society at its best is a very imperfect machine, and in need of constant repairs and improvements, Christianity will naturally be on the side of all reforms and improvements which tend to lift the relations of the different classes of society into an atmosphere less dominated by the selfish interests of the privileged few, than is wont to be the case even in the best oligarchies. In opposition to all narrow and selfish policies, it will adopt to the full the famous democratic maxim of Bentham—of which, indeed, Christianity, not Bentham, may be regarded as the proper parent—THE GREATEST HAPPINESS OF THE GREATEST NUMBER, and sing in full chorus with Burns that, whatever significance stars and garters and crosses and high-sounding titles may possess in the outward blazonry of the social organism, always and under the mask of all social forms,

> "The rank is but the guinea stamp,
> The man's the gowd for a' that."

Only one difficulty remains. Some one may say—Well, we grant that Christianity, though presenting historically a quiet and submissive face to all constituted authorities, and slow even to strike the first blow against red-hand usurpers, does nevertheless contain within itself the seeds of a sturdy individualism, which, with time and favouring circumstances, will naturally blossom out into democracy. But is a Christian man, though he may accept democracy when it comes, and even quietly work for it as the ripe fruit of a Church essentially democratic, entitled to take the sword in his hand and violently overturn an existing government—the corner-stone of the existing social order, the key-stone rather of every possible social order? The answer to this is twofold: Whatever rights a man has as a man, he must continue to have as a religious man, unless the religion which he professes expressly interdicts him from the exercise of any human function; as the Mohammedan faith, for instance, prohibits wine, and the Popish religion, with the Essenes and old Egyptian ascetics, forbids marriage in the person at least of its officiating ministers. Now, Christianity does not prohibit self-defence, or the repulsion of force by force as a general law; the fact that our Saviour on a notable occasion forbade the use of the sword is only a fact valid, like so many other facts, for the time, place, and person to whom it refers, and no more near to a general restrictive law than the negation which the wise Minerva in the *Iliad* puts upon the hasty hand of Achilles, when she appears behind him and seizes his yellow hair, and checks his unseemly stroke of violence in the bud. Christianity does not forbid war, any more than it forbids marriage; but it may dissuade from war, as from a perilous, a sorrowful, and an expensive game, whenever it can possibly be avoided, and it may dissuade from marriage as in certain circumstances cumbersome and inexpedient. Wars of wanton aggression and vainglorious conquest,— as in the case of Cæsar's invasion of Britain, or the great Napoleon's overriding of Europe with French sovereignty,—as springing out of pure selfishness, can, of course, find no place in a religion, one of whose most distinctive precepts is to respect your neighbour's rights as you respect your own. But if the use of armed violence in favour of selfish aggrandisement is forbidden, no less is that tame and cowardly temper discouraged which holds out a bribe to every kind of rapacity, and feeds the flame of overbearing insolence. In matters of conscientious conviction, particularly, there is that in the bosom of every Christian, as a member of a higher citizenship, which instinctively revolts against all intrusion by secular force into a properly spiritual domain, and makes him on every such occasion boldly launch forth his sacred protest in the language of the Apostle Peter

(Acts v. 29), WE MUST OBEY GOD RATHER THAN MEN. This right of moral protest was exercised on the grandest scale by the Hebrew prophets, who could walk up fearlessly before the throne of a guilty potentate and say, *Thou art the man!* And though, when his spiritual domain is invaded, a witness of Christian truth may oftentimes judge it wise, for the sake of peace, to retreat from the field and occupy less disputable ground, yet there are occasions on which such a retreat is either morally base or locally impossible. And on such occasions, as when large permanently localised bodies of men are threatened with moral slavery or annihilation by the intrusion of an extraneous force, then of course the alarm bell of revolt may righteously ring, and the sacred right of insurrection be, with all most pious devotedness, asserted. It never can be the duty of any Christian man, whether in civil or religious matters, to allow wrong to riot reinless over the world, and to look on Justice bleeding at the foot of Violence without a stroke.

The conclusion which we have now come to with regard to the political attitude of Christianity is simply this: In its social action the religion of Christ is neither Whig nor Tory, neither Conservative nor Liberal, aristocratic nor democratic, in the common sense in which these words are used as representing antagonistic political forces. But, like the philosophy of Aristotle, it strives always after a golden mean in asserting the proper balance of liberty and authority according to the needs of time and place, and in thus establishing a reign of justice in the social organism, where joint shall work into joint smoothly by the motive power of mutual love and esteem among all classes—always, however, in doubtful cases with a decided leaning towards the party of authority, order, and subordination, rather than to the party of restlessness and discontent, the self-assertiveness which scorns conciliation, and the lust of liberty which frets against the restrictions of necessary law.

The application of the principles of Christian politics to the great questions of national establishments, toleration, Sabbath observance, and such like, where the Church and State, generally moving on distinct lines, are forced for mutual convenience to co-operate, or for mutual annoyance to collide, are of too wide a sweep and too serious a significance to be discussed here. Only two general cautions may wisely be given to all persons who are ambitious to pass a true judgment on the action of Christianity in the political world. The Church must in no wise be confounded with the clergy; nor the social tone of Christianity judged by the temper of parties as it is displayed in the struggles of political partisanship. In some countries, no doubt, as in Rome, it may almost be said that the clergy are the Church; they have assumed to themselves, and by the connivance of centuries have been allowed to assume for themselves, the character of special vessels or conducting wires, through which the vivifying influences of divine grace are distributed to men; and in such cases those free independent spirits, who do not accept the priesthood as the representative and guiding organ in the Church, generally desert the Church altogether, and, as their temper may be, stand to it in an attitude of indifference, or half-sincere acquiescence, or declared hostility. In all Protestant countries, however, the clergy are merely members of a profession, like other professions; and, like members of other professions, they are liable to be seduced into that "idolatry of the tribe" to which Bacon has given so prominent a place in his Temple of Fallacies; and which must in nowise be confounded with the Christian spirit of which the profession in such case is the exaggeration or the caricature. A potent thing, beyond all question, is this professional idolatry, from which no profession that I know is altogether free; and the more a man keeps himself free from it, the more completely does he represent the normal type of manhood, gentlemanship, philosophy, culture, and true religion. Partly this professional type, as a stunted exhibition of the grand human type, arises from the exclusive exercise of functions necessary to the profession, or the exclusive habit of looking at things only from the professional point of view; as when Vulcan, in Homer, has thin shanks, great athletes small brains, and great diplomatists little truthfulness; partly, also, from a pecuniary interest, which the professors of all arts may often have while acting in a direction exactly contrary to the public good; as when lawyers make more money by cumbrous forms of pleading, and prolonged stages of process, when physicians, acting as their own apothecaries, become rich by administering many drugs, and keeping their patients as long as possible under their action, and when professors in universities keep their teaching at as low a level as decency may allow, because there are more students to pay fees for low teaching than for high. Similarly in the church: the shibboleth of an unintelligible creed, which the practice of his ministerial function teaches him constantly to repeat, may become more dear to a man than the most vital principles of gospel morality; and the body on whom an evangelist is dependent for his living and for his social position—whether the State, as in the Established Church, or the congregation, as among dissenters —may easily cause his moral compass to vary by a noticeable aberration from its true pointing towards that star which guided the footsteps of the pious Magi from the East. All these disturbing influences of course must be discounted before saddling Christianity with any exhibition of narrow-mindedness, bitterness, jealousy, ill-temper, or unsanctified utterance in any shape, of which Church courts have not unfrequently been the scene. The attitude of Christianity in all matters of political and social significance is always the attitude of the clergy, less that amount of uncharitableness, bigotry, petty jealousy, spite, dogmatism, insolence, and pride, which the practice of the clerical profession so often induces in its members. Then, again, as to party politics, apart from their accidental connection with Churches, they represent a sort of internal war between antagonistic forces in the social body, and are to be judged from a Christian point of view on the same principles that guided our judgment with regard to war generally. Christianity, as it denounces aggressive conquest and wanton war betwixt nation and nation, so it must nip in the bud all those bitter rivalries, fierce contentions, and fretful struggles between different classes in the body politic, which proceed from a love of power and place, and which form no small part often of what, in modern political language, is called the history of party. The devil, in fact, always and everywhere, has three great baits,—power, pleasure, and pence; and the greatest of these three is power, partly because whosoever possesses this commands the other two, partly because it affords the largest scope, and calls forth the most powerful energies, of the strongest minds. Of course there is a legitimate antagonism of parties within the State, as much as a legitimate antagonism of one State to another; but even when the antagonism which begets parties in the State is natural and salutary, the spirit in which it is conducted is too apt to degenerate into that combination of variance, selfish rivalries, wrath, and strife, and divisions, which St. Paul (Gal. v. 20) enumerates among the works of the flesh. The mere love of power as a motive of action is in its root essentially selfish, and, as such, is condemned as severely by Aristotle and Plato as by St. Peter and St. Paul.[1] And whosoever looks impartially into the elements of social struggle as they are worked up into a chronic ferment by the violence of political parties in a free State, will be bound to confess that, whatever freedom may do for the organism of society, it too often fails either to inspire patriotism or to inculcate moderation. The unscrupulousness of men engaged in a hot political contest, leading to the creation of what are called faggot votes, and other the like questionable devices, is proverbial. In democratic countries, where the struggle for power and place at short intervals is constantly recurring, the moral tone of public men is often so lowered, that persons of independent character and pure heart are forced to withdraw themselves altogether from the service of the State; and the atmosphere which the opposition party, whether Liberal or Conservative, in constitutional governments frequently breathes is so strongly impregnated with bitterness, exaggeration, misrepresentation, and all sorts of unreasonableness, ungenerousness, and uncharitableness, that a man of lofty thought and pure evangelical sentiment must turn from it as from a hot tropical swamp and thick floating tissue of rank vegetation, reeking with malaria and fever. Certainly the daily outflow of our periodical pens that write in the service of party, and whose great principle seems to be that their party is always in the

[1] Hence the bad sense of Φιλοτιμία—literally *love of honour*—which at first sounds so strange in the chapters of the great Greek moralists.

right, and the other party always in the wrong, must be pure gall and bitterness to the man who has sucked the milk of divine love from the Gospel of St. John, and whose heart has grown warm with deep draughts of the mellow wine of human charity, which St. Paul has stored up for all good Christians in the thirteenth chapter of the First Epistle to the Corinthians.

VII.

THE DIGNITY OF LABOUR.

"My Father worketh hitherto, and I work."—JOHN v. 17.

IN this age of multifarious movement, when everything is talked about, discussed, debated, disputed, and denied, some persons have been found curiously to ask the question, "What is the meaning of life?" and others, of a more negative character, have even written discussions with the title, "Is life worth living?" This last question need not be answered; life is certainly not worth living to those who, in all seriousness, propound this question. But the other question may be answered simply by saying that the meaning of life is WORK—reasonable, calculated, vigorous, dexterous, and effective work,—work also which, while complete within its own sphere, at the same time plays concentuously into the great harmony of that miraculous product of divine workmanship which we call the universe. This is the work the contemplation of which filled the soul of the large-hearted Hebrew psalmist with ever-increasing admiration, and made him compare the most glorious factor in the energising drama of creation, the Sun, to a giant that rejoiceth as a strong man to run a race. A similar reverent contemplation of the same great work led those stoutest apostles of the manliest manhood, the Stoics, to declare that the end of man is "contemplari atque imitari mundum," to contemplate and to imitate the universe, to feel the power of the mighty working of God in the grand whole of things, and then to make some feeble approximate imitation of it in our own small sphere, as a burning-glass repeats the sun. And Aristotle, at once the most comprehensive and the most sagacious of all the wise men who, in wise Greece, discoursed on human duty and destiny, assumes, as a matter of course, that the excellence of everything that exists is to be measured by its work (ἔργον), and the virtue of man by his excellence in that kind of work which specially belongs to him as a reasonable soul. Thus the virtue of a dog consists in running well, of a fish in swimming well, of a bird in flying well; and in the case of men, the virtue of a soldier consists in fighting well, of a ploughman in ploughing well, of a ditcher in delving well; a Mazzini shows his patriotic virtue by prophesying well, a Garibaldi by risking well, and a Cavour by managing well; but always, and under every phasis, by some kind of work. There is neither excellence, nor praise, nor virtue, nor any such thing in the universe without work.

The divine workmanship, we have just said, is the world, a piece of work which, in this mechanical country, some persons have been willing to look upon as a manufacture, taking up, literally perhaps, Dr. Paley's well-known simile of a watch; but the Doctor's simile was only a simile, not a proposition, and used by him only for his immediate purpose, and so far only as it applied. He saw reason and calculation and design in the watch and in the world, and he saw with discerning eyes. But the work of God in creation is not a manufacture, but a growth; both are products of reason; the one the product of the secondary human reason, and dead; the other the manifestation of the primary divine reason—the λόγος of St. John—and alive. As like as a portrait by a great master is to the original, so like is a piece of dead machinery made by Arkwright or Watt to the great living machinery of the universe, the perpetual glorious manifestation of the Divine Architect of all things. That grand piece of dead machinery called a steam-engine, with all its cunning, can do no work of any kind without calling in the aid of steam, or water, or some other of the moving forces of the world, which come directly from the primary unexhausted fountain of all motion, and the source of all working power, which we justly call God; but the machinery of the biggest star that wheels or the smallest flower that grows is essentially vital and essentially divine. I have often stood before a steam-engine in wonder at the quiet and easy sway of the ponderous beam which, with no apparent exertion, not so much as a child would require to lift a pebble, sets in motion so many hundreds of whirring looms and so many thousands of busy hands; but there is a divine secret in the living tissue of the universe which makes the biggest work of British engineers or Egyptian temple-builders appear small before the meanest lichen on the crag. These things were made, but this thing grows; these were the product of human reason, this of divine. Wisely, indeed, did Emmanuel Kant, the great German philosopher, say—condensing into a sentence the fourteen verses of the sublime Nineteenth Psalm —"Two things fill me with never-ceasing wonder and with ever-increasing worship, the starry heavens above and the moral law within!" In this moral law we behold the second great field of the divine workmanship, less measurable, no doubt, to our finite faculties, but not less certainly a work of definite object and measurable proportions than the smallest yellow starlet that peeps out from a grassy carpet in the spring, or the lightest feather of a fern that looks forth timidly into day from the hard embrace of the rock. This wonderful work of God in the evolution of the moral law through the long process of the ages is doubtless what the Great Teacher alludes to more particularly in the words of our text, "My Father worketh hitherto, and I work"—that is, in the succession of dispensations, or œconomies, as our theologians have been used to call them, by which man, in the stages of reasonable moral growth called history, is educated up from step to step of social advancement till his greatest possible excellence as the elect organ of God's moral work shall have been achieved. To seek out reverently, and modestly to expatiate on the ages of this great life of God, so to speak, in the soul of society, is a theme the most worthy on which divine philosophy can expend its energies; but this demands the compass of a history like Livy's, or of an epic poem when a greater Milton shall one day arise; so, for our present profit, I shall content myself with setting down in order some of those significant hints which the contemplation of the great process of divine work in the macrocosm supplies to us for the right conduct of our human work, each in his own proper microcosm.

First, then, let us fling overboard the sickly idea—more like the lazy dream of a water-lily at mid-day in a slimy pool than the thought of a human being—the notion that there is any absolute bliss in rest. The world is a working world, and man is a working creature; and he who does not understand this is plainly out of place here. Epicurus, no doubt, sitting in his leafy Attic garden, with fragrant honey-laden breezes from Hymettus fanning him on a summer's day, might fancy his Olympian gods doing nothing through all eternity but drinking nectar, and sipping ambrosia, and laughing at lame Vulcan; but this certainly was not his serious thought; he was merely shunting the Celestials of that day off into a corner, like an easy David Hume, not to be bothered in any wise with what he could not altogether comprehend; and he was busy himself all the while writing books, in which sort of work he

Q

was extremely prolific, having written not less than three hundred volumes in his day. Buddha, likewise, the great Oriental Quietist, if all that is written of his "Nirvana" be true, is the prophet of an extreme kind of stupid holy life, which never can be a model for a healthy Occidental man. Historians and travellers prove most abundantly that at all times and in all places a man is most a man when he has most to do. The savage in a hot tropical climate works little, works violently, and works by starts; our civilisation in this temperate western zone is all built up of a higher potency, a more cunning division, and a more persistent continuity of work. We are all working men, those who work with the brain often a great deal more so than those who work with their hands. Who more assiduous in work than a well-employed barrister? Who more the minister of another man's needs than a skilful country surgeon? Who more hardly worked than a conscientious clergyman in the most populous and least prosperous districts of one of our large towns? Let no man, therefore, sit down and fret over his work because it is work, and envy the rich who have nothing to do. The richest men are often those who have worked, and who do work, the hardest; and if there be rich men, as not a few there are in this country, who live upon the inherited produce of other persons' work, with nothing specially to do for themselves, they are a class of men to be pitied rather than to be envied. Work enough there is for them, no doubt. Plato would not have tolerated them in his well-ordered republic, nor Alexander Severus in his palace ;[1] but they have, unfortunately, no spur for action; and being inspired by no high feeling of the dignity of work in the universe, they will be found too frequently sitting down and rotting their lives away, living on their rents, or filling up the vacuity of their hours with degrading pleasures and unfruitful excitements. For such we must be heartily sorry; and, if they can be of no other use in the world, they may at least teach us not to fret over our daily task, but rather to rejoice in it. The yoke at times may press rather heavily on our necks, but we have always in our hearts the consolation that we are fellow-workers with God in a working world; that we see some fruit of our good work growing up around us daily; and that the great Master of the vineyard could not come down upon us, as he might upon the class of idle gentlemen, saying, "*Pluck them up, for they are cumberers of the ground.*"

How then are we to work, and what are we to do? This is the great question which meets every one on the very threshold of active life; and every one should set himself with all seriousness to find an answer to it. In the best circumstances the answer will find itself; and the best circumstances are when a man of strong character, lofty purpose, and encouraging opportunities, after having had time to look about, consecrates his life

[1] Nec quemquam passus est in palatinis nisi necessarium hominem."
—Lamprid. *Vit. Sever.* 15.

to a single great object, to which his whole nature points, and from which he would sooner die than swerve. An illustrious example of this kind of noblest life-work we have in the well-known German statesman, theologian, and scholar, the late Baron Bunsen,[1] not many years ago Prussian Minister at the English Court. Known to the English reading public principally as an Egyptologist of speculation sometimes more daring than wise, this man, of "kingly and all-ruling spirit," as the poet Schulze calls him, had started on the various and rich career of his noble life with the firm resolution "to bring into his own knowledge and into his own fatherland the language and the spirit of the solemn and distant East;" and from this resolution, whether amid the seductive solicitations of archæological study in Rome, or the distractions of political and social duties in London, he never relaxed, till it ripened into that grand combination of learning, philosophy, piety, and patriotism, the far-famed *Bibelwerk*, or translation and commentary on the Christian Scriptures,—the noblest offering perhaps ever laid by a layman at the foot of the Christian altar. But it is not every one that knows his work in the world so well as Bunsen did, and fewer still who have the strength and the firmness to carry it to a triumphant realisation. In this case a man must be content to turn his hand to what he can get to do; and there is happily an adaptability in human nature, which from the most unfriendly

---

[1] *Life of Bunsen.* 1868. Vol. i. p. 51.

THE DIGNITY OF LABOUR. 229

work will witch a pleasantness, if the witchcraft be plied in right earnest. Occupations, moreover, are like other things; they are not to be judged by their outside; the pleasure and the pain which cleave to them can be known only when they are tried. It is the fault of the man in most cases, and not of the business, if assiduous culture shall not cause sweet flowers to grow in what appeared to him a barren wilderness. Barring the choice of a favourite profession, and the gratification of some delicate fancy, the only rule for a fair start in life is to grasp with a firm hand the task that lies nearest to us, and to work at our cottage garden, or our little strawberry bed, with as much devotedness as if it were a botanic garden of all rarities. No half-purpose ever produced a whole deed; and only a whole deed can produce that complete satisfaction in the act of doing which it is the meed of victorious energy to achieve.

And this brings me to the second great practical rule of all life-work. Whatever you do, do it well; and if you wish to do it well, do it honestly. Let it be true work. Learn to consider what that means, ποιεῖν τὴν ἀλήθειαν, to do the truth, not merely to speak the truth.[1] Many a man does bad work in his trade, who would sooner cut off his right hand than tell a lie. But all bad work is a lie. Why? In two respects: first for the worker, because he is not doing what he pretends to do, or only does it half; second, and more seriously, for those who may

[1] 1 John i. 6.

have to do with his work, in the way of exchange or otherwise. In the first case the worker is an incongruity, a discord, a thing altogether out of place in this world of realities; in the second place he is an impostor and a swindler; for no more reputable epithet may suit the falsity of his pretensions and the hollowness of his productions. You come to weed my garden; and instead of pulling the weeds up by the roots, you content yourself by snipping off their heads. What right have you in this case to your half-crown, or whatever the wage be which I have paid you for your work? Strictly speaking, the wage is not due, because the work is not done; and if your performance is flagrantly and flaringly behind your contract, 'tis like enough you may find a contractor some day who understands his rights, and will teach you to expect nothing in exchange for work that amounts to nothing. But in only too many cases it happens that work insufficiently done is so varnished over with a fair show of sufficiency, that the sin is not discovered till it is too late. That this is a case of gross falsehood and swindle there can be no doubt. But worse than swindle, it may be murder, or to speak more gently, homicide; for how many men may lose honest lives because you put in a dishonest plank on a platform, or a dishonest mast in a ship? If ever there was an age and a country in the world where this doctrine of the truthfulness of labour requires to be preached, it is here in England, at this place and in this hour. Thomas Carlyle now is not the only prophet who, with a cry of grim reproach, setting the mediæval past in the face of the modern present, insists upon telling us that with all our boasted enlightenment, and all our flaunting Liberalism and loudly-trumpeted progress, we are not so very much brighter than "the dark ages" in all respects as we are apt to conceit ourselves. I read in London newspapers sometimes startling revelations to the effect that English wares are not now greedily sought after in all parts of the world as the most substantial wares, as the wares that for an honest price may be relied on to give the most honest piece of work. Our tissues, they say, have no fibre, our masonry no firmness, our steel is not true. So far as these things are said not without cause, it is in vain to talk of the dignity of labour or the social value of the so-called working man. There can be no dignity of labour where there is no truthfulness of work. Dignity does not consist in hollowness and in light-handedness, but in substantiality and in strength. If there be flimsiness and superficiality of all kinds apparent in the work of the present day, more than in that of our forefathers, whence comes it? From eagerness and competition, and the haste to be rich. Hasty work can never be good work; nay, even slow work, done from any less true motive than doing the best work possible, never can be good work. A man of genius no doubt will not seldom dash off a brilliant song or ballad at a heat, as Burns did "Tam O'Shanter;" but that dash was possible only as the bursting of a blossom prepared by long years of moral growth. For the common work of talent in the world, deliberation and calculation and cool survey and the sober advance of unspurred forces are essential conditions; whoso does otherwise must drug his conscience with a posset, sell his intellect for a silver penny, and hand over this fair marshalled world, so far as his work is concerned, to Chaos and old Night and blank nonentity—a consummation in which only Mephistopheles and his minions will rejoice.

Again, whoso would do work that may help him to feel the dignity of labour, must do his work not only vigorously and honestly for the hour, but systematically and persistently for the day, and for the week, and for the year, and while breath remains in his body. The man who plunges into work by random fits has no conception of the permanency of the quiet enjoyment which an active mind may achieve by the continuity of systematic work directed to a noble end. Under such wisely regulated activity the barren desert shall become a Paradise, and the air of the dullest town impregnated with the most lively interest.

No person would go to Kirkcaldy, I presume, in order to achieve a perfectly happy and enjoyable existence. Under the real or imagined dulness of such a small provincial town many a person of mighty conceit would fret his hours away like a caged eagle; but one of the greatest and wisest of Scottish men spent his days for ten years in this little Kirkcaldy, more happy than he had been in the most brilliant circles of rank and fashion in the great French metropolis. This was Adam Smith, who, in a letter to David Hume, written in the year 1767, has left on record these remarkable words:—"My business here is study, in which I have been deeply engaged for about a month past. My amusements are long and solitary walks by the seaside. You may judge how I spend my time. I feel myself, however, extremely happy, comfortable, and contented. I never was, perhaps, more so in my life."[1] Occupation— regular and systematic and persistent occupation—is the one vital magic that gives enjoyment to all existence, the one power that gives permanency to all work and dignity to all labour, and seasons dignity likewise with that pleasantness which is not wont always to follow in its train.

Finally, if your labour is to be with fruit, and your work with permanence, and the putting forth of your strength not without dignity, you must not only be persistent in all you undertake, but moderate; you must not only be without rest, but, according to Goethe's famous motto, at the same time without haste. If you cast your eye round about you on that marvellous action and counteraction of divine forces which we call the world, you will see plainly enough that those forces which exhibit their presence in incalculable outbursts

[1] *Life of Adam Smith.* By Horatio Macculloch. Edinburgh, 1855. Privately printed. P. 20.

of sudden, turbulent, and explosive energy—earthquakes, volcanoes, storms, tornadoes, inundations, conflagrations, and such like—are not plastic powers in any sense, but rather powers of destruction; not creative, vital, and organic, but at best only the preparers of a soil and an atmosphere in which organic vitality may flourish. In contrast with these wild forces, all organic growth is moderate, calculated, noiseless, and scarcely perceptible. There is a thing in these days much talked about which is called LAW. Law is not a force or a power, much less a god; it is only a steady, wisely-moderated method of operation; not a deed, much less the cause of a deed, but only a way of doing; the sure procedure of the self-existent, self-consistent, and self-persistent working Reason which shapes forth the universe; a method of operation to which we willingly pay all reasonable homage, addressing it in the words of the poet—

"Thou dost preserve the stars from wrong,
 And the most ancient heavens through thee are fresh and strong."

And what the omnipresent, ever-working reason of God does in the universe by the calm process of regulated work which we call law, even this thing it is the problem of our human life to achieve, by the formation of what we call character. Character, said Novalis, is a perfectly trained will; and a perfectly trained will is only a well-calculated and a well-regulated working power. The excessive energy put forth to-day, as it is generally the offspring of laziness yesterday, so it is sure to end in languor to-morrow. "My Father worketh hitherto, and I work." But how? Not with much observation and blare of trumpets, but like the seed which swells beneath the soil, with an increase which no eye can measure when it is doing, but all must admire when it is done.

VIII.

THE SCOTTISH COVENANTERS.

> "Others had trial of cruel mockings and scourgings, yea, moreover, of bonds and imprisonment: they were stoned, they were sawn asunder, were tempted, were slain with the sword: they wandered about in sheep-skins and goat-skins; being destitute, afflicted, tormented; (of whom the world was not worthy:) they wandered in deserts, and in mountains, and in dens and caves of the earth."—HEBREWS xi. 36-38.

> "Put not your trust in princes."—PSALM cxlvi. 3.

"HAPPY is the people whose annals are blank," said some one: happy, I should rather say, is the people whose history is full of heroes. The man who expressed that sentiment was thinking no doubt of a certain fashion of chronicles rich in the records of strife, and in whose gaunt columns one year differs from another only in the greater or less atrocity of the battles by which it is signalised; the less of that, of course, in one view the better; it is no pleasant spectacle to behold large communities of rational beings turning themselves periodically into tigers, and devouring one another with fierce greed, and calling it great glory to do so. But this is only the dark side of the picture; war is not always or only a theatre of mere fierceness and ferocity and human tigerhood; it is a school of mettle and of manhood, the nursery of heroism, and the cradle of nationality. Peace is, we all know, a good thing, and a very good thing; so is rest; but as rest is certainly fully enjoyable only after labour, so it may be that the blessings of peace can be reaped largely only by a people who were bred in the school of war. The world is agreed in worshipping heroes; and no hero that we read of, from Theseus and Romulus to Bruce and Wallace and John Knox, was the product of peaceful times; they grew strong in the element of strife; even as the mountain pine that rises in the face of the rough blast is stronger than his brother that adds a gentle grace to the luxuriance of a sheltered garden. Peace can cover the land with portly landlords, astute lawyers, fat farmers, enterprising merchants, and thrifty shopkeepers; but heroes are always the product of struggle and of antagonism—come to the foreground only when there is something to be done that will not be done peacefully; for without resistance to overcome, struggles to make, and victories to achieve, how could they become heroes? We shall not expect, therefore, to find the Scottish Covenanters, of whom we are now to say a few words, made of any softer stuff; they were all warriors; and to them, as trained in the great school of stout struggle for liberty of conscience against a perjured monarch, a pretentious clergy, and a venal ministry, we owe the greater part of that moral inheritance which makes the

Scot a notable type of sturdy manhood and vigorous achievement among the most advanced men of this nineteenth century.

In order that the champions of the right may have a field on which to display their prowess, it is necessary that a great wrong should first be done, and that mighty Nimrods of evil-doing should begin to perform their hunting before the Lord in some notable fashion. The mighty Nimrods of misgovernment who brought the Covenanters on the scene were the Stuarts; and the special Stuart who was destined to bring about this result by a continuous process of force and fraud and sheer brutality, of rare example in history, was Charles II. We must go farther back, by a century, however, before we can get hold of the germ of insolence, self-will, and vain conceit, out of which that crop of bloody blossoms so luxuriantly grew. That a people has a right to have a conscience in matters of religious conviction, and that no civil governor, however absolute he may be in other matters, has a right to impose his personal faith forcibly on an unwilling people, is a proposition that ought never to have been doubted by any European sovereign sitting on a Christian throne. For though man as man, contradistinguished from the brute, always has boasted of his conscience or his point of honour in some sort, it was not till Christianity appeared that a moral association called the Church, springing out of the absolute self-assertion of the individual conscience, planted itself cognisably in the face of the secular power, and publicly disowned all right of State interference or coercion. "My kingdom is not of this world," was the watchword which at once described the character of the new religion, and ensured its progress. The Roman governors generally were too wise to interfere with the assertion of religious convictions, so long as they did not in any way impede the action of the regular machinery of the State;[1] and when ultimately they did sanction systematic persecutions against the rising strength of the sect of the Nazarenes, it was only because Church and State in Greece and Rome were, from the earliest tradition, so intertwined, and radically, indeed, in some of their most important functions so identical, that the profession of a different religion,—at least of a religion so peculiar as Christianity,—necessarily implied an abstention from some of the recognised functions and services of good citizenship. The Cæsars flung the Christians into the jaws of wild beasts not because they were heretical religionists, but because, by their usages, they were bad citizens; the Stuarts gibbeted the Covenanters because they denied the right of a civil sovereign to frame liturgies, and to impose constitutions on a spiritual association. The Roman Nero or Antoninus, who persecuted the Christians because, when serving in the army, they would not perform homage to the statue of the Emperor as to a god, was justified, according to the then notions of policy, in treating the recusant as a rebel;

[1] Acts xviii. 14; xxvi. 31.

the first and second Charles, when they persisted in forcing a hated form of Church government and Church ceremonial down the throat of the Scottish people, were walking altogether out of their proper domain, and usurping a jurisdiction in a matter with which they had as little in common as police regulations have with the propositions of philosophy. That the Scottish people, body and soul of them, from the lowest to the topmost classes, were in the main a Presbyterian people, and that of a very distinct and emphatic type, had been sufficiently declared to all the world by the Act of the General Assembly of the Church, 1560 ; and, had there been wisdom upon the throne in the period intervening between that date and the Revolution Settlement of more than a hundred years afterwards, the whole of that blind tussle of blunders which we call our great civil war would have been spared to history ; but of course we should have lost our heroes also ; and therein lies the comfort. As it was, the Stuarts had conspired, in England in the main, against the political rights of their subjects, and in Scotland more prominently against the rights of conscience : in either case they were traitors, and guilty of high treason against their people, and had no right to complain when they suffered the natural penalties of disownment and decapitation. The loss of a single crowned head, indeed, was a very small matter in comparison of the mountains of misery which, in their foolhardy insolence, they had persistently heaped on hundreds and thousands of the most innocent and the most noble-minded of their subjects. One cannot, indeed, say that they were wicked men, or generally much worse than their neighbours; individually, only one was utterly worthless—Charles II.—and employed the most wicked and unscrupulous men to carry out his purposes; but they started and pushed on the most wicked projects, for which, according to the necessary course of human affairs, they must expect to pay the penalty. A man cannot raise a fire about my ears in my house, and say that he only meant to clear the chimney; he must suffer for fire-raising, whatever the motive was.

It has been written that Charles the First was "the most unfortunate of men." I am willing, for charity's sake, to pass no more severe judgment upon him. That he was perfectly honest and honourable in his intentions, though perhaps somewhat shuffling and unreliable in his manœuvres, I willingly grant; and it is not at all difficult, and not a little instructive, to observe what the sources were from which he got his head infected with that pernicious crotchet of royal absolutism which drove him blindly to his ruin. Even in private a man with a fixed idea in his head is an uncomfortable inmate and an unpleasant acquaintance—what we call a bore; but on a throne, or at the pilot's station in the ship, he is perilous, and under critical circumstances may lead to utter ruin. He does not see the beacon-light ahead, where the hidden reefs are; he sees only the phantom-star in his own conceit, and follows that

R

for a guidance. Poor Charles! he had a sad inheritance of false doctrine to deal with; his father was a fool before him, and that is a great misfortune to anybody, specially to a king. King James was a writer of books,—a much easier matter than the government of human beings,—and in one of the most notable of his discourses, the *True Law of Free Monarchies*, he announces his views as to the absolute right of kings in the exact letter and spirit of the old Roman law with regard to the *patria potestas*. The monarch, as the father of the State family, has an absolute right over his children, but his children are absolutely devoid of all right as respects the father. If the monarch, as the State father, abuses his powers, and becomes a sanguinary tyrant, he is answerable to God; but his children have no remedy, and must content themselves, like the Church in the days of the Roman persecutions, with *preces et lachrymæ*,—prayers and tears.[1] With this milk of autocratic orthodoxy young Charles, the future framer of State-sanctioned liturgies, was doubtless largely nourished. But there was something more potent than that. The Protestant divines of that age, in their rage for Scripture authority for all things, with a certain Bibliolatry, or worship of the letter, of which the operation is even now distinctly visible, were accustomed to quote the whole sacred volume at random, as if it had been a collection of statutes codified into a homogeneous body of divine law; whereas the Bible is really not a book, but a

---

[1] *Works of King James VI. of Scotland.* London, 1616, p. 205.

literature, and contains a law obligatory in its final conclusions, but not in its initiatory and progressive stages. In obedience to this vicious style of hermeneutics we find James in that same treatise,—and no doubt the whole army of prelatic theologians with him, —claiming to himself, as of divine right, whatsoever power, civil or ecclesiastical, was vested by Samuel in Saul at the constitution of the Hebrew monarchy.[1] This was no trivial mistake. As far as Asia is distant from Europe geographically, so far do the fundamental principles of civil government applicable to the East stand apart from those which are the natural growth of the West. The Greeks, who are the earliest and the most illustrious representatives of European as opposed to Asiatic civilisation, were in the spirit of their institutions essentially popular and democratic; so thoroughly, indeed, that Aristotle, in his philosophic review of the forms of civil polity,[2] sets down monarchy —that is, the absolute monarchy of ancient States—as a thing of the past, and fit only for the inferior civilisation of the barbarian East. And most unquestionably here, as in other matters, "the great master of those who know" was right. Monarchy has never led to any great results on European ground, except when tempered by a democratic atmosphere, and limited by popular institutions. This we see plainly enough now, looking back on the great volume of the history of the last two

---

[1] 1 Sam. viii. 10-22.
[2] *Politics*, l. iii. cc. 16, 17. See Congreve's note 17. 18.

thousand years, as it has unrolled itself grandly before us; but however gross the anachronism and the incongruity may appear of an Egyptian, Babylonian, or Palæstinian type of autocracy at Edinburgh or London, as we see it now, there were many things two hundred years ago all over Europe which blinded the eyes of men to so obvious a political difference. The social atmosphere was poisoned by an element derived partly from the precepts of mediæval Popery, tending in all things towards slavish submission, and partly from the maxims of Roman law, which had been built up in times when the power of the emperors assumed Titanic proportions over the ruins of popular liberty all over the world. Rome was the mother and the type of policy to all governors; the emperors at Rome and Constantinople had exercised without question, during the long period which elapsed between the fall of the ancient and the rise of the modern kingdoms, a power almost unlimited in ecclesiastical as well as in civil matters; and what a Trajan and an Antonine, as mighty masters of polity, did in their day for the good government of the whole world, surely Charles in little England, and James in half-savage Scotland, might be allowed to do without blame. And there were modern examples too, and prosperous types apparently, of European autocracy quite close at hand. Louis the XIII. in France, with his great minister Richelieu, had commenced, under apparently the most favourable auspices, that grand experiment of governing one of the most forward States of free Europe on the autocratic principle of *l'Etat c'est moi*, which was destined to attain speedy perfection in the brilliant epiphany of his magnificent son—a principle useful indeed in the early stages of the unification of an ill-compacted aggregate of social units, but in its after stages pernicious, as stunting the growth of the outer limbs and smothering the soul of manhood throughout the whole body of the community. It was the natural ambition of our English sovereigns of the seventeenth century to follow in the same brilliant track of self-aggrandisement; but they had to do with more tough materials; and in the attempt, with the spur of privilege and the bit of raw authority, to ride triumphantly on the back of the stout steed of British liberty, found themselves unhorsed shamefully, and, after a prolonged period of uncomfortable kicking and snorting, were left to die in the mud. The whole history of this ill-starred mimicry of Continental Absolutism it is not my business here to tell. We have only to mention in a preparatory way that James VI., though he held personally the divine right of kings with as fixed a persuasion as any of his most thorough-going successors, had Scottish caution and practical sagacity enough to see that theoretical ideas of the sacrosanct rights of crowned gentlemen on a throne had to be stripped of their pretensions considerably as soon as they were applied to practice; and guided safely by this instinct, he contrived to keep his head on his shoulders, though no doubt plotting secretly in his heart, and in various curiously tentative ways, no less than his unfortunate son, against the liberties of the Scottish Church. Nothing is more safe for a one-sided thinker in practical matters than a little inconsistency. Perfect consistency achieves great things only with great men and on great occasions; in small men, the natural narrowness of sympathy in which it originates is sure to generate an utter incapacity of dealing with the contending claims of antagonistic parties, which, as the natural process of social growth at certain recurrent periods, are sure to come to the foreground. What James said of Laud in this regard is highly interesting. "I keep him back because he hath a restless spirit. Not content with the five articles of order and decency which I had obtained from the Assembly of Perth, he assaulted me again with another ill-fangled platform to make the stubborn kirk stoop more to the English pattern. But I durst not play fast and loose with my soul. *He knows not the stomach of this people.* But I ken the story of my grandmother, who, after she was inveigled to break her promise to some mutineers at Perth, never saw good day after that."[1] Laud certainly, as history shows him, was one of those men of small notions, meagre sympathy, and strong volition, who, when perched misfortunately on high places, are always found driving right ahead to some terrible catastrophe; in theory full of sublime conceptions, but in practice an

---

[1] Hachtel's *Williams*, page 14, in Stanley's *Church of Scotland* London. 1872.

impertinent intermeddler and a stickler for buttons and buttonholes, and a particular cut of sacerdotal millinery, at a time when the cry was for warm clothing at any price, and a ready protection from the cold weather, according to the fashion of the country. With a pedant of such magnitude, who would stake a kingdom for the cut of a Churchman's cope, and goad a whole nation into rebellion by standing out for the proper angle of a genuflexion or the orthodox intonation of an Amen, it was the evil fortune or the innocent unsuspicious choice of poor Charles to be associated, when he entered upon the perilous task of carrying out his father's Episcopising schemes and theories in a more thorough-going way; and with such a comrade at home, a far-reaching Richelieu on the banks of the Seine, and the Pope in Rome, with his army of Jesuits all over Europe, sowing the soil with conspiracies for the recovery of his lost spiritual domination, it required a more cool understanding and a more sound training than a royal Stuart could have in those days, to keep himself free from that intoxication of power which is the besetting sin of the head that wears a crown. The atmosphere everywhere—in France, in Germany, in Italy, and Spain—was either raging with social fever or sowing the seeds for its speedy eruption. Under such lowering clouds of social electricity, England could not hope to escape the contagion; and where the gunpowder that might lead to an explosion in the inflammable stuff of Scotch hearts was largely spread, two such pertinacious and persistent theorists as King

Charles and Priest Laud were just the men to apply the spark.

It does not belong to the drift of the present discourse to give any detailed account of the progress of the great civil war which ran its natural course in England, without any exceptional amount of sanguinary surgery, during the ten years that elapsed from the solemn swearing of the Covenant by the representatives of the Scottish people in 1638, to the judicial decapitation of the royal originator of the fray in 1649. All that our subject requires for the clear understanding of the strictly Covenanting period is distinctly to mark at the outset the starting-point and the issue of the great struggle; and the consequent condition of the hostile parties, at the commencement of the great persecution which was carried on with more or less continuous atrocity from the unhappy epoch of the Restoration in 1660, to the settlement of contending claims by the glorious Revolution of 1688. The solemn swearing of the Covenant in Greyfriars Churchyard on the first day of March 1638,—one of the grandest acts of national self-assertion recorded in history,—was the direct result of the determination displayed by Charles from the moment of his succession to force Episcopacy, with the whole weight of its lordly pretensions and rigid ceremonial, upon the conscience of the people. On his first visit to Scotland in the year 1633, instead of paying respect to the religious convictions and even prejudices of his subjects, which a king is bound to do, he made an offensive display at Holyrood of white rochets and white sleeves and copes of gold, and other articles of sacerdotal frippery, calculated to remind his Presbyterian subjects of Popish mummeries happily cast off, and even of the procession of the priests of Isis on the banks of heathen Nile. This folly took a more serious shape in the summer of 1637, when the monarch, with his pedantic adviser, actually took upon himself to manufacture a prayer-book for the Church, and to make it treason for a pious Presbyterian to pray to God otherwise than in the words of a formula dictated by a clique of semi-Popish priests in London. What might have been expected as the result of such impertinent intermeddling in sacred matters actually took place. The congregation in the High Church on whom this king-made liturgy was pompously imposed rose in revolt; and the perpetrators of such an act of rude insult to the conscience of a godly people were driven shamefully out of their usurped ministrations by a rattling tempest of the stools on which the indignant people had been sitting; and the lady who threw the first stool at the head of the officiating Dean, no matter whether Geddes or Main—the name is of no consequence—became thenceforward a person as notable in the history of Scottish independence as the she-wolf that suckled young Romulus when his watery cradle had been stranded at the base of the Palatine Hill. A popular riot of this kind is a revenge of nature, instantaneously striving to liberate herself from the bonds with which a junto of Lilliputian politicians had assayed to bind her. But the warning was given in vain. Laud was not the man to understand a hint which implied retrogression from the mouth of a volcano, or confession that in any the minutest point of petty ecclesiastical formalism he could possibly have been wrong. He was a perfect type of that class of whom the proverb has been spoken : *Whom God wishes to destroy, him he first makes mad.* The hint was not taken ; and so the riot ripened suddenly to a civil war ; and the rashness with which the priest-ridden monarch had provoked an internecine war with his people was equalled only by the inadequacy of the means at his disposal for carrying it on. His splendid phrases and his cunning shifts were equally in vain against a people who had sworn solemnly not to be juggled out of God's greatest gift to man—a personal conscience. The civil war, on the part of the unhappy monarch, turned out to be, even in England, an affair of attitudinising, without backbone, and ended, as affairs so got up always do, in complete discomfiture. After the bitterness of defeat, and the bursting of all those bubbles of hieratico-monarchical absolutism with which his youthful fancy had been fed, he delivered himself a captive into the hands of his people, and met with the natural fate which his high-handed conspiracy against the civil and religious liberties of the country deserved. It may well be that tears of pity were shed over his fall by the recording angels, but they shed tears also over many thousands of uncrowned traitors. It was a just judgment nevertheless,—whether politic or not in the circumstances is a different question,—unless, indeed, we are prepared to maintain in the face of all conscience that kings have no duties and people no rights; and that, while for the grossest violation of what are commonly esteemed kingly duties, no punishment can follow, the slightest assertion of right on the part of the people incurs the penalty of high treason against the monarch. But this is a doctrine which cannot be preached in the atmosphere of these islands, nor indeed anywhere now, except at Constantinople. In the English Prayer-book, among not a few formulas utterly destitute of any moral significance, Charles I. is called a martyr. This, of course, is the language of pure partisanship. He was a martyr only as the drunkard is to his drink; a martyr to the intoxicating virtue of the Circean cup of absolutism prepared for him by his foolish father, and cunningly mingled with sacerdotal drugs by the arch-pedant Laud; he was a martyr as Alexander the Great was when he became a murderer, and, heated with wine, pierced his dearest friend through the heart with a spear;—only the Macedonian, we read, was afterwards pierced with many a pang of sorrow for his offence: Charles, I fear, never was. He died a martyr in his own conceit, as many a fool has done before him. This pious imagination in the circumstances was his only possible consolation.

The execution of Charles I., though an act of the

most manifest political justice, might, as we have said, have been an act of bad policy; at all events, so far as Scotland was concerned, it was followed by one very bad consequence. The Scotch, though a sturdy and an independent, were a pre-eminently loyal people; they had inherited from a long train of ancestors, what might be called even a superstitious reverence for their kings and the blood royal; so, whether they did or did not approve of the penalty paid in England by the great disturber of the peace for his usurpation of religious rights in Scotland, they could not see their way to a government without a throne, or to a throne without a king's son upon it. With these principles of loyal devotion to the Stuart family, considerations of human pity and human kindness in the breasts of the mass of the people were no doubt largely mingled. The people in general feel much more kindly to their royal masters in misfortune, than their royal masters in prosperity generally feel for them. It seemed a hard thing to disown and disinherit the son because the father had done a foolish thing, and paid for his folly with his life; and this Scottish loyalty and human pity, acting together, brought Charles II. to Scone in the year 1649, and crowned him there the sworn head of a free and a Presbyterian people. Never was the generosity of a noble nation more vilely thrown away than on this crowned reprobate,—a wretch to whom honour was a word without meaning, and with whom the most shamelessly paraded lies were looked on only as stepping-stones to a throne on which he might sit, indulging in any amount of frivolity, baseness, and swinish sensuality on which a diseased imagination might feed. He swore to the Covenant, and accepted the crown from the hands of the acknowledged chief of his Presbyterian subjects, with the reservation in his mind that, on the first convenient occasion, the head of that chief should be demanded as a sacrifice to his father's treasonable schemes, still closely hugged in the bosom of the son; a combination of ingratitude and falsehood happily rare even among that class of men—kings and politicians —in whom the noblest feelings of humanity are most readily frozen in the chill atmosphere of selfish ambition, or strangled in the meshes of a base expediency.

Charles left Scotland very soon, with a crown on his head and a lie in his breast; but he had few friends in England; and a strong man was there, against whom a bolstered-up composition of rottenness and lies like this second Charles could no more stand than an army of straw against a phalanx of flesh and blood. Cromwell was now in the field, and Cromwell was master of the ground. How did this affect our Presbyterians?—just as weakness and division always are affected where decision and unity seize the helm. The death of the king and the pitiful sympathy with treacherous loyalty had split the free people of Scotland into two parties: one more moderate, willing to come to terms with the existing government; the other, though still clinging to the form of kingship, distrustful of royal promises, and determined to stand out more stiffly for the original principles of the Solemn League and Covenant in all their consistency. Moderation and compromise are very good things in peaceful times; but in critical moments of great and perilous antagonism, by sowing divisions, they create weakness and lead to defeat. This is the explanation of the part played by Cromwell in the important decade of years between the decapitation of the traitor father and the restoration of the perjured son. In these times of violent commotion and general confusion, it was necessary that a strong hand should seize the reins and deal with incipient anarchy in somewhat of an arbitrary fashion, till order should be restored. This was Cromwell's mission; and in the year 1653 he drove the General Assembly of the Church out of its session, at point of pike,—a rough procedure, for which the circumstances and the ideas of the age must form his excuse. In the main, as Burton has it, he performed the function of public constable, keeping the peace in Scotland very creditably; only his character as keeper of the peace not having any sentimental halo about it, and not being free from a few sharp memories, tended rather to nourish the smothered flame of loyalty in Scottish hearts than to starve it out. The severe regimen of the Protector unquestionably favoured the growth of that reaction in favour of the exiled Stuarts, which allowed the Scottish nation, at the Restoration in 1660, to throw itself on the faith of a worthless monarch with a facility equally unwarranted by the experience of a very recent past, and the dictates of a reasonable expectation for the future.

The restoration of an overthrown Government or an exiled dynasty is, in the nature of the case, always a reaction, and not only a reaction, but, as human affairs go, generally also a revenge,—the restored party, however guilty in the eye of the impartial spectator, always considering themselves as the injured party, and interpreting the act of restoration to mean a public confession that they had from the beginning been in the right. Nobody, therefore, will be surprised to find that the restoration of Charles II., however from various causes published through the length and breadth of the land with loud bells of rejoicing, was interpreted by the wise and thoughtful to be the knell of some of the most valuable results gained by the struggle of the great patriotic party during the last twenty years. The danger of losing their dearly-bought liberties was peculiarly great in Scotland, remote as it was from the central seat of government, exhausted by the magnitude of a struggle in which it had played a part beyond its natural strength, and weakened yet more by the division in its own ranks, the fruit of its own excessive loyalty. The Scots, however, did not rush altogether blindly into the arms of a monarch who, they had the best reason to know, had, as has recently been said of the Bourbons, forgot nothing in the dark days of his adversity, and learned nothing, and—what was not said of the Bourbons—was ready to swear anything. Accordingly they sent up to London one of the most accredited of their number to negotiate with the restored monarch with regard to the liberties of the Scottish Kirk. This accredited negotiator was the notorious James Sharp, who sold his conscience, his country, and his cause, for an archbishop's mitre, and sits to all eternity in a special niche of the Scottish historical gallery as the manifest type of a TRAITOR.[1] How many murders of sainted men and noble patriots this mitred poltroon was the cause of by this gross act of betrayal of trust we shall see immediately. In the meantime the careless Charles, having shuffled off this disagreeable business from his shoulders, or rather allowed it to be shuffled off by the violent Episcopalian councillors who possessed his ear—for himself was a poor creature of straw, as Macaulay well remarks, equally incapable of great revenge as of small gratitude—proceeded to deal with Scotland in the way that in a few years afterwards he dealt with the glory of the British arms and the honour of the English people. Plunging himself in his palace, into a whirl of frivolities and sensualities, enringed with

---

[1] Burton, by no means a fervid friend of the Covenanters, admits this designation to the full (*Hist. Scot.*, chap. 77). A writer in the *North British Quarterly Review* (vii. 45) says that he was not properly a traitor, but only "a self-seeking man who took the winning side when it was offered to him," flinging his friends overboard at the same time, he ought to have added. The distinction between this and traitor is like the distinction between red heat and white heat—both burn.

a base chorus of buffoons, courtesans, hollow witlings and greedy place-hunters, totally absorbed in that succession of carnal stimulants which men of his kidney call pleasure, he allowed the conduct of Scotch business to drift into the hands of the most worthless, unprincipled, and unscrupulous persons, who showed themselves the most eager to seize the reins. In Scotland, under the then electoral qualification—an inadequate inheritance from the Middle Ages—nothing was more easy than to pack a Parliament, that is, to bring together a conclave of slaves with sounding titles, ready to perpetrate any iniquity or commit any absurdity which a royal nod or a ministerial menace might enjoin. But easy as this was, the Episcopising zealots and recreant time-servers into whose hands Charles had allowed the administration of Scottish affairs to fall, were not content with the concurrence of fair chances in their favour. Some of them knew well "the stomach of this people;" and, though the risk of anything like a national uprising as in 1643 was now very small, nevertheless the renewed attempt to thrust Episcopacy violently down the throats of a Presbyterian people required to be made with all precaution against possible serious consequences. The way to make sure here was by intimidation. First cut off one or two heads of the principal ringleaders, and beneath a bleeding scaffold very few men would be willing to enter as deputy to a Parliament where consistent adherence to patriotic and Presbyterian principles was already proscribed as high treason. The victims selected were, among the laity, the Marquis of Argyll, and among the Churchmen, James Guthrie. These men had committed no crime except that they submitted to the Government of Cromwell when submission was a social necessity, and that they had consistently protested against the usurpation by the civil magistrate of the inalienable rights of conscience, and the sacred functions of the Church. Argyll, as the most prominent name of the patriotic and Presbyterian party from the signing of the National Covenant in the Greyfriars Churchyard downwards, was the first person singled out for a display of royal ingratitude and ministerial perfidy, the best calculated to forewarn the nation of the twenty-seven years of iron oppression and sanguinary atrocity that an unprincipled Government was now preparing for them. Of course a political massacre of this kind would find apologists and laudators among the partisan politicians of the time,—the scutcheon of a restoration is always blazoned on a ground of blood ; but it is strange to see how, even two hundred years after the passions of partizans have cooled down, it is still a favourite fashion, with a certain school of historical writers, to hold up this great man and consistent patriot as a vulgar compound of ambition and cowardice, while, on the other hand, his great opponent, Montrose, is held up as the model of chivalrous sentiment, brilliant soldiership, and self-devoted loyalty. The "master-fiend Argyll" may be a very proper phrase for the background of a historical ballad artistically conceived for the glorification of his brilliant antagonist and unfortunate fellow-martyr; but in plain prose Argyll was simply a man of policy, and a very wise and consistent one; and, what is better, he exercised his practical wisdom in defending the political and ecclesiastical liberties of his country, which Montrose, in his brilliant way, did his best to destroy. The character of a dashing soldier is always popular; but when the dazzling effect of the hour is over, the sober judgment of history must pronounce that it is better in political matters to have policy without sentiment than to have sentiment without sense. The Marquis of Argyll was executed at the Cross of Edinburgh on the 27th day of May 1661, the proto-martyr of the Covenanters, the sop which did not satisfy but only stimulate the sanguinary Cerberus of restored Episcopacy. In the next month followed the clerical victim, James Guthrie, first at Lauder and then at Stirling, one of the far-sighted of Presbyterian prophets, who had seen from the first how hopeless was the expedient to deal in compromise and half measures with such incurable crotchet-mongers, slippery intriguers, and self-willed absolutists as the Stuarts. His high moral worth, of course, was the star on his breast which marked him out as a victim for the band of executioners whom Charles had sent north to butcher his loyal Scottish subjects into a sanguinary submission; and his fidelity to his country and to his Church were the unpardonable offences which the lordly despots of the law construed into high treason.

The treason was all on the other side; and the true character of the bloody exhibition of the wrath of man in this case shines now emphatically forth for all times in the pictured page of the stout bard of the Covenanters.

THE DEATH OF JAMES GUTHRIE.

Slowly, slowly tolls the death-note, at the Cross the scaffold stands :
Freedom, law, and life are playthings where the Tyrant's voice commands :
Found in blood your throne and temple ! foretaste of a glorious reign ;
Though the heavens were hung in sackcloth, let the Witnesses be slain !

'Tis the merriest month of summer, 'tis the sweetest day in June,
And the sun breathes joy in all things, riding at his highest noon ;
Yet a silence, deep and boding, broods on all the city round,
And a fear is on the people, as an earthquake rocked the ground.

Slowly, slowly tolls the death-note, at the Cross the scaffold stands;
And the Guardsmen prance and circle, marshalled in their savage bands ;
And the people swell and gather, heaving darkly like the deep,
When, in fitful gusts, the north winds o'er its troubled bosom sweep.

Now the grim Tolbooth is opened, and the death-procession forms,
With the tinsel pomps of office, with the vain parade of arms ;

Lowly in the midst, and leaning on his staff, in humble guise,
Guthrie comes, the Proto-martyr ! ready for the sacrifice ;
Guthrie comes, the Proto-martyr ! and a stern and stifled groan
Travels through the eager throng ; but patiently he passeth on ;
And the people stand uncovered, and they gaze with streaming
    eyes,
As when of old the fiery chariot rapt Elijah to the skies.

On his staff in meekness leaning, see him bend infirm and
    weak ;
Man in youth, and old in manhood, pale and sunken is his
    cheek ;
And adown his shoulders flowing, locks grown prematurely
    gray,
Yet the spirit, strong in weakness, feels not languor nor decay ;
And a loftiness is on him, such as fits a noble mind,
Like the oak in grandeur rising, howsoever blows the wind ;
On his lips, though blanched with vigils, sits the will to dare
    or die,
And the fires of grace and genius sparkle in his cloudless eye.[1]

The people being now cowed, and all things prepared for the second grand crusade of the Stuart conspirators against the conscience of the Scottish people, execution in sweeping style commenced. The royal commissioner who called the two first Parliaments of Charles II., was John, Earl of Middleton, a soldier more than a statesman, and like not a few of the other more prominent instruments of Episcopalian oppression, an apostate from the Presbyterian faith. But the remarkable thing about this man and his Parliamentary

---

[1] *Lays of the Covenanters.* By James Dodds. Edinburgh, 1880.

fellow-workers was that they had so little regard for common decency and propriety of conduct, that when they were performing the public business they were generally in a state of intoxication, so as to get the accredited name of "The Drunken Parliament." Drunk indeed they certainly were, in a double sense,—drunk with wine to cloud their understandings, and with blood to infuriate their hearts. Their performances were principally three—among the most foolish and ill-advised ordinances of a blind reactionary impulse that ever appeared in a statute-book of men calling themselves civilised. Their first act was the formal restoration of Episcopacy—an act deliberately ignoring the well-known convictions of the Scottish people, and directly calculated to smother every spark of manhood in their bosoms. Then there came what are called the Acts rescissory; that is, Acts declaring null and void all that the best men of the nation had thought, felt, and solemnly declared, from the moment they had got quit of the crowned conspirator and his minions, up to 1662. There is something ludicrously sublime in the wholesale style in which these bibulous statute-mongers went about their work. They must make a *tabula rasa* of all previous rational legislation, before their own untempered folly could parade itself in full livery, before they could be free to play the Episcopal fox, the Episcopal tiger, and the Episcopal fool again, without even the ghost of an old parliamentary paper to trouble their blood-bolted consciences. So far apparently well—

at least from Middleton's point of view. But it is seldom that men who swill the wine of faction largely, and taste the blood of persecution, know when to stop. Middleton was determined to fool it to the top of his bent; so, going to Glasgow, in which region the most zealous Covenanters were wont to congregate, and insisting on the instant literal execution of his despotic decrees against the religion of the people, he found, to his no small astonishment no doubt,—for the men who have no honour in themselves are ever slow to believe its existence in others,—that, instead of violating their consciences by submission to a usurped authority, four hundred honest men were prepared to leave all their worldly emoluments, to sacrifice their social position, and walk out into the wilderness!

And they did walk out—a sight worth seeing, and compensating to our human feeling, in no small degree, for the dismal sequence of blood and blunders which this sad epoch of our history records. Middleton, soon after this hasty provocation of the stout old Scottish stomach, fell into discredit, went abroad, and died soon afterwards in a manner worthy of his exploits, by falling down a stair, drunk. At home the rudder of Scotch affairs was seized by a man of rather more sense, perhaps, but considerably more brutality than himself; and, at the head of an irresponsible Privy Council, and with a chosen band of servile politicians, worldly Churchmen, and rude soldiers at his command, Lauderdale managed to carry on the public business of the country with a reasonable amount of persecution, and without the encumbrance of a Parliament, till more serious symptoms of the eruption of the suppressed disease of Presbytery called for a new exhibition of sanguinary authority. To dispense with Parliament after the Continental fashion inaugurated by Richelieu and Mazarin was always the ideal of the Stuarts; and the man who could dispense with them altogether for a season, or twirl them round his little finger with lies and cajolery, was esteemed the most accomplished statesman.

In the year 1666 occurred the futile insurrectionary movement commonly known as the Pentland Rising. Futile it was, for the present at least, and for a long space afterwards; because it is only in very rare cases that an ill-concerted insurrectionary revolt, suddenly bursting out, produces any other result than only more firmly to rivet the chains of the oppressed. It is not necessary for our purpose to follow out the details of this unpremeditated encounter. Originating in the west country, where the inflammable material of the Presbyterian party was most abundant, it gathered to a point at a spot called Rullion Green on the south slope of the Pentlands, some ten or twelve miles from Edinburgh. Here, as was to have been expected, the hastily-got-up band of self-sacrificing patriots was, notwithstanding a fair display of military courage, with little difficulty scattered and blown to the winds by the power of the Government and the arm of an experienced old soldier whom they employed as a fit instrument for the savage sort of work which their oppressive system demanded. This was Dalziel of Binns, a famous Royalist, and a rough campaigner, who had learned in barbarous combats with Turks and Tartars those arts of atrocious cruelty which he was soon to practise on his own countrymen.[1] He acted the Muscovite, Burnet says, a little too grossly; but this was only in Burnet's estimation: no grossness could be too great for the service of Lauderdale and his accomplices in the shedding of innocent blood. The necessary consequence of the fatal issue of the Pentland rising was the execution of a select lot of the most eminent men of the patriotic party; they had been recusants before, and liable to fines and other petty oppressions; now they were rebels in the eye of that Devil's law which in Scotland at that time had usurped the throne of Justice; and there was no help for it, so long as the Episcopising conspirators sat in the chair where kings faithful to the religion of the people only had a right to sit. Where wolves are both judge and jury, for the poor innocent lambs there could be no hope. The most distinguished victim brought forward at this period to glut the appetite for blood of that infuriate Government, was a young man, dear to all Scotsmen, called HUGH MACKAIL. It is one of the saddest things connected with all insurrectional uprisings against usurped authority, such as the revolt of

---

[1] Dodds's *History of the Covenanters*, chap. iv.

the Milanese against the Austrians, that the noblest and best of the land, the choicest and most select spirits, are most sure to fall the first victims to the revindicated yoke of the oppressor. Young MacKail, when yet fresh from the University, and not more than twenty-two years of age, had preached a sermon in Edinburgh, in which, with the fearless instinct that leads the best young men to harbour no sentiments in their breast which they are afraid to confess with their mouth, he had lamented the then sorrowful estate of the Church of God in Scotland, with a Pharaoh for a king, a Haman at the helm, and a Judas in the Church.[1] From that moment he was a marked man ; and having been drawn from mere local connection accidentally into the Pentland fray, he was suspected of being one of the ringleaders of the insurrection, and, despite of the failure of the boot to extract anything further out of him, by the insatiate bloodthirstiness of Sharp, and other traitors to their old Presbyterian faith, he was condemned to undergo the last penalty of the law, and was accordingly executed on the market cross of Edinburgh on the 22d December 1666. The details of his last hours, preserved in that noble Scottish Plutarch, the *Scots Worthies*, are not to be read without tears, and some of them are signally significant of the fine tissue of the youth's mind,—a mind gentle, liberal, and refined, and altogether in keeping with the grace of his manners and beauty of his person. The last words he spoke at

[1] *Scots Worthies.* By John Howie, of Lochgoin. Edinburgh, 1870.

supper on the evening before his execution, showed his true estimate of the superior value of the moral to the intellectual qualities in all that constitutes the nobility of human nature. "*Notions of knowledge,*" said he, "*without love are of small worth, evanishing in nothing, and very dangerous.*" His last words—words of holy triumph and exultation—on the scaffold, were: "Farewell, father and mother, friends and relations; farewell, the world and all its delights; farewell, meat and drink; farewell, sun, moon, and stars; welcome, God and Father; welcome, sweet Jesus Christ, the Mediator of the New Covenant; welcome, blessed Spirit of grace, and God of all consolation; welcome glory; welcome eternal life; welcome death!"

The Episcopal thirst for blood having been now satiated for a season, Lauderdale, who was not a tiger altogether, but only a coarse compound of a fox and a bear, perhaps not without a hint from above, bethought himself of trying the effect of more moderate counsels. There was, in fact, a change of Ministry in England, of which the chief feature was a public separation of the king from the Anglican, or what we would now call the High Church party, and an adoption of apparently a more conciliating policy towards dissenters, with a view no doubt of favouring the Romanists, to whom Charles and all the Stuarts had a secret predilection. Clarendon, a High Churchman, was discarded; and a new conclave, composed of five such worthless and slippery men as suited the genius of the monarch, stepped into his shoes under the name of the Cabal. Of these five, says Macaulay, only one had the slightest pretensions to be called an honest man, and the worst of the bad was Lauderdale. Worthless as the men were, however, their want of principle in the meantime tended decidedly to relax the strictness of Episcopalian persecution in Scotland. Sharp, the arch-Pharisee of those times, was no longer allowed full swing for his sacred rancour and sacerdotal spite; and men were taken into counsel who even went so far as to call to severe account the blood-stained underlings of the late outrageous persecutions.[1] No stretch of charity, however, can induce the impartial student of those times to attribute to Lauderdale's personal influence any temporary relaxation of the general harshness which characterised his Scottish administration. His future conduct amply testified to the permanence of the inhuman and savage element in his constitution. Out of the same fountain flow not bitter waters and sweet. His portrait, as sketched by the men of the time, presents no redeeming feature but that of a well-stored brain-chamber, hung round, according to the fashion of the age, with all sorts of Greek and Latin and even Hebrew trappings, which indeed saved him from the shame of intellectual nakedness, but could not teach him to think soundly, to act wisely, or even to behave with common decency in a drawing-room. "I knew him very particularly," says Burnet; "he made a very ill appearance: he was very big, his hair red,

---

[1] See the details in Dodds, chap. vi.

hanging oddly about him; his tongue was too big for his mouth, which made him bedew all that he talked to; and his whole manner was rough and boisterous, and very unfit for a court." The hint here given is taken up by Dodds, who, in the pages of his noble vindication of our Covenanting heroes, gives the following full-length portrait of their great persistent persecutor:—" His portrait, though touched up by the refining fingers of Sir Peter Lely, attests to this day the accuracy and the pungency of the traits by which he is described in the political ballads of the time. The low brazen forehead, the loose baggy cheeks, the thick insatiable lips, the satyr's eye, the huge brutish person, bring before us in their combination as gruesome a carle as can well be fancied. He was a man of immense erudition, but not a man of thought, or of any fine natural ability. Buckingham, who was a wit, and had the wit's felicity in hitting off a character, called him a man of a blundering understanding. He was always setting out with a wrong idea, or getting upon a wrong track, or doing even right things in a wrong way. And it was in vain to correct him; this only drove him into further freaks of folly. But it was not his intellectual, it was his moral, or rather, his immoral, qualities which gave him his high place in the confidence of the king, and consequently in the counsels of the nation. As to the utter rottenness of his character, there is not one dissentient voice. Amidst the accumulation of vices charged on his memory we can trace the one single type to which all of them may be reduced—unredeemed selfishness, total want of principle, corruption insatiable as the horse leech with her two daughters crying eternally, *Give, Give!* Even in that age of bold bad men, he was pre-eminently vile. He was swelled out with ambition, not from the grand impulse of a noble mind, not to realise some lofty conception of government, but for the low paltry gratification of being what is styled the *great man* of the country. He sought to conceal his treachery and his cunning under a roaring noisy bluntness. To his inferiors, and even his peers, he was haughty beyond expression; to those above him or who could serve him, an abject loathsome flatterer. His friendships were squared to his interest; his enmities were deep, burning, and unappeasable. His paroxysms of rage were terrific—Satanic—the madness of a foul distempered soul. At first he affected a kind of austerity of manners, and pretended to despise all worldly grandeur; but anon he plunged headlong into the flood of iniquity which set in with the Restoration. His sensuality was that of the sow wallowing in the mire, unaccompanied by any of that refinement which half veils its grossness. He rushed into a course of the wildest extravagance, and would be guilty of any baseness to wring out money for the support of his magnificence. Enriched by the bribes of Louis, a panderer to the lowest vices of Charles, grovelling at the feet of his mistresses and blubbering for their favour, drawing his strength from every species of wickedness,—he turned round and defied all the assaults of those who sought to overthrow him, whether from envy or from patriotism. In the earlier part of his life he seemed under religious convictions, and courted the friendship of such men as Richard Baxter; but after these impressions wore off he was capable of the most awful falsehoods and blasphemous appeals to God, and the favourite exercise of his coarse humour was to pun upon texts of Scripture, and mimic his old doings amongst the Covenanters. For his mess of pottage he sold himself, soul and body, to all the monstrous projects of the Court." [1]

Such is the man who, by a strange freak of fortune, for a moment stands prominent as the introducer of more moderate counsels for the management of the Scottish recusants. In 1669 an Act of Indulgence was put forth, bearing grace and kindness on its front; but it was not the benignity of an angel, but the fair-faced calculation of a fox, from which it proceeded. The indulgence was an act of concession, granting to the Presbyterians a certain limited freedom under royal superintendence; meaning something like this:—I will not throw you into prison, nor confine you on the Bass Rock, nor banish you from the country, nor treat you as a traitor, provided you walk quietly, and do a permitted part of your work within certain prescribed bounds. In other words, I keep you still as my servants, and sworn to my system, but remove certain restrictions so as to

---

[1] *The Scottish Covenanters.* By James Dodds. Edinburgh, 1860. Pp. 191-194.

make your service more easy, and your burden more light. The acceptance of such a concession could be a matter of course only with those who had been half-hearted in the great struggle between the country and the king for liberty of conscience, and who were more concerned for their own personal comfort than for the assertion of a great public principle. To serve in any shape under an Episcopal establishment was to admit the right of the State to dictate in religious matters, and practically to take all virtue from the noble national protest made in the Greyfriars Churchyard by the heads of the people in the year 1638. The men of mark and manhood, accordingly, the leaders and typical men of Scotch nationality at the time, rejected the Indulgence. The measure, however, did not fail of its calculated effect. The effect was twofold: *First*, To cause division in the ranks of the recusants, and by division to introduce weakness; and *Second*, To give a new stimulus to the suppression of what were called conventicles; that is, gatherings of pious people on the hills and in the glens of their native country for the purpose of worshipping their Maker freely in the fashion that commended itself to their consciences as most agreeable to the divine will; for in the mouth of the persecuting party it seemed only reasonable to say, that if greater liberties had been permitted with regard to worshipping within doors, so much the more unreasonable was it to persevere in the rebellious practice of praising God outside. And so, in spite of all the fair grace of this

Episcopalian concession, the royal practice was still continued of scouring the whole country with dragoons, in order to fill the pockets of their unlicensed marauders with fines imposed on persons who refused to worship according to the recognised limitations of royal absolutism. Add to this, that shortly after the granting of the Indulgence by the influence chiefly of the Countess of Dysart, who ruled Lauderdale, the men of moderate counsels who had been associated with him after the affair of Rullion Green were dismissed, and the old system of systematic exhaustion of the severely bled patient resumed in full vigour. Where imprisonment and punishment could not be practised, fines did the work, with scarcely less severity, all over the country. In one small county alone—Renfrew—the fines imposed upon proprietors for various acts of sympathy or connivance with the people in their endeavours to escape the scent of the omnipresent heresy-hunter, amounted to little short of £90,000, according to the present value of money; and the Marquis of Athole, a creature of Lauderdale, who had a gift of certain fines, made by them in one week upwards of £5000.[1] This state of matters was not made better but rather worse by the fall of the Cabal, and the return of the Anglican party to power in the year 1673. Under any ministry Lauderdale knew how to care for himself; and Sharp, for a season in the background, was again in a condition to pursue his old policy against the

[1] Dodds.

faithful of the land—a policy founded literally on the model of St. Paul, before his conversion, when, to use his own words (Acts xxii. 4), he persecuted the Christians "unto the death, binding and delivering into prisons both men and women." Every pious and patriotic Presbyterian man was now put under ban; to harbour such an interdicted person, to give him a morsel of bread when hungry, or a glass of water when thirsty, or a night's shelter from the wintry storm, was a crime which, according to the various hue of its fictitious enormity, might lead to the Tolbooth, to Barbadoes, or to the Bass. Under this system of sucking out the strength and stamping out the manhood of the nation, a state of utter enfeeblement and prostration ensued, which sought to relieve itself—but alas! for the time ineffectually—by desperate plunges of spasmodic revolt. Of these wild plunges the violent death of the arch-traitor Sharp, which took place at Magus Muir, not far from St. Andrews, on the 3d day of May 1679, was the first, and forms a notable turning-point in the further development of this sanguinary drama. With regard to the violent thrusting aside of Sharp, I am sorry to see that even sensible writers at the present day seem to feel themselves bound either to make apologies for the act, or, as their leanings may be, to declare that neither apology nor palliation is possible.[1]

[1] "Surely it may be confidently hoped—let us say it may be at once believed—that at this day, no man sane and intelligent, making himself acquainted with the nature of the deed, would have a word to say in vindication or even in palliation of it."—BURTON.

But a little consideration will convince any impartial thinker that these judgments proceed either from an incapacity of all historical appreciation, or from an amount of prejudice which renders all appreciation impossible. It is the word assassination, I imagine, that is the bugbear here. But assassination is a word that may cover acts as different in character as lust is from love, or superstition from religion. No doubt, in quiet times of regulated life, when the rulers of the world perform their normal functions tolerably well, and know to reign by the one only right of divine wisdom, and to send forth their decrees in conformity with the immutable law of eternal justice (Prov. viii. 15), nothing can be more uncalled for, and few things more reprehensible, than an act of vulgar assassination. Such an act, by taking the law into the hand of the individual, actually abolishes all law, and brings society back into the most savage and unsocial state, when every man for every crime was his own judge and his own avenger, when justice was done, if done at all, in an extravagant and unwarrantable way, not by the cool award of an impartial arbiter, but under the spur of momentary passion or deep-seated rancour; and this too, often under circumstances of secresy and of helplessness, of which an honourable man would scorn to take advantage. The assassin stabs his enemy, defenceless, in the dark and on the back, because he dares not face him by daylight with an open challenge. King David refused to make away with King Saul in the cave, because, had he done so, he would have disgraced his nobility by manifesting the spirit of an assassin and a poltroon. But there are occasions on which the individual may justly take the law into his own hand; and among such occasions may most certainly be numbered those abnormal and monstrous conditions of society, when law is not only the inadequate expression of justice, as frequently will happen with the imperfection of all human arrangements, but when these two regulators of all common action amongst reasonable beings are systematically opposed; when the poles of the moral law are inverted; when the magistrate sits on his seat literally as a terror to good men, and a praise and a protection to those who do evil; and when the existence of government in the country is known to the people principally by a sequence of legalised robberies under the name of confiscations, and a system of legalised murders under the name of treason. In such circumstances every lover of his kind,—every man who has faith in God and in the moral government of the world, in opposition to the crouching and cowardly submission preached by the Stuarts and their priestly satellites,—is bound to maintain the sacred right of insurrection; and in cases where a general insurrection is not possible, a special dealing with a notoriously infamous individual, in the shape of what may be called assassination, may become perfectly justifiable. Sharp was not only a man whose head might at any time, by an impartial jury (had any such then been possible), have justly been held up to public execration, with the phrase, *Behold the head of a traitor!*—but he was a systematic persecutor, a priest who had abused his sacred function to salve the civil oppressor with holy phrases to mask his atrocities; and who had waded knee-deep, for nearly a generation, in the blood of Scotland's most heroic and most sainted sons. How it should be accounted a crime to give such a man a taste of the bloody justice which he had dealt so plentifully to others, I find it difficult to understand. Law and legality are not words which possess any virtue to hide from me the radical instincts and the inalienable rights of nature,—rights which these specious names have so often served to overlay and to smother for a season. There is no iniquity of the most outrageous kind, as the pages of history largely declare, which has not been perpetrated under the fair name and with the authority of law. When, therefore, the moral life of a nation has been cramped, and its breathing stifled, by a tissue of those artificial sanctions to villany which a conclave of robbers and conspirators call laws, Nature, who will not allow herself to be choked or stamped out by any conclaves, however pretentious, bursts these invasive fetters some fine morning volcanically, where she can best find vent; and the eruption may be in the form of what smooth and respectable people, living in quiet times, shudder at, and call ASSASSINATION. It is another question, of course, whether either a popular insurrection against a tyrannical government, or a popular assassination against an infamous individual, at any time, and under any given circumstances, is politic or not. Of the right of Nature to avenge herself in both cases, in my opinion, there can be no question. I have the most perfect sympathy with the godly sincerity of the men who went to that bloody work with a prayer on their tongue and a sacred sanction in their breast. It was a work which was forced upon them by the gross offence of the times, and for which they were not answerable; but whether the blow which descended judicially with full right on the head of the traitor was dealt wisely, with a view to immediate results and future consequences, I do not decide. The general law reigns, as stated above in reference to the affair of the Pentlands, that the failure of an insurrection will always be the signal for an increased severity of oppression, and always supplies the existing authorities with a fair excuse for those severities. That this may have been the case with the bloody taking off of that mitred offender, on the roadside between Ceres and St. Andrews, I have little doubt; still my sympathies beat warmly with the assassins. It seems most unreasonable to expect calm policy from a people smarting for years under such an intolerable combination of civil and sacerdotal violence; and therefore I insert here some verses which I wrote on the subject full thirty years ago, while standing on the very ground where that deed of red retribution was committed, and which, I feel convinced, express my deliberate convictions on the subject more firmly and more effectively than I have now endeavoured to do it in the more loose medium of prose.

LINES WRITTEN AT MAGUS MUIR.

Lament who will the surplice rent,
    And mitre trampled low,
I cannot think the blow misspent,
    That felled our priestly foe.

Who sent him here?—A perjured king.
    His work?—With Churchman's art
To bind young Freedom's mounting wing,
    And crush a people's heart.

Ill-omened priest! for courtly place
    Well made, and cold propriety;
But here thou found'st a fervid race,
    Whose sternly-glowing piety

Scorned paper laws. Their free-bred soul
    Went not with priests to school,
To trim the tippet and the stole,
    And pray by printed rule;

But they would cast the eager word
    From their heart's fiery core,
Smoking and red, as God had stirred
    The Hebrew men of yore.

And thou didst come, a cassocked slave,
    With windy proclamation,
Parchment and ink, and wax, to brave
    The spirit of a nation;

And with rash plume didst brush the flame,
    And wert consumed, poor fly!—
So perish all who join the name
    Of Christ with tyranny!

Prate not of law and lawyer's art!
    When kingly sin is rife,
The law is in a people's heart
    That whets the needful knife.

O Scotland! O my country! thou
    Through blood hast waded well;
From glorious Bannockburn till now
    The tyrant hears his knell

Rung from thy iron heart. And we,
    In lone rock-girdled glen,
Or purple heath, erect and free,
    From harsh, knife-bearing men

Inherit peace. Lament who will
    The mitre trampled low;
Not all are murderers who kill;
    The cause commends the blow.

The blood of the mitred time-server had scarcely dried when the long-suppressed popular indignation suddenly broke out among the gray moors and black peat bogs that lie thickly in the hilly ground between Ayrshire and Lanarkshire. This was the strong ground of the Covenanters, who, in spite of constant dragooning and terrible declarations of treason and its red consequences, persisted in praising God in their own way and causing the heather braes to resound with the billows of a manly and free-breasted psalmody. As field worship was a capital crime in the eyes of a sacerdotal Government, who believed the worship of God was acceptable only when conducted within certain walls of stone and lime, and by persons bearing certain arbitrary titles, and dressed in certain prescribed robes, those sturdy worshippers were obliged to fence their meetings round with armed watchers, ready for a surprise. At one of these armed conventicles, as they were called, a young rising soldier, of less brutal character than the Turners and Dalziels who had preceded him—John Graham of Claverhouse—suddenly came upon the Covenanters as they were celebrating worship beneath the shade of Loudon Hill near the sources of the Avon, with the thought that he could easily disperse them. But it turned out otherwise. They were singing the seventy-sixth psalm—a psalm full of war and judgment and victory; and the striking words of the verse—

> "When thy rebuke, O Jacob's God,
> Had forth against them pass'd,
> Their horses and their chariots both
> Were in a dead sleep cast"

seemed to have inspired them with a strength to which even the tried tactics of a gallant young soldier, trained in the schools of France and Holland, proved unequal. Claverhouse was routed; and the little remnant of patriots, saved from the discouragement and demoralisation of a twenty years' persecution, had at last achieved a memorable success. But the success was momentary. In a few weeks DRUMCLOG was followed by Bothwell Brig. There the natural strength of an established government against a sudden insurrectionary force was aided by most unwise division among the spiritual leaders of the patriotic army, with an utter want of that generalship which alone can in war lead to permanent results. The Covenanting strength was a second time completely broken; Bothwell Brig was even a more complete failure than Rullion Green. The last desperate struggle to shake off the oppressive yoke of civil and sacerdotal absolutism had been made in vain. Prostration was now complete, hope extinguished, and the reign of blood inaugurated anew.

I will not enter upon the disgusting and disheartening details of coarse, spiteful triumph, and malignant, crushing revenge, that followed on this defeat. The horrors of an African slave ship and the life in death of a Calcutta Black Hole were enacted here on the bodies of the only people in whom a spark of manhood had been left strong enough to resist the smothering influence of pervasive tyranny in the land. But though Scotland now lay bleeding under the mitred insolence of the Stuarts, as Greece did under the iron hoof of the Macedonian, the same God who raised up a Demosthenes to fight the battle of national independence in the midst of general prostration and corruption, raised up a prophet and a protector for Scotland in the hour of her utmost need—and that prophet was RICHARD

CAMERON. On the 22d day of June 1680,—the very day of the anniversary of the Bothwell Brig prostration,—the gray old burgh of Sanquhar, with its picturesque castle and winding water amid the ridges of wild heathy hills towards the sources of the Nith in Dumfriesshire, was startled by the sudden tramp of a body of horsemen, who rode straight up to the market-place, and there, after singing a psalm and offering up a prayer, two of them dismounted, and amidst the holy hush of the multitude read forth the following declaration :—" WE DO BY THESE PRESENTS DISOWN CHARLES STUART, THAT HAS BEEN REIGNING, OR RATHER TYRANNISING, ON THE THRONE OF BRITAIN THESE TWENTY YEARS BYGONE, AS HAVING ANY RIGHT, TITLE TO, OR INTEREST IN THE CROWN OF SCOTLAND FOR GOVERNMENT, AS FORFEITED MANY YEARS SINCE BY HIS PERJURY AND BREACH OF COVENANT, BOTH TO GOD AND THE CHURCH, AND BY HIS TYRANNY AND BREACH OF THE *leges regnandi*—THE VERY ESSENTIAL CONDITIONS OF GOVERNMENT IN MATTERS CIVIL. WE DO DECLARE WAR AGAINST SUCH A TYRANT AND USURPER, AND ALL THE MEN OF HIS PRACTICES. AND WE HOPE NONE WILL BLAME US, OR BE OFFENDED AT OUR REWARDING THOSE THAT ARE AGAINST US, AS THEY HAVE DONE TO US, AS THE LORD MAY GIVE US OPPORTUNITY." This is one of the most manly, stout-hearted, noble-minded, and courageous protests in the name of civil and religious liberty that ever was made on the blood-stained floors of history. We all remember when, at no distant date, a strong man marched over Europe, shaking the oldest and best established thrones by the tread of his terrible foot, and proclaiming by his mere word to the astonished nations that this and the other mighty empire had ceased to exist, and this and that famous crowned head was no longer numbered among the princes of the earth. But these were acts of mere violence. With some hundred thousand men at his back, and no danger visible before, such fiats could be largely fulminated without raising any sentiment higher than vulgar fear and astonishment. But the act of Richard Cameron was an act not only of grand prophetic instinct, but of courage and moral nobility, not surpassed by the most celebrated acts of self-sacrifice in the annals of Greek and Roman patriotism; and if the name of this Scottish prophet is not as well known in the annals of civil and religious liberty as that of Socrates is in the records of moral progress, it is to be attributed not to the inferior moral dignity of the act, but to the less public stage on which the act was exhibited, and the want of classical recorders of his virtue. Had the life and deeds of Demosthenes come to our ears through Macedonian writers, as the life and deeds of Cameron came to the general public in these islands from the pen of Episcopalian and Royalist historians, many people would have acknowledged the great Athenian orator with as scanty and grudgeful a meed of praise as they now may dole out to the great Scottish prophet of the glorious English Settlement of 1688. Morally, Cameron was as great a man as Socrates, and a greater than Demosthenes. The Declaration of Sanquhar, it may be said by those who would be blind to its heroism, was the most foolish and futile of public protests that was ever put forth by political or religious fanaticism. Foolish it certainly was, if the preservation of their own lives had been the object of the protesters; futile it certainly was not, as it served to sound through the length and breadth of the land the important fact that, in spite of all the innocent blood that had been shed, and all the noble lives that had been sacrificed, the spirit of Scotland was not yet crushed; and there survived a soul in the plaided prophets of the hills, before which, at no distant period, the blood-bolted minions of tyranny would flee in precipitate dismay, like the myriads of Xerxes before the faithful little bands of Marathon and Plataea. Foolish the Declaration of Sanquhar certainly was in a worldly sense, even as was also the death of Socrates; but if foolish in one estimate, not the less noble and not the less wise in another. Socrates might have escaped with his head on his shoulders, if he had pleased; that is a well-known fact; but he was more anxious to seal his mission with his death than to save his life by some legal subterfuge or some affected respect. Exactly so Cameron; he published the Magna Charta of the Revolution Settlement at the time when he knew that such publication was death to all who took any part in it. He chose to die as Patrick Hamilton and George Wishart had died at the opening of the great struggle of the Reformation, because he knew that the germ of

Scottish liberty, civil and religious, had grown up from the watering of that blood, and could not be restored to its own greenness and sturdiness by any element less precious. He lived the life of a patriot and a prophet; and he died the death of a patriot and a soldier on the bloody field of Airds Moss, where his gray memorial now stands. Blessed is the people that can bend a loyal knee and breathe a pious prayer before the monument of such a man!

Richard Cameron is gone to his rest; and we must now turn our eyes on a less pleasant spectacle than the stage of a patriotic defiance, and the field of a devout battle. Instead of the battle-field we now look again at the scaffold; and instead of something like a fair fight, we must, for a few years longer, behold treachery and butchery in league to exterminate, if it might be, the small remnant of moral nobility in the land. The most notable personage in the first scene of the last act of this long-protracted bloody drama is ROBERT BAILLIE of Jerviswood. Here we are introduced to a new form of atrocity, as if the infuriated despots of these times had wished to exhaust every possible variation of tigerhood in the guise of humanity. In Hugh MacKail they had fleshed their teeth with the youngest and most delicate and most gracious of Scottish youth; Baillie of Jerviswood, a frail old man on the verge of the grave, and a gentleman of good social repute and the highest respectability, was the victim whom they now picked out to glut their ripe appetite. It is needless to state with what crime he was charged, or to inquire curiously what proofs were brought forward to support the charge. His crime, of course, was that he was a Presbyterian, and could not be expected to cherish any very warm feelings of loyalty towards a perjured monarch, who followed one consistent idea through his base life—to root out all religious conscience and all moral dignity from the land; but Baillie had been moderate and discreet in his utterances; and, had not justice been equally trampled out with liberty under the iron foot of absolutism, the condemnation of such a man would have been impossible. But in a land where law and prosecutor and judge and jury were one, and all leagued in an infamous conspiracy to crush conscience and manhood out of the breasts of Scottish men, any slightest shadow of a proof, or no proof at all, in the case of involved persons, was sufficient to substantiate a charge of what the lawyers of those days, in the slang of their profession, called constructive treason. It was a sight to move tears even in the eyes of the most hardened of Claverhouse's dragoons, when that venerable old gentleman was brought before the Court wrapped in his dressing-gown as he had risen from his sick bed, and attended by his sister-in-law, daughter of the celebrated Warriston, who from time to time administered cordials to keep up his fainting strength. Mackenzie of Rosehaugh, the king's advocate, commonly called "the bloody Mackenzie," pressed the charge with the usual violence characteristic of the partisan prosecutors of those times; but Jerviswood not only denied every charge in detail with the utmost precision, but appealed in open Court to the prosecutor with the startling question, how he could in public so violently accuse him, when in private he had confessed to him that he did not believe him guilty? To which the advocate, accustomed to act professionally as a mere speaking-trumpet to the conclave of conspirators by whom the country was ruled, pointing to the Clerk of the Privy Council, then present, coolly replied: "I spoke to you then as a private individual; what I say here I speak by special direction of the Privy Council; he—the clerk—knows my orders." "Well," replied Jerviswood, "if you have one conscience for yourself and another for the Council, I pray God forgive you; I do."[1] The law of course, as law was in those days, took its course; and one of the noblest of Scottish gentlemen was forthwith beheaded and quartered and mutilated, and hung up to public exposure through the land like the vilest of malefactors.

Another notable figure that looms forth conspicuously at various stages through the bloody mist of those "killing times" was ALEXANDER PEDEN, commonly called Peden the Prophet, who, however, by some happy chain of circumstances, had the singular luck in those days to die in his bed. When the heady eagerness of Middleton had caused the secession of the four hundred

---

[1] Hetherington's *History of the Church of Scotland*. Edinburgh, 1841. Vol. ii. p. 493.

brave recusants, Peden was minister of Glenluce, in a remote corner of Wigtonshire, and at once chose his portion with the party which expressed the manhood and independence of the country. After preaching his last sermon, on leaving the pulpit he shut the door emphatically behind him, and giving it three stout raps with his Bible, said—" I hereby arrest you, in the name of my Master, and solemnly enjoin to allow no man to preach here who does not enter by the authority of the King of kings, freely and unconditionally, as I did!" And from that time, history records, there never was a preacher opened his mouth in the pulpit till the day of the Revolution of 1688, when the servile curates and glib venal talkers (whom Peden in his picturesque phrase used to call the Devil's rattle-bags) gave place to the free and independent evangelists of the National Church. This well-known incident sufficiently indicates the mixture of dramatic emphasis and moral divination in his attitude which gained him the name of Peden the Prophet,—a designation in reference to which, no doubt, many exaggerated stories were told, and it may be also, as Wodrow asserts, not a few manifest forgeries launched into circulation,[1] but which indicates, in the most expressive way, the presence of an original character of great depth of feeling and vividness of imagination. How a man who was always in the midst of the persecuted, roaming often at large between " one bloody land and another"—Ireland and Scotland, as he phrased it

---

[1] Wodrow, book iii. chap. x.

—should have escaped so long the multitudinous spies and scouts, informers and bloodhounds in human shape, to whom so many less notorious actors in the same bloody drama fell a victim, might look almost like one of those special providential provisions to which the godly men of those times were fond of attributing all the chances of personal as of national life. He did not escape the Bass, however, and was in fact sent up to London in 1678 to be shipped off to Virginia, or any other of the American plantations. But in London he had the good fortune to meet with a ship captain of a very different sort of conscience from that of the hard lawyer who used his venal rhetoric to procure the execution of the Laird of Jerviswood. This honest seaman, on being informed that, instead of a gang of thieves and robbers and evildoers, he was expected to convey into banishment a company of grave Christian men, exiled for obeying God rather than man in matters of religious faith, bluntly said "he would sail the sea with none such;" and there being no other ship there ready to sail, and little money in the Government chest to pay the expense of keeping them in London (there were sixty of them in all), they were set at liberty without any imposition of bonds or oaths; and some good Christians in London showed them great kindness.[1] Thus singularly preserved for the land which he loved, and in whose speedy redemption he potently believed, this faithful servant of Christ contrived to wander in deserts and in

---

[1] *Life of Peden.* London, 1774.

mountains, and in dens and caves of the earth, till, worn out with many sorrows, he died in his native parish among the hills of Sorn in Ayrshire, aged eighty-six years, only two years before the glorious Revolution Settlement; but not till he had the satisfaction of leaving his blessing and his mission with the last of the sacred band of Scottish Covenanting martyrs, the noble-minded Renwick. It ought to be mentioned, as a fact strikingly characteristic of the brutality of that age, or rather of the men who gloried to stamp the age with their atrocities, that the soldiers in the pay of the Episcopising Government, disappointed that they had never been able to strike their fangs into the body of the living man, determined to wreak their vengeance on his corpse, which they accordingly dug out from the grave beneath his paternal plane trees, and hung it upon a gibbet on a hill above Cumnock, where the common gallows stood.[1]

JAMES RENWICK, on whom the last stroke of the Episcopal axe was destined to fall, but who, as Dodds well remarks, ought rather to be known in history as the PRE-MARTYR OF THE REVOLUTION SETTLEMENT, was born in Minniehive, a beautiful village in the heart of the Covenanting country, in the year 1662. He was consequently a mere youth, not above three-and-twenty years old, at the death of Charles II., when James VII. came openly forward with his long-cherished scheme of establishing Popery in these islands, which he introduced in a very subtle way, by sending forth edicts

[1] Dodds, chap. x., who is particularly good on Peden.

of general religious toleration. Toleration from the Papists! rather a strange sound! Enter the devil with a cup of holy water in his hands, but his hands are black nevertheless, and his whole body smells of blood. Renwick was a young man of remarkable capacity, of fine feelings, and of good education; he had studied both in Edinburgh and in Holland; and with the clear glance of an uncorrupted mind and an unbribed conscience had seen clearly that all compromise with Episcopising and Romanising Stuarts on the throne was impossible. He accordingly joined himself to the followers of the noble Cameron, who, under the name of the "Society men," had formed themselves into a widespread association, the watchword of which was the formal renunciation of James VII. as lawful sovereign of the kingdom of Scotland. Of course they were right in all this; for James had usurped absolute power in a free country, and conspired to introduce Popery into a Protestant country. But in the meantime he sat there; and Renwick knew very well what he was doing when he put himself at the head of these patriotic and constitutional convocations; whatever he might be before God, and by Scottish public-law, when public law was in the land, he was now in the eye of the Popish Government a rebel and a heretic of the extreme type; and, as the Cameronian Societies were specially exempted from the Toleration Acts, he could expect no safety, except so long as he might dwell with the wild birds on the bleak hills of

Glencairn. But skulking about in that way did not suit his temper. So, after he had been preaching in Fife, and, coming across to Edinburgh, happened to be lodging with a friend on the Castlehill, the Harpies of the law surprised him, and pursuing him down the Castle Wynd to the head of the Cowgate, came upon him, when he fell several times, and got him securely in their fangs; and shortly after, on the 8th February 1688, had him tried before the Justiciary. Of course, though there might be pity in some eyes, there could be no mercy. Not a few even of the persecuting party wished to save the life of the handsome, high-spirited youth who had thus thrown himself straight into the arms of death. Even in their eye the bloody game was being played too grossly. One word would have saved him; but, like Socrates, that one word he would not speak. He would not admit the justice of his condemnation in order to gain what in his conviction would have been a dishonourable acquittal. He could as soon have sworn that the Evil One had a right to sit upon the throne of God, as that James VII. could lawfully sit upon the Protestant throne of this country. He would as soon have said that the new-born babe had no right to breathe, as that Scottish Presbyterians had no right to worship God on their native hills according to the dictates of their conscience. He resisted all attempts to make him sign any shadow of a recantation of his constitutional principles. He would not swear fealty to a tyrant, a traitor to the

Scottish liberties, and a usurper of the divine rights of the Christian Church. He was executed in the Grassmarket, as Socrates was in the Athenian prison, with the words of manhood and courage and consolation in his mouth. The cruel drums of the sacrificers drowned a great portion of the cheerful words of constancy and hope and ultimate victory which he gave as his last bequeathment to his country; but they could not stop the tears that flowed copiously from the eyes of the surrounding multitude.

"Weep! Scotland, weep! but only for a day,
Frail stands the throne whose props are glued with gore;
For a short hour the godless man holds sway,
And Justice whets her knife at Murder's door.
Weep, Scotland! but, let noble Pride this day
Gleam through thine eye with sorrow streaming o'er;
For why?—thy Renwick's dead, whose noble crime
Gave Freedom's trumpet breath an hour before the Time!"

What remains of this bloody history—the few months from the murder of this noble boy to the Revolution Settlement—belongs to the British Empire generally, not specially to Scotland. The open profession of Popery by James, and his pig-headed persistency in running a-muck against all parties in the State, crowned his isolation by its natural fruit, a formal disownment; and the stamp of legality and public right was now placed on the prophetic disclaimer of the Cameronians. I have only one word to say in conclusion. Though the acerbities and soreness and unworthy jealousies which, as an inheritance from the bloody times which we have been sketching, have long ceased to be felt between Episcopalians and Presbyterians in Scotland, it still remains a fact that our society, in the matter of religious sentiment, exhibits the spectacle of two distinct strata, which refuse at various points to interflow. A considerable section of the upper classes are Episcopalians by conviction and by inheritance, while not a few latterly, whether from marriage with English families, from peculiar æsthetic sensibilities, or from mere fashion and vulgar notions of worldly respectability, have joined the same body. These classes, though not formidable in numbers—for Presbyterianism is still unquestionably the backbone, and Episcopacy only the dress-coat of Scotland—exercise a social influence, and communicate a certain tone to popular sentiment, which has acted most unfavourably to the memory of our great Presbyterian heroes, the Covenanters. The historic traditions of the Episcopalians also lead them to devote themselves with special love to historical study ; and so it has happened that the historical literature of Scotland has received a strong tinge from men who, in common with our great popular novelist, and our singers of Jacobite ballads, were more disposed to see the ludicrous than the heroic aspect of the plaided prophets of the hills. And even among those whose sense of justice forced them to confess that the stern men of the Covenant were not only morally noble and constitutionally in the right, but worthy in some sense of a niche in the Pantheon of the select and the elect of the earth, there is wont to be a qualification given, to the effect that in point of principle the one party was not one whit better than the other, and that the Covenanters would have persecuted, and in some cases actually did persecute, the Episcopalians, with no less intolerance, where only they might find an opportunity. This judgment is given without a proper historical discrimination. Neither the Covenanters, nor the Episcopalians, nor, in fact, any people in Europe in the seventeenth century, had acknowledged the doctrine of religious toleration as it is now almost universally acknowledged. It is by no means an easy matter to define in every case where the action of the State should cease, and all compulsory forces in moral matters be disallowed. It is only the other day that religious tests in universities were abolished ; and it was no fault of the Covenanting theologians if, in the days of Cromwell,—when, by the way, statutable intolerance was intensified by civil strife and party hatred,—a zealous presbytery here and there exacted fines from a pious Episcopalian lady for not attending the parish church.[1] The motives from which this conduct proceeded were based on the general law of Europe, and could not be eradicated from the clerical mind till the hot blood of the great civil war had

---

[1] See *The Abbey of Paisley from its Foundation to its Dissolution*, by Dr. J. Cameron Lees. Paisley, 1878. Chapter 24 ; The Abercorns and the Kirk.

cooled down, and the world had time to consider anew to what conclusions the great Protestant doctrine of private judgment must necessarily lead. But what the patriotic men who signed the Solemn League and Covenant in the Greyfriars Churchyard in 1638 solemnly declared, and what with no less solemnity, and with much greater boldness, was solemnly declared after them by the Cameronians at the Cross of Sanquhar, was simply this :—Every distinct people has a right to its national conscience, and no civil magistrate or foreign ruler has a right to impose a creed, a liturgy, or a church government on an unwilling people. The king, as head of the social organism, according to the acknowledged ideal of the century, is a representative man, who, if he does not personally belong to the National Church —which is the most fitting and natural thing in the case—must at all events swear to its maintenance, and do nothing that goes directly to undermine it. Against this plain proposition of public right the Stuarts and their prelatic advisers rebelled; and, after long-continued attempts to trample on popular liberty and strangle the national conscience, they were cast out of the stomach of the country as an intolerable and indigestible morsel. The Covenanters were the men in Scotland who maintained this internecine struggle in its darkest days, and through its most hopeless stages ; their noble resistance fought out for us the platform on which we now stand ; maintained for us the erect attitude of freemen which is our pride ; and left for us the noblest inheritance that fathers can leave to their sons, a retrospect of courage, consistency, and unspotted honour. From the glory thus belonging to them, no secondary faults, arising whether from the imperfection of human nature or the necessarily slow growth of the social harmonies, can be allowed to detract; and on calm consideration of the whole matter, every true Scot who loves his country will give his full assent to the words of the great lyrical exponent of our best feelings as Scotsmen—

> " The Solemn League and Covenant
> Cost Scotland blood, cost Scotland tears;
> But Faith sealed Freedom's sacred cause;
> If thou'rt a slave, indulge thy sneers!"

These words were written by a man, from his station in society and his paternal traditions far better able to take the true measure of the heroes of the Covenant than either Walter Scott with his wonderful wealth of chivalrous lore, or Professor Aytoun with the fervid flash of his aristocratic fancy, or Burton with his rough justice and hard political appreciation. History to be understood must be written and read in the same spirit in which it was acted. Unsympathetic record is always untrue.

IX.

ON SYMBOLISM, CEREMONIALISM, FORMALISM, AND THE NEW CREATURE.

"In Christ Jesus there is neither circumcision nor uncircumcision, but a new creature."—GALATIANS vi. 15.

THAT vast and variously-massed army of speaking things which we call the world and the universe, from its largest manifestation in a sun-centre of revolving spheres to its minutest in the scarcely visible insect that flits for a moment in the summer beam and dies, falls everywhere under the double category of FORM and FORCE: FORCE, an internal power, felt but not seen, which, with whatever name it may be specialised, is at bottom that self-existent, self-energising, plastic reason which we justly call GOD; and FORM, the outward expression or external planting of that force which we are accustomed to call Body or Matter. These two things, though in their nature contrary and antagonistic, are not therefore necessarily separable; on the contrary, it stands before our eyes patently as part of the divine mystery of the universe that in some degree or other they always co-exist, like show and substance,[1] and even in their extremest divergence cannot be divorced. The most solid form of matter—the white quartz rock, or the close-grained metal—is still drawn towards a centre, and powerfully held together by the force called gravitation; while, on the other hand, the subtlest forms of energy which we know—Light, Electricity, and Thought—either operate through an extremely attenuated ether, or demand a machinery to make their existence felt. There is no motion without a moving medium; no thinking without brain; no stroke without muscle. But though, so far as our senses can testify, inseparable, these two contrasted elements of all existence are by no means of like dignity and importance. Coeval they may be in the absolute nature of things, but not coequal. The one stands to the other manifestly in a relation of dependence and subordination, as the clay does to the potter, as the fuel does to the fire, as the word does to the thought of which it is the exponent. The whole significance and virtue of things, the magic of vitality, the charm of beauty, the sovereignty of intellect, lies in the force—a force which always strives after an embodiment that may be more or less expressive of its highest virtue, but which, in whatever degree, always lends to the form the only value which gives it a place in the great account of things. The value of things, whether material or moral, in fact, always depends upon the

---

[1] "Der Schein was ist er dem das Wesen fehlt?
Das Wesen wär es, wenn es nicht erschiene."—GOETHE.

quality and quantity of the force which is in them; or, to use the language of religion, which is always the most philosophical, on the quality and quantity of the divine inspiration which breathes through them. The form in itself is utterly worthless; without the force a mere ossification or fossil; either absolute death, or something that leads straightway down to death; as that well-known evangelic text plainly indicates, THE LETTER KILLETH, BUT THE SPIRIT MAKETH ALIVE.

In the moral world, with which alone we have to do in this place, the domain of form, under various aspects, is well known under the names of symbolism, ceremonialism, formalism, and generally externalism, or outwardness of different types. Now all these things, of course, are necessary to the sensuous manifestation of that kind of moral force, the action of which forms a society or a church; but of course, also, they derive all their value only from the kind and amount of actually energising force which they express; and the moment they are tempted to assert themselves as having an independent value, or *locus standi*, as the lawyers say, in the social world, that instant they lose their virtue; ossification of the heart commences; the jewels are being stolen out of the casket; the expression departs from the fair face of the woman, and only the features of a doll remain. The tendency towards this assertion of an independent existence by the form is to be found in the history of moral societies of all kinds, specially, however, in all Churches; as plentifully everywhere, indeed, as weeds are in neglected gardens, or rather worse; for where weeds grow in a garden the gardener loves to pluck them up or to trench them down; whereas, in the garden of the moral world the spiritual gardener not seldom makes a business of cultivating the rag-weed and neglecting the rose. The reason of this strange phenomenon seems to lie partly in the fact that the symbol and the ceremonial are the things seen, and thus act more potently on the senses than the unseen force behind; and partly in the weakness of human nature— οἱ πολλοὶ κακοὶ—which makes it difficult for not a few persons to feel and to think themselves back into the deep inward wells of thoughtful sentiment out of which the symbol sprang, and so they cling to the outward; by which act, indeed, they contrive to save themselves from drowning in the seas of doubt and discomfort where poor humanity is often tossed, but fail to extract any true spiritual nourishment for their souls. Hence the necessity of preachers, philosophers, prophets, apostles, poets, orators, and men of all kinds, strong in the original vitalities of Nature, to act upon the poor starving dead-alive masses by strong moral stimulants, direct from the divine Source of life, and the first fountain of all excellence. Hence revolutions, reformations, and revivals of all kinds, both in the political and in the religious world. Hence Oliver Cromwell, Mirabeau, and Bismarck; hence the Apostle Paul and Martin Luther, John Knox and John Wesley—men all divinely missioned, though in the most diverse ways, to give the sleeping world a shake, and to teach politicians that no State can be well governed which does not honestly strive to support the weak against the strong, instead of making the strong stronger, and that no Church can be called Christian which makes itself known more by magnifying the privileges of the office-bearers than by working out the salvation of the people.

The text which we have chosen as a starting-point to our present meditations, after casting a rapid glance at the formalism of the Jews, against which St. Paul had to carry on a life-long protest, leads us to point out some of the more salient forms under which formalism parades itself in the existing life of the Christian Churches; and then to consider what the apostle indicates as the great restorative force by which life was to be breathed into the dead bones of Hebrew Ceremonialism and self-righteous Pharisaism in his days. This form he makes intelligible under a simile well known in Oriental theology, called the new birth or the new creature, or, as our scholastic catechisms have it, regeneration.

The special badge of distinction on which the Jew of St. Paul's day based his claim of superiority before God and man was circumcision. With this as a mere fleshly peculiarity of hygienic or other significance, acknowledged by the Egyptians and a few other eastern nations,[1] but unknown to the Semitic neighbours of the

[1] Herodot. ii. 104.

Jews on the sea-coast, as well as to the Greeks and Romans, we have nothing here to do. It was not as an operation of any sanitary virtue or medical significance that St. Paul found himself forced to stand in an attitude of continual protest against the advocates of circumcision. If circumcision, in the estimation of the Jew, placed him on a high vantage ground of preference above the uncircumcised Gentiles, it was because he inherited this peculiarity as the descendant of Abraham, the father of the faithful, and the elect head of the people whom God, at an early period, had chosen as the repository of the great truth of the divine unity, to be revealed in due season to the whole world. This is just, in an old Semitic dress, what we are only too familiar with in our modern British life—that species of empty self-glorification called the pride of pedigree. Now this, of course, like all deeply-seated and widely-experienced feelings, has its root in human nature; and, as so rooted, unquestionably has its justification as a beneficial force in the organism of society. To be able to look back on a noble ancestry, conspicuous from generation to generation for its practice of all those virtues that make the good citizen and the eminent patriot, is one of the greatest blessings that can belong to a human being born into this world; for persons so born are not only launched into the great sea of life under the most favourable circumstances and with the most auspicious omens; but they must be altogether base, and of a clay inferior to the great mass of humanity, if they do not feel the honour of this descent acting within them as a constant spur to a career that may not show itself as an open degeneracy from the noble precedents out of which it sprang. No sound-minded man likes to fall down in public estimation from the point of his starting, but rather to rise. And in accordance with this feeling in all the great social struggles in which humanity has been engaged,—from Moses to the Greeks and Romans, and from the Romans to the most stout asserters of national independence in modern times,—we find that no appeal has been more potent to fire the blood and to nerve the thews of a lofty patriotism than simply this, not to act unworthily of our forefathers. But here, as in the case of money and other external advantages, a good thing misunderstood, or not wisely used, becomes not only a bad thing, but one of the worst, as the proverb has it, *Corruptio optimi pessima;* and the corruption commences here, as in other cases, the moment that the virtue of which the external badge is only the bearer is forgotten, and the badge is used either as a thing of value in itself, or as a means of procuring things which are utterly without value. Thus money is an effective symbol, token, or tool, the possession of which may enable a man to fling out stimulants to beneficent activity in hundreds of ways from which a penniless man is altogether barred ; but the moment this natural use and significance is forgotten, it may be used as a necromancer's wand for raising all sorts of evil spirits, and selling the soul of the conjuror to the

x

Devil. Or, to speak more plainly, it may be used—as, unfortunately, we see it used every day—to purchase poison instead of food. Even so the pride of pedigree becomes ridiculous and pernicious the moment it turns the noble retrospect, which is the soul of it, into a vain boast instead of an effective spur. To be born of a noble father, and to live a shameful life, is a double shame, and not an honour to the person who so drags his paternal laurels through the mire. Properly speaking, indeed, a man should not be proud of pedigree at all, but only thankful for it—thankful to Providence for having started him in life with a stock of reputable memories, that, if well used, may lift him to platforms of political importance and social significance, of which otherwise, with ten times the amount of talent, he could not have dreamed. The place of pride in pedigree is not before, but after, the use has been made of it. And it was because the Jews, like some of our modern worshippers of rank and title, prided themselves on their external descent from Abraham, without being at all anxious to know and to reproduce in their own lives the spirit and the character of the great patriarch, that St. Paul, in the preaching of the gospel, felt himself morally bound to encounter them with the most aggressive hostility. There could be no compromise between a gospel inspired and permeated by the pure inwardness of moral motives, and a claim of superiority before God, founded on external observances, accidental advantages, or ancestral traditions of whatever kind. To advance such claims was to starve the children by giving them the shell to feed on instead of the kernel. It was worse than nothing; it was making a virtue of that which was devoid of all virtue; and not only so, but a formal barring of the door against the entrance of all real excellence by the preoccupation with an imaginary merit. An empty house might be furnished with useful furniture, if the possessor of the house only were not besotted in the habit of its emptiness; but a house filled to the ceiling and crammed to the door with the craziness and mouldiness of all sorts of ancestral lumber, cannot be trimmed into a state of comfortable equipment till the old rubbish be clean swept away. So of circumcision, titles of honour, and such outward badges of inherited distinction, there must be a complete clearance in the soul before a spiritual gospel can have room to come in. To the born Jew, accordingly, who had circumcision to boast of, it was plainly said that he is not a Jew who is one outwardly in the flesh, but inwardly in the spirit; while to the Christian who was not born a Jew, but who nevertheless wished to be circumcised—as we see from the Epistle that the Galatians did—it was indignantly answered that to seek for circumcision in his case was to give plain evidence that the seed of an essentially spiritual religion had never taken firm root in his heart.

So much for the Jews. Our next and our more proper business is to inquire against what manifestations of a soulless, unevangelical, and unfruitful externalism, noticeable in the life of the Christian Churches at the present day, may the voice of St. Paul in the text before us be considered as uttering a solemn protest. And the most common type of formalism which meets us here is undoubtedly what our preachers call trust in ordinances. By ordinances are meant certain symbolical acts or commemorative celebrations, in which the faith of a nation rejoices to declare itself and unfurl its banners solemnly before the world. Such a great national act of religious symbolism we find in various seats of polytheistic worship amongst the ancient Greeks, under the name of Mysteries, as at Eleusis, Samothrace, and elsewhere; and the virtue of these sacred celebrations consisted simply in their revealing, by a vivid presentation to the eye, and a serious exercise of the soul, some pregnant phase of the action of divine forces in the universe, tending to elevate the soul above the grossness of mere sensual perception, and to ennoble human life by the powerful stimulants of high memories and hopeful aspirations. Thus, at Eleusis, a reverence for the divine mystery of life, whether, as visibly displayed before us in the processes of vegetation and generation, or as prophetically indicated in the solemn mystery of death, viewed as the passage from a lower to a higher life, was worked into the soul by the contemplation of the legendary history of Demeter, mother Earth, or the divine Mother; and this reverence, in the case of a moral being like man, natur-

ally connected itself with the possession of a certain moral purity, which rendered exclusion from the Mysteries the natural penalty of an immoral and a vicious life. In this way the hierophant at Eleusis, if he was no mere worldling, but deeply conscious of the divine significance of the rites which he administered, might justly take into his mouth the words with which the Hebrew Psalmist has expressed the character of a worthy worshipper in the holy hill at Jerusalem :—
"Who shall ascend into the hill of the Lord? or who shall stand in his holy place? He that hath clean hands and a pure heart, who hath not lifted up his soul unto vanity, nor sworn deceitfully." Closely analogous to this consummating act ($\tau\epsilon\lambda\epsilon\tau\acute{\eta}$ from $\tau\acute{\epsilon}\lambda$os) of old Hellenic piety was the solemn Commemoration Supper of our Lord with his disciples, of which the institution is told with such pathetic simplicity in the Gospels—an analogy, indeed, so striking, that the word in common use for the most sacred ceremony of Greek religion ($\mu\upsilon\sigma\tau\acute{\eta}\rho\iota\upsilon\nu$) was by an instinctive feeling of the early Greek Church transferred to the memorial supper. For the outward symbols, however different in the two cases, equally implied the participation in a higher moral life by the partaker. Without this participation the whole ceremony in both cases became a vanity and a profanation, or, as St. Paul more strongly expresses it, a condemnation to the unworthy participant. The sacrament, as a social act performed by a body of Christians, was in itself simply a badge; and, like other badges, valuable only in so far

as it truly expressed the sentiments, character, and conduct of the person who wore it; otherwise, it became not only unmeaning, but a lie and a treachery and a snare, insomuch as a false friend is always more dangerous to any associated body than a declared enemy. The condemnation which such a hollow profession naturally brings with it has exercised through large sections of the Church in Christian countries its proper and purifying influence by causing a systematic abstinence from the consummating rite of their religion by persons of wavering faith or inconsistent conduct; and though in some sections of the Christian Church, as in the Scottish Highlands, this abstinence may have been carried too far by a sort of superstitious terror and tender scrupulosity, there cannot be the slightest doubt that this extreme is far more honest and far more healthy than that trust in the magical operation of the ceremony to which the Christian Church, on the whole, has rather inclined. For in this matter the besetting sin of the religious man to trust in rites, and of the priest to magnify the virtue of his function, conspired out of a single act of pious commemoration to develop a mystery and a magic of sacred symbolism, which overtops anything that the annals of religious absurdity contain. The commemoration was turned into a mystification, of which, in its extreme form, the greatest result seemed rather the prostration of reason than the pacification of the passions or the elevation of the soul. Anyhow, whether with the unblushing nonsense of transubstantiation, or the milder juggle of consubstantiation, or the plain common sense of a symbolical commemoration, the sacrament was often taken as a mere outward badge of respectability, and people were encouraged to take a certain pride, and to feel a certain comfort, in the performance of this external act, as if Christianity were in some sense a religion of magical operations, and not of divine motives. To such sacramental formalists St. Paul would certainly have said in his broad way:— *In Christ Jesus there is neither going to the supper nor refusing to go, but a new creature.* No doubt, to go to the sacrament is good ; but it is not the act of going to it, nor of coming from it, that is good ; it is the spirit in which the act is performed. If you go to the Lord's table from a sincere desire to realise the person and the power of Christ and his work in the moral world of which you are a part, well ; if you go otherwise, better is he who abstains from going altogether, like the good Quaker from a crotchet of anti-symbolism, than you who go. God will have a living soul always in his worship, not a dead body ; a glowing manifestation of spiritual life, not a painted mask.

As with the commemorative supper, so with the symbolical water, the bias of the clergy and the weakness of the people have conspired to change a simple and significant rite into an outward act of magical operation, devoid equally of rational meaning and of moral effect. The baptismal regeneration which the High Church Anglican clergy have juggled out of the simple symbolism of water as significant of moral purity, is in its nature not a whit less repugnant to reason, or rather to common sense, than the mumbo-jumbo of transubstantiation with which the Romanists have so befooled religion and strangled reason in the mass. That men who never in common life or in literary interpretation are so stupid as to translate a simile into a fact, should perpetrate this stupidity where religion is concerned can be accounted for from the simple fact that all extreme passion for the moment to a certain extent blinds reason; and if it be the professional proclivity, as it certainly is, of the priesthood not only to exaggerate such passion, but to stamp it with permanence in liturgical forms, there will result from this combined action those monstrous dogmatisms of which our creeds and theological books make much parade, but which resolve themselves lightly, at the touch of reason, into the soulless crystallisation of a simile, or the senseless misunderstanding of a symbol. Here, as in all other matters, it is the undue value given to the external act that degrades the spiritual into the sensual, and empties religion of all reasonable contents. Whether it be the High Churchman, who makes a mystery of a plain symbol by the magic of a sacerdotal benediction, or the low Dissenter who displays the hyperscrupulosity of a verbal conscience by making curious inquiries whether the verb $\beta\acute{\alpha}\pi\tau\omega$ means to *dip* or to *sprinkle* or to *plunge* overhead in water; in both these cases,—the one at the extreme pole of sacerdotalism, the other at the opposite pole of what has not insignificantly been called bibliolatry, or a cleaving to the literal letter of Scripture,—the same tendency to magnify the external, and to idolise the ordinance, is plainly operative ; and to all these varieties of faith in the outward symbol, as a thing apart from the virtue which it symbolises, St. Paul would certainly have replied as to these Judaising Galatians : *In Christ Jesus there is neither baptismal regeneration, nor dipping, nor sprinkling, nor plunging, nor any such fashion of outward purification, but a new creature.*

Closely allied to the trust in ordinances or traditional institutions is the trust in orthodoxy or traditional creeds. What is orthodoxy ? I have called it a traditional creed ; but let us inquire a little more curiously. Etymologically, and on the face of it, orthodoxy signifies a right opinion, and in theological language,—to which, in the usage of the English tongue, it is confined,—a right opinion concerning God and divine things. Now this may mean either a right opinion absolutely, as when we say God is the self-existent uncaused cause of all things, which is a universally accepted truth among all sane-minded thinking beings, as much as that two and two make four ; or it may mean a right opinion about some attributes of the Divine Being or the laws of the divine administration not necessarily obvious to every thinking creature, but either as entertained by some thinking individual for himself, or, what is the general acceptation of the term, as handed down through a train of generations from some primary tribunal believed to have been in possession of insight in such matters, what we have just called a traditional creed. Now the primary tribunal from which the received right opinion concerning God and divine things always emanates in such cases is the Church, that is, the clergy; for, though the Christian Church in its original character was no doubt a congregation, and as such, justly designated by the democratic term of Athenian origin ἐκκλησία, yet in point of fact it has always been the case that the laity or the great mass of the congregation who have made no special studies in philosophical or historical theology, but are what the Greeks called ἰδιῶται in such matters, have taken their traditional creed, with absolute assent, from the professional expounders of Church doctrine, just as they take their medical opinions from their medical adviser, and their legal opinions from counsel learned in the law. To trust in orthodoxy, therefore, is to trust in a certain tabulated form of opinion concerning God and divine things drawn out by some school or council of theologians some hundred or a thousand and more years ago, thinking and speaking under the influence of whatever principles of pious speculation might at the time be pervading the atmosphere of the religious world. Now it is needless to say, in reference to such orthodoxy, whether a general orthodoxy representing a type of thought accepted by the Universal Church, as the orthodoxy of the Nicene Creed formulated in the year 325 after Christ, or the narrower orthodoxy of a special time or place, like the Calvinistic orthodoxy of the Dutch Church in the seventeenth century, which made itself so unhumanly conspicuous by the banishment and imprisonment of such eminent theologians as Limborch, Grotius, Episcopius—in reference to all such orthodoxies, I say, it is manifest that even if Christian faith consisted mainly in rightness of intellectual conceptions rather than in the nobility of a moral life, they are as a prop to lean on of a very brittle and crazy character indeed. For, in the first place, does it not imply an immense presumption in the case of mortals compassed round with infirmity such as we are, to dogmatise curiously on certain attributes of the divine nature, or certain principles of the divine procedure in the government of the world? "*Who can by searching find out God? who can find out the Almighty unto perfection?*" Enough for us that we have evidence of self-existent and self-energising power and goodness in a thousand shapes within us and without us, to warrant our faith and to compel our obedience. And again, what reason have we for thinking that the men who formulated creeds at Nicæa, or Trent, or Dort, or Westminster, in any given century, were in all points the wisest and best Christian thinkers of their time? or, if they were, which in the main, I fancy, we are safe to grant, who can guarantee that the type of theological thought that, from any temporal or local causes, dominated the minds of a certain majority of Churchmen at a certain numerous gathering of clerical notabilities some centuries ago, and which gave, we shall suppose, adequate expression to the religious needs of the time, was such as that it might safely be accepted for ever, in ages when other notions possessed the brain, and other feelings stirred the hearts, of the more earnest part of the religious communities? Religious creeds, however solemnly published, and with whatever venerable memories connected, we may depend upon it, fall under no other law than that which regulates the formal assertion and the venerable tradition of opinion in other matters. If in law and legislation, in politics, in medicine, in scholarship and science, the movement of opinion in many matters of difficult solution is often so great that progress in the future can be secured only by the complete overthrow of the most pretentious architecture of the past, how much more in theology, when what men assert is often of things the farthest removed from the possibility of exact human cognition, and concerning which they are often the wisest who, like Simonides, the longer they ponder the more piously they pause. We may say, therefore, with all certainty, that to lean upon Nicene or Athanasian Creeds, or upon the Five Articles of the Synod of Dort, or upon the metaphysical Calvinism of the Scottish Confession of Faith, is of all resources of intellectual externalism the most slippery and the most deceptive to which a poor bewildered religious thinker can recur. Christian faith no doubt implies belief in those broad and salient features of the divine nature and administration which are shortly indicated by St. Paul in the sixth verse of the eleventh chapter of the Epistle to the Hebrews, "He that cometh to God must believe that he is, and that he is the rewarder of them that diligently seek him." But it is not even this faith, broad and simple as it is, taken intellectually, which is the stuff out of which the heroes of the moral world are made; for "the devils also believe and tremble;" but it is this faith carried out in a moral conviction, with regard to the function of man in the system of things under which we live, and a course of conduct in the world of social action corresponding thereto. In contrast with this living faith of the heart and life all merely intellectual or head orthodoxy, however perfect, is in the eye of the Apostle Paul a piece of externalism as vain as circumcision or any other outward sign, divorced from the spiritual need which gives it significance. To talk of salvation by belief in any such articles is at bottom just as extrinsic to all saving faith as the belief in any proposition of mathematics with regard to the properties of curves, or any principle of physics with regard to the statical or dynamical action of forces. In Christ Jesus certainly, in this sense, there is neither heterodoxy nor orthodoxy, but a new creature; and unless this new creature exist along with the intellectual orthodoxy there is great danger that the very orthodoxy of the head may lead to a heterodoxy of the heart, which ossifies the fine fibres of human pity, and poisons the flow of a healthy human blood in the veins.

For a trust in curious points of intellectual orthodoxy, as the damnatory clauses of the Athanasian Creed, which Richard Baxter refused to sign, naturally leads to a false self-satisfaction in the man who believes, and a false contempt of his unbelieving brother; nay more, it may lead, and whole pages of Church history written in blood prove that it often has led on a large scale, to persecution and condemnation, and what we must call the perpetration of murder under legal forms, and with alleged divine sanction; for murder is not the less murder in the eye of Nature because it is committed with the usurped sanction of a monstrous infallibility and the unreasoned acceptance of an unreasoned tradition. And even without the possibility, as in those times, of such a bloody outcome of a Christian faith falsely so called, it is rare that a man laced tightly in the stays of a stiff orthodoxy can be found who is not more or less deficient in those graces that make society sweet and humanity lovable.

A third form of Externalism which at certain epochs in the history of the Church played a notable, and alas! also, sometimes a tragic part, is the trust in forms of Church government. On this a few words will suffice. Of all forms of Externalism which the sense-bound intellect of man has dreamed of substituting for a spiritual religion and a noble life, this is at once the most unreasonable, and, from a Christian point of view, the most unpardonable. It is, in fact, to assert that the framework is a necessary part of the picture, the binding an essential part of the book, and the particular kind of hive which you happen to patronise in your garden a necessary condition of the honey. The honey depends upon the bees, and upon the season, and upon the heather bloom, not upon your hive at all. And yet the hive is necessary for you in a sense. Without the hive you could not get the bees, nor manipulate the honey; but there are various kinds of hives, and each will have its own special advantage; so, if you are a lawgiver, you will not think of making a law that all honey-manipulators shall have one kind of hive, and whosoever may not choose to use this kind of hive shall not be allowed to have any honey. A form of Church government belongs to a religion just as a hive belongs to the bees, or a camp and its disposition to an army; but the forms and furnishings of hives and of camps are always matters of external arrangement which depend upon circumstances, and which, therefore, no wise man will prescribe by an anticipatory regulation for all times and all places. Accordingly we find—however ecclesiastical men in the heat of controversy may have battled and blundered on the point—that there is no form of government laid down in the New Testament as a constituent element of the Christian Church; and whatever plausibility may have been given to such a carnal conception of the character of the early Christian Church arose from the confounding of accidental circumstances belonging to the growth of an infant institution with the essential formative principles of the institution itself. There are not a few things mentioned as facts in the New Testament records which are not to be construed as precedents ; and thus, though it may be quite true—as I for one am strongly convinced—that the most important notices of the form of Church government in the New Testament point rather to Presbytery than to Episcopacy, I do not for that reason feel in the least degree moved to maintain the thesis that Presbytery is of divine institution ; much less that I am entitled, as an administrator of divine law in the Church, to force that form of government down the throats of all Christian congregations. On the contrary, the wisdom of the founders of the Church appears in nothing more than in this, that they left not only forms of Church government but much more important matters, such as slavery, to adjust themselves according to the consuetude and the convenience of time and place where the gospel might be accepted ; and in fact, not only Presbyterianism and Independency and Episcopacy, but even Popery, as a mere form of ecclesiastical administration, may exist, and has existed, in the Church, without the slightest prejudice to the energetic action of Christianity as the great engine for the moral regeneration of society. There is no reason in the nature of things why the three great types—democratic, aristocratic, and monarchical—which stand out everywhere with characteristic and marked features in civil government, should not, by a necessary law of social action, assert themselves with equal emphasis in the outward body and visible presentation of the Church ; and that they have so asserted themselves lies before us as an undeniable fact in the records of the last eighteen hundred years. Pure democracy stands represented in Independency ; democracy, less loosely aggregated, in Presbyterianism ; broad aristocracy in Episcopacy ; and a more narrow aristocracy, limited by the monarchical element, in Popery. And as it is not the form of the administration of the laws, but the quality of justice in the laws, and the character of justice in the administrators, that makes a good civil government, so in Church government. Pope and bishop and presbyter, so long as they confine themselves purely to the machinery of administration, are mere bottles out of which the wine and the oil are poured that make the heart of the Church glad, and its face to shine. No doubt the office-bearers of the Church, whether monarchical, aristocratic, or democratic, have a tendency to interfere with the form of doctrine and the liberty of worship which belong to the Church inherently, independent of all administration, by divine right, and by the charter of its original institution. But this is in all cases a usurpation and a trespass into a forbidden field, for the existence of which generally the ignorance, tameness, laziness, and cowardice of the Christian people are not less to blame than the ambition and the insolence of their officers. Unquestionably Pope Pius, when by his recent famous bull he stamped the character of an authoritative dogma on the immaculate conception of the Virgin Mary, previously only a floating sentiment in the popular mind, went beyond his function as the mere administrative head of a monarchico-aristocratical form of Church government; and not less certainly did Charles II. abuse his function as civil ruler and head of an Episcopal Church in certain external matters, when he plunged Scotland into a prolonged civil war in order to assert his insolent claim of framing an Episcopal liturgy for a Presbyterian people. But these vices, which historically have manifested themselves in connection with certain forms of external arrangement in matters ecclesiastical, do not belong in any wise essentially to the form. They are the accidental result of a vicious moral tendency, and an error of judgment on the part of the persons holding office under that form.

These remarks will have sufficiently indicated the essentially unchristian character of all contentions among the Churches tending to give any form of Church government a position of importance or of primary significance in the constitution of a Christian Church. The direct consequence of all such perverse assertiveness on the part of unwisely zealous Churchmen is to supply artificial stilts to that natural self-importance which among all classes is only too apt to rear itself proudly upon some accidental externals of privilege and position. Instead of encouraging this sort of ecclesiastical Pharisaism, the leaders of the various Churches should direct all their energies to induce all the Churches to act together, like the different corps in a well-generaled army, provoking one another, as the Apostle has it, not to strife and to denominational jealousy, but to love and to good works; for in Christ Jesus there is neither circumcision nor uncircumcision, neither a Church of bishops nor a Church of presbyters, neither a Free Church nor an Established Church, but a new creature.

But what is this new creature? Well, of course, it is in the main a thing quite the reverse of all those vanities of Externalism which we have just been condemning; it is essentially an inward and a spiritual thing—a thing of motives and aspirations and purposes, not of observances and rites and ceremonies. It is not so much a deed, or a series of deeds, as a power; it is a power instinct with that divine mystery direct from the primal source of all energy which we call LIFE; it is a root of moral spontaneity, out of which, by the divine process of evolution which we call growth, is sent forth a rich crop of green shoots and spreading branches in a constantly enlarging ring; it is a well-head out of which living waters, heaven-fed, are ever discharging themselves with an unforced fulness of bright overflow; it is the full tide of a rich moral life in the soul. About its excellence and superiority to all mere Externalism and Ceremonialism there can be no question; the only question that will naturally be put is, Whence this strong simile—the new creature? The simile is strong, no doubt, but it is in every way apt and adequate; nor is it, as some may imagine, a way of viewing the higher moral life peculiar to Christianity, but a favourite phrase with the Hindoos to indicate the transition from the secular life of the common man to the spiritual service of the Brahman. And the appropriateness of the simile will appear when we consider the familiar phenomena of the stages of life in human beings. The life of man asserts itself in three platforms, rising gradually one upon the other, like geological strata, in an invariable order; the sensuous or observant nature first, the intellectual or comparing and generalising nature afterwards, and last of all, the crown and top of human excellence, the moral nature. However clever a child may be, and however good, we cannot talk of its moral nature in the proper sense of the word. One child may be more pliable than another, more easily moulded, more open to all the gracious and kindly influences of which the family is the divinely-appointed nursery; but what the child does it does not by self-projected plans, purposes, and resolutions, by any sort of internal dictatorship, but by instincts and emotions, just as a hound pursues a hare, or a hawk a pigeon. There must be, therefore, a new birth, an awakening to a perfectly different form of existence, before the moral life can be properly said to have commenced. By good training and habits of obedience a child may grow up into a most engaging amiability; but all this has been done for it, not by it. A tree has flourished greenly in the nursery, but now it has to be transplanted into the open air, and learn to grow into independent hardihood in the face of the buffeting blasts and the drenching rains of an unregardful climate. The moral life of man, the regeneration—παλιγγενεσία— more properly so called, commences with a similar change. It commences with an awakening to the full consciousness of the dignity and lofty destiny of man as a moral being, and with a deliberate purpose and plan to carry it out to its legitimate consequences in the life of an essentially social animal. This is what in the New Testament narrative of apostolic preaching, and in many well-known religious biographies of recent date, is called *conversion;* and there can be no doubt both of the necessity and the reality of such a process. Those who are unwilling to admit this are either persons of a low moral type, who have never thoroughly escaped from the bonds of sensualism and selfishness which our theologians call the Old Adam, or persons whose lives have run on in such a smooth and even tenor, and so free from all noticeable transitions, that they are inclined to look with suspicion on all accounts of sudden conversions and startling experiences in the moral life, such as might be expressed by the emphatic image of a new birth. But neither are sudden conversions to be desired, nor in all cases to be insisted on, as if they were a necessary step in the process of the upbuilding of an ethical life. On the contrary, as in the physical world all growth is gradual, so there is every reason to expect that in the moral world it shall be the same. Even in the case of physical birth, though the forthcoming of the child from the dark shelter of the maternal womb into the large freedom of the open air is a very marked phenomenon to the bystanders, there can be little doubt that the conscious change of state after delivery is much greater to the mother than to the babe. To assert that a young person like the evangelist Timothy, brought up from his earliest years by a pious mother on the milk of the gospel, must necessarily be able to point to a moment in his history when, like the jailer at Philippi, he called in an agony of conviction, *What must I do to be saved?* is to indulge in a onesidedness of theological dogma as contrary to Scripture as to fact. The moral heat of nature is too variously dispersed to be always leaping from a fixed freezing point to fixed boiling point in this monstrous fashion. Betwixt the night and the day there must no doubt always be a sunrise; but the sun rises in divers ways, and with very different aspects in different countries, and in the same countries at different seasons. Let no man, therefore, as Baxter reports of himself in his biography, be painfully anxious to put his finger on the exact moment of his conversion from sin to holiness. After all, conversion, when it is most striking, most undoubted, and most deeply engraved into the living tablets of the memory, is only a start—only the awakening to the fact that there is a race to run; not the race itself, much less the goal. The great question is not, When did you begin, and how did you begin to be what you are? but WHAT

ARE YOU? How do you stand affected to our Lord Jesus Christ, as the grand ideal of moral perfection which it is your constant endeavour to realise in your own life? How do you answer the question, *What is the chief end of man?* Have you any end in life at all? or do you live at random like a boat without a pilot, a compass, or a chart? Or, to adopt the Platonic simile, do you hold the reins of your chariot firmly, or do you sit easily, or dreaming, or perhaps even drunk, upon the chariot seat, at the mercy of the wild steed, which at any moment may dash you on the granite pavement or leave you floundering in the mire? That is the one thing needful. No matter who put your timbers together, and where or when you were launched; but once fairly out on the stormy ocean of human life, take your bearings seriously, and know what you are about. Nevertheless, there are such things as sudden conversions, not only in individual cases, such as the well-known instances of Colonel Gardiner and Brownlow North, accompanied by very singular and striking circumstances, but in great gushes, so to speak, and spring-tides of popular emotion; for in all political, social, and religious movements there is an element of contagion which acts as beneficently as in the case of infectious diseases its action is pernicious. The Acts of the Apostles in the first constitution of the Church, and the records of "Revivals" so common in later times, are equally proofs of this influence. Had the masses of the people at Stewarton, Cambuslang, Kilsyth, and other parts of Scotland, been in any sound state of Christian vitality in the first half of the last century, no such sweeping storms of moral appeal would have been required to stir the stagnant and clear the turbid waters of their soul. But the age was flat and the people were low, and were just as much in need of the contagion of a sudden conversion in mass as the Aphrodite worshippers of Corinth were in the days of the Apostle Paul, or the slaves of a sacerdotal tyranny at St. Andrews in the days of John Knox. Similar sweeping blasts of regenerative virtue occurred about the end of the century, in the remarkable mission of the brothers Haldane, and the preaching of MacDonald of Ferintosh, the Apostle of the North. And if these revivals were at times accompanied with strange screamings and faintings, and hysterical agitations of various kinds, that was merely a matter of nerves and temperament in a few, which could not in the least discredit the reality and the soundness of the great change. Many wild things were done and said at the great French Revolution which have passed away as fire and smoke, like the show scenes in an operatic spectacle; but the principles of that great political earthquake and overthrow remain to the present hour, impregnating the atmosphere, ventilating the lungs, and purifying the blood of every social organism in Europe. God does nothing in vain.

In conclusion, we may remark that the great doctrine of a new birth, brought into such prominence by the phraseology of the New Testament, is not in anywise peculiar to the religious world, but is found manifesting itself vigorously in every manifestation of the higher life of man. In ART, for instance, the ancient Egyptians attained to a certain excellence of form and expression, but there they stopped, and, instead of a rich expansion into various forms of graceful development, such as we see in the works of God, stiffened into the formal rigidity of a hereditary type. Here, as in the case of the Jews, the conservatism natural to all religious traditions came in to co-operate with the sterility of human genius and the servility of artistic execution; but, however caused, this phenomenon in the region of plastic art was one precisely analogous to the formalistic superstition in religion against which our text protests. To these old Memphian artists, when in the days of their decadence under the Persians they bescrawled the walls of their shrines and sepulchres with the thousandfold repetition of a cow-headed Athor or a hawk-headed Ra, a Greek Phidias, working out in marble the chaste dignity of a Pallas, or the awful serenity of a Jove, might have said in the spirit of the Great Teacher to Nicodemus : " *Verily, verily, except ye be born again, ye shall not enter into the kingdom of true art.*" And in the same manner POETRY has had its ages, when the tyranny of a fashionable type fettered the freedom of rhythmical expression, and a dexterous manipulation of certain artificial flowers of rhetoric was accepted as a substitute for the green exuberance of a spontaneous vitality. To put an end to such an epoch of pedantic formalism and meretricious decoration, a radical change, or, in the language of our text, a new birth, is absolutely necessary; a new birth, of which in this country at the end of the last, and at the commencement of the present century, Cowper and Burns and Wordsworth were the great apostles,—men to whose powerful propulsion we owe whatever of true and pure, and healthy, strong, and natural, still remains effective amid the somewhat overstrained and over-ornamented poetical productions of our time. So in PHYSICAL SCIENCE the name of Bacon marks an epoch of regeneration and conversion from empty speculations about Nature to fruitful inductions from Nature; even as in scholarship, the arid verbalism and stylistic prettiness into which the sound and muscular erudition of the sixteenth century had degenerated was elevated into the brotherhood of philosophy and poetry by the cosmopolitan genius of Wolf, Boeckh, Lepsius, Grimm, Bopp, and the other hierarchs of the great German philology. In all things, but specially in religion, we must watch and pray against the lazy shift of cleaving to the form when we ought rather to rouse the spirit; of mistaking a long custom or a hoary statute for an eternal rule of right, of seeing God indirectly through human creeds instead of directly in his Word and works; and making our religion consist rather in the strictness of some external observance than in the fervour of a habitual piety. Religious observances are useful, and sacerdotal theologies are ingenious, even as painted glass is beautiful ; but as vision is not in a normal state to him who enjoys the light of the sun not amid the fragrant vegetation of green and golden Nature, but only through the gay motley of the glass, so neither will useful observance nor subtle theology beget a reasonable piety in the man whom the new birth has not redeemed from the slavery of human traditions into the perfect liberty of the sons of God. This is the alpha and the omega of all evangelical doctrine.

APPENDIX.

THE METAPHYSICS OF GENESIS I.

THE first chapter of Genesis was not intended to teach metaphysics any more than physics. It is neither historical nor metaphysical; it is philosophical or theological, or, from another point of view, mythical; not, of course, in the sense in which St. Paul uses the word μῦθος in Titus i. 14, when he advises the youthful superintendent of the Cretan presbyters or bishops to beware of Jewish *myths* or *fables*, but in the sense in which a parable or fictitious narrative is used in the New Testament as the fittest medium for the expression of profound moral truth. In this sense there can be no doubt that the Mosaic account of the creation is a philosophico-theological myth;[1] and the philosophico-theological truth which it pictures forth is not of the nature of a formal metaphysical proposition propounded by a learned University professor, or spun out of the subtle-brooding brain of some solitary Spinoza; but contents itself with stating simply in a few firm lines such salient features of a reasonable theory of the universe as under normal circumstances will satisfy the demands of a fully awakened human mind; and it expresses this theory in a language neither studiously avoiding a conflict with any possible metaphysics or any probable science, nor carefully forecasting an agreement with the same, but in such style as most aptly to convey to unsophisticated men the great truths which it enunciates. What I mean to

[1] "*Historische Data wird niemand heut zu Tage mehr darin suchen;* DAS GANZE IST BLOS PHILOSOPHISCH."— BUTMANN, MYTHOLOGUS. Berlin, 1828. Vol. i. p. 122.

discuss in this Note, therefore, is not the metaphysical or theological doctrine of Moses in scholastic form, for no such doctrine exists; but rather the subtle metaphysics and curiously concatenated theology which the doctors of the Christian Church, from their misapprehension of the nature of early mythical teaching, have imported into it. Metaphysically and scientifically there may be some disputable points in the Mosaic narrative when pressed curiously; but, as this curious pressing is altogether impertinent in the interpretation of a theological mythus, written in early times for an early Oriental people, the flaws imagined to be found in the composition of the mythical writer fall properly to be charged to ignorance and want of intelligent sympathy on the part of the interpreter.

(I.) "*In the* BEGINNING."—That is, at the beginning or start of the present order of things; not an absolute beginning of which theologians may talk or dream, but of which Moses certainly was not thinking. An absolute beginning of creative energy in the Supreme Reason is, in fact, impossible; because, if there had been an absolute beginning of a created universe, there must have been previously to that beginning an absolute eternity of divine existence devoid of all energy or plastic manifestation; that is, an infinite period of imperfect divine existence; for unrealised thinking, or thoughts not shaping themselves into deeds, can never be looked on as anything more than a step in the process of perfect existence—a step which may, no doubt, be predicated of finite man, whose plastic function is altogether derivative and secondary, but not of God, whose thoughts are essentially and necessarily deeds; as the great poet-thinker has it—"*Im Anfang war die That.*" And here I must dissent from Joannes Damascenus,[1] and, I imagine, also from the great herd of so-called orthodox theologians, when he says distinctly that benevolence led the Creator to create, he being otherwise perfectly complete in the thinking of his own thoughts:—

[1] *Damasceni Theologia Orthodoxa.* Paris: Stephan. 1512. Lib. ii. ch. 2, *De Opificio.*

"*Quia ergo Deus bonus et superbonus,* NON CONTENTUS EST SUA IPSIAS CONTEMPLATIONE, *sed super abundantiâ bonitatis complacuit ut fierent quædam quibus benefaceret, et quæ ejus participarent bonitate ; et ex nihilo ad esse deduxit atque condidit universa visibilia atque invisibilia.*" Of course Moses, being neither a theologian nor a metaphysician, but only a monotheistic lawgiver, knows nothing about this ; and we have simply to repeat that he knows as little of an absolute beginning of the universe. He only says that the present order of things on this earth had a beginning, with its natural sequence,—a growth and a development,—a proposition which no sensible man will dispute.

(II.) The next metaphysical point which arises out of the Mosaic narrative is the nature of MATTER, specially in its relation to GOD, or self-existent, self-energising, self-plastic MIND. Now, the vulgar opinion in the Christian world, and the opinion stamped as orthodox by a long chain of Jewish and Christian authorities, undoubtedly is, that matter is a distinct and separate entity, altogether diverse and discrete from MIND. In the words of Philo Judæus, "Matter is a substance without order, without quality, without life, full of all heterogeneousness, incongruity, and discord ; but it is capable of receiving from the Supreme Reason virtues the opposite of itself—viz. quality, vitality, likeness, identity, congruity, harmony, and whatever belongs to the dominance of the most excellent idea."[1] Now there seems no doubt that this vulgar opinion is founded on one of the strongest conceivable contrasts, presenting itself to the daily and hourly observation of all men—viz. the contrast between a hard granite rock or a heap of ice, and a thought, a fancy, or a dream. No subtlety of argument, no ingenuity of puzzling, will ever convince any sound-minded man that these two glaringly contrasted things are identical, or, to use Spinoza's language, modifications the one of the other. But, however far they may be from being identical, it is another proposition altogether to say that they are separable ; and if they are never found separated in

[1] *De Mundi Opificio,* 5.

Nature as the system of things now is, the fair conclusion seems to be, that they never did exist independently, and never can so exist. That this is true with regard to the spiritual pole of the contrast is plain from the fact that no man can think without a brain, or live without blood ; and with regard to the material pole of the contrast, while it is on the one hand true that many forms of what is vulgarly esteemed matter, such as electricity and light, are more swift and more subtle even than human thought, it is on the other hand no less true that the different forms of matter, such as the granite rock, or the Arctic icebergs, are constantly acted upon and kept in their consistency by two omnipotent forces called the attraction of cohesion and the attraction of gravitation. May it not therefore be true that what we call matter is not a distinct separable substance, but a substance standing to mind in the same relation that our nails stand to our souls ?—altogether different indeed from a thought or a fancy, but indissolubly bound up with the compact totality of the creature man, and partaking in a certain low degree of his vitality so long as they remain a part of the body. And if this indissoluble bond, as it seems, really exists, it never can be said in a literal sense that God made the world by both making the material out of which the world was made, and putting that material into shape ; but we shall more properly say, as Plato indeed has it in the *Timæus*, that the world is a divine animal, and that what is vulgarly called matter is simply the Body of God.[1] Call this Pantheism if you please ; it matters nothing, so long as Pantheism does not merge the one in the many, and is rather the highest and most effective form of theism than any form of materialism ; for this

---

[1] I cannot agree with Bentley (*Siris's* Works, ii. p. 476), that "to conceive God as the sentient soul of an animal is altogether unworthy and absurd." It is only not agreeable to our habitual modern associations. Had it been essentially unworthy or absurd, Plato certainly was the last man to have used it so gravely. Plato was no Pantheist ; but when the Finite talks about the Infinite similes, more or less inadequate are the only propositions possible.

Pantheism simply denies the existence of matter altogether, as a substance capable of existing independently of the great self-existent, all-present, all-plastic intellect which we reasonably call GOD. And here we clearly see the reason why Aristotle, Ocellus Lucanus, and, I fancy, all the great philosophers, taught what Christian theologians are fond to number among great heresies—the eternity of the world; for, as all philosophical speculation among Polytheistic peoples naturally assumes a Pantheistic form, the eternity of the world is merely an outside phrase for the eternity of God: what we generally call the world being, in fact, merely the face or external manifestation of that soul of the world to which Christian theologians, in their nomenclature of extreme spiritualism, confine the name of God. But however these things may be understood, or argued about in a round of pretentious logomachies, it is plain that they travel altogether outside of the broad common-sense utterance of the first verse of Genesis; and though we may perhaps see cause to agree with Tuch (*Commentary on Genesis*, p. 12), that the creation out of nothing (ἐκ τῶν οὐκ ὄντων, 2 Maccab. vii. 28) was the orthodox Jewish doctrine, rather than the creation from amorphous matter (*Wisdom* xi. 18; ἐξ ἀμόρφου ὕλης),—supposing matter somehow or other to have had an independent existence,—the sound-minded interpreter of the Bible can look upon all these problems with as much indifference as he does upon the question whether Moses really taught that the earth was the centre of the cosmic system, or only used that language in conformity with vulgar parlance—as we talk of the sun rising, when we believe only in the earth moving. As a popular teacher Moses was not, and could not be, commissioned to take note of any such unpractical, and, from his point of view, altogether unprofitable speculations. Enough, that with the wise Greeks he set the unity of the universe upon a firm basis for all times, by planting the one Sovereign, νοῦς and λόγος, where Polytheism by the assertion of many antagonistic gods had cherished intellectual and moral anarchy; this being sure, the whence and the whither of Matter as a medium for the manifestation of the divine excellence, are to him a speculation of perfect indifference.

(III.) The most important question connected with the existence of Matter arises from the bearing which it necessarily has on the exercise of the faculty called VOLITION in the Divine Mind. Was the world created by a sovereign and, so to speak, arbitrary act of the Divine Will, or did it grow, as it were, from a Divine Necessity in the Supreme Nature? Here we come upon debateable ground of a much more serious character; for while, on the one hand, theologians of the high Augustinian type have been forward to magnify the Divine Volition, so as to make it move in an altogether uncontrolled fashion, within the range of infinite possibilities, Pantheistic philosophers, like Spinoza, have denied volition altogether to the Divine Mind, and practically, with Shelley, made NECESSITY, I will not say a blind, but certainly not a free mother of the world.[1] Now the first point of the theologians here is certainly one that I find considerable difficulty in conceiving, viz. that a cause called MIND, having nothing in common with a substance called Matter, should by a single act of omnipotent volition be supposed to have brought such a substance into existence. If this be accepted as an act of Divine causation, it is a kind of causation quite contrary to anything of the kind of which the constitution of the world gives us any indication; for in every result or chain of results of which we have experience, there is always something in the force which precedes the result naturally and necessarily calculated to produce the result. I say, therefore, judging modestly from analogy, and not rashly from presumptuous speculation, that the creation of dead matter by omnipotent Divine volition is a proposition which we have no right to lay down; and as to volition generally, whether in the Supreme Being or in a finite Nature, we have every warrant for saying that it must ever be exercised in a manner conformable to the nature and excellence of the Being in whom it resides; in other words, it can neither

[1] "Necessity, thou mother of the world."—QUEEN MAB.

be arbitrary nor omnipotent;—not arbitrary, because arbitrary volition means determination without reason; not omnipotent, because no all-wise Being can do anything that is contrary to the essential function of His own all-wise Nature. Let us now see what Spinoza says on this point; for he is the great prophet at present in fashion with those who delight to relegate the wisdom of Moses into the limbo of silly legend and infantile conceit. Spinoza was no doubt a profound thinker and a wise man, and a man essentially noble in practice as well as in theory; but no more than other mortals may we expect to find him free from the great law of reaction, by which all the processes of change in the moral as much as in the physical world are controlled. As Locke's system of sensational externalism was not planted scientifically against the ideal internalism of Plato, but arose occasionally in the way of reaction out of the illegitimate theory of innate ideas held by certain contemporary writers, so we shall fail correctly to estimate the proper significance and drift of Spinoza's theology if we do not view it as an emphatic and thorough-going protest against the great body of what we may call volitional theologians, whose dogmas he found himself unable to digest. But, in the first place here let us not forget prominently to put forth the real character of Spinoza as a metaphysical theist. To him, as to all Christians, God is God, a Being and a Substance, not, according to the senseless phraseology of certain of our modern agnostics, only a name for an order of things, of which it is useless to ask for a cause.[1] Again, our modern British philosophy since Hume has earned for itself a cheap originality by confounding the idea of cause with that of invariable sequence; but into the profound and serious and reverential thought of Spinoza such a superficial sophism could never enter. He does not, indeed, formally define the word cause, but he allows that word to stand where, by the necessity of

---

[1] *Per* DEUM *intelligo* ENS *absolutum hoc est* SUBSTANTIAM *constantem infinitis attributis quorum unumquodque æternam et infinitam essentiam exprimit.*—Ethic I. def. 6, and proposition xi.

human thought, it always has stood, and always will stand, as the expression of a precedent force, which, by an inherent virtue, necessarily produces a corresponding result called an effect; and in this view God is not only the order of things, an infinite series of invariable sequences, but He is the alone ultimate cause of all the causes which make that invariability possible. Farther on (Prop. xvii.) he lays it down emphatically that "*God is the only* FREE *cause*," or in other words, "DEUS EX SOLIS SUÆ NATURÆ LEGIBIS ET A NEMINE COACTUS AGIT,"—a proposition which, as thus simply stated, seems perfectly reasonable, but about which we may feel at first inclined to hesitate, when in the exposition of it we are told flatly that God is a Being, of whom, properly speaking, neither intellect nor will can be predicated. How are we to understand this? Happily on this point he is so clear that it is our own fault altogether if we misinterpret him. His proposition is, he tells us, directed distinctly against those who, to magnify the divine omnipotence, have chosen "*Deum ad omnia indifferentem statuere nec aliud creantem præter id quod absolutâ quâdam voluntate voluerit.*" Now this compliment from the orthodox party, meant to be paid to the divine omnipotence, reveals its absurdity in a moment when applied to an absolute human governor; for, if to be determined by mere unreasonable will in the human case is the attribute of a senseless, arbitrary, and oppressive tyrant, surely such conduct can never be attributed to the Supreme Source of all wisdom and goodness. The great Pantheist is therefore right when he says that the Divine Being, though absolutely free from any external compulsion, is not free to act otherwise than according to the necessary laws of His own excellence. And in this sense no sensible man will have any hesitation in saying that neither intellect nor will, used in such arbitrary fashion, can be predicated of the Supreme Excellence. So far well. But Spinoza was fond of mathematical similes; and every simile limps, as the proverb says; and so, in illustrating this doctrine, he uses two similes, which can be accepted only with a deduction. He says, in the first place, that all things flow by the same necessity from the divine nature, that the bi-rectangular measure of the contained angles of a triangle flows from the essential nature of a figure so circumscribed. Then, again, he asserts that human intellect and human will differ *toto coelo* from the divine intellect and the divine will, agree, in fact, only in name, having nothing in common beyond what the dog-star in the celestial constellations has with the terrestrial barking quadruped which we call a dog. Now these are startling propositions, and, taken literally, lead to very questionable conclusions. Every human being feels that, when he comes, for instance, to the parting of two walks in a public park, he may take the path to the right hand or that to the left from no necessity of his nature, but simply and absolutely from the motive of proving his freedom of choice in the face of any one who may controvert it. This is what we call volition in man, and is a quality which can no more be confounded with the necessary outcome of spatial limitation in geometry than a granite rock with a song of Robert Burns; and if this be true of the extremely limited and circumscribed sphere of absolute volition in man, it appears most absurd to enchain the divine will in a more dependent fashion. Again, when it is said that there is nothing in common between the human intellect and the divine—a notion ventilated also in his easy way of dealing with deep things by David Hume—this is true only of the method of action in the divine intellect, not of its essential nature and quality; just as we might say that there is nothing in common between the creative genius of Shakespeare and the receptive criticism of his commentators. God acts from the centre downwards, plastically; *man* from the periphery upwards, receptively; and these two methods of action have, no doubt, nothing in common. Nevertheless, to say that the writer Shakespeare and the readers of Shakespeare have nothing in common, would be glaringly false; for, if they had nothing in common, they could not appeal to one another, or enjoy one another, any more than Beethoven with his symphonies, or Mozart with his masses, could appeal for sympathy to the braying capacity of an ass. We shall therefore take the liberty of dealing here with Spinoza as we do with the familiar paradoxes of the Stoics, and some paradoxical sentences in the New Testament: we shall suppose they are meant to be seasoned with common sense, and, unless so seasoned, they are simply a more ingenious sort of nonsense.

Only one remark in vindication of Spinoza we may justly make. It is supposed by some, naturally enough, that because choice and volition belong to the highest excellence of human nature, they therefore must belong in a higher sense, and with a wider range, to God; and in a certain sense, no doubt, as we have indicated, this is true; but we must always bear in mind that, though a wise choice and an effective volition are the highest things in man, the necessity of making a choice and forming a volition with human beings, does for the most part arise out of their ignorance and the forecasting of chances, which this ignorance, by a laborious process of calculation, renders necessary. But such choosing and such determination cannot for a moment be conceived of in Him who is the fountain of all knowledge and the controller of all chance. And if in this sense only Spinoza meant to deny reasoned choice and volition to God (and at bottom I can scarcely think he meant anything more), we can only thank him for his heterodox protest, and leave all orthodox dogmas about the possibilities of an arbitrary omnipotence to float about in the inane of those cobwebby speculators whose stomachs are not strong enough to digest any more substantial nutriment.

(IV.) On Teleology, or the doctrine of design, I have stated my views so fully in the text, that I have nothing to do specially here but to prove, from an examination of the famous chapter in the Ethics of Spinoza (Prop. xxxvi., Appendix) that the recent fashion of planting that profound thinker as the antagonist of Socrates and the Stoics in respect of this doctrine, is altogether a mistake. The argument from design, indeed, as John Stuart Mill clearly saw, is so deeply rooted in the intellectual instinct of every normally constituted mind, that any objections to it, however pretentiously paraded and echoed for a year and a day, will pass away as certainly as darkness from the face of the sun after an eclipse. Spinoza, with all his greatness, could not as a finite creature shake himself free from the destiny that follows all apostolic and iconoclastic activity in this world; such activity must, by the nature of things, be one-sided, and, however effective as a blow, fail to be decisive if taken as an ultimate verdict. But, on a careful examination, I am not inclined to think that the great Jew had any thought of an ultimate verdict here, such as a cool, comprehensive, and judicial Aristotle, for instance, would have given; however absolutely he lays down the proposition in words, it is plain to whosoever follows the thread of his whole language from beginning to end, that he is writing as a reactionist, and that his one end is not to deny a large design in the grand scheme of creation, but to expose the fallacies of conceited and presumptuous men, who would dwarf the largeness of that design down to the measure of their petty personal utilities. The proposition, " OMNES CAUSAS FINALES NIHIL NISI HUMANA ESSE FIGMENTA " is introduced as the summation of a statement that men generally are of opinion " *Deum omnia propter hominem fecisse,*" and that they consequently " *Omnia naturalia ad suum utile media considerant.*" " *Unde factum ut unusquisque diversos Deum colendi modos ex suo ingenio excogitaverit, ut Deus eos supra reliquos diligeret, et totam naturam in usum cœcœ illorum cupiditatis et insatiabilis avaritiæ dirigeret.* This is a slashing passage; but it is a passage to which the most intellectual Socratic philosopher, believing in design, will be as willing to subscribe as the most one-sided British physicist, who delights in exposing the so-called barren virginity of final causes. For what does it substantially mean? Not, as we have already said, that there is no design in creation, but that men err greatly in supposing that that design is limited and confined, or in any way influenced, by a respect for their petty utilities and vain imaginations. And what does he go on to say? He states his belief antagonistic to this debased and degraded form of teleology in the words, "*Omnia naturæ æterna quâdam necessitate summâque perfectione procedere,*" which means that God, by the necessity of his own most excellent nature, cannot do otherwise than manifest himself in a procession of absolutely perfect forms, that is, as parts of a grand whole, and not by forming special purposes or designs, with a one-sided partial reference to the convenience of his creature, man. And observe, further, in this view the very peculiar language which he uses in apparently controverting the Socratic exposition of a miraculous divine design in the structure of the human frame. After stating that the will of God is habitually used by a certain class of ill-instructed and pious people as "the asylum of ignorance," he continues, "*Sic etiam, ubi corporis humani fabricam vident, stupescunt et ex eo quod tantæ artes causas ignorant, concludunt eandem non mechanicâ sed divinâ vel supernaturali arte fabricari.*" This antithesis between mechanical art and divine or supernatural art plainly shows that the writer is fighting against a class of ignorant and superstitious persons, with whose imaginations the idea of design in the mind of the highly intellectual Socrates could have nothing in common ; for it is precisely the perfection of the mechanical art which Socrates admires, and it is not ignorance but knowledge of the nature of mechanical art that leads all sound-minded persons to attribute such structure to intellectual design. After this, in the next paragraph, he reverts to his original starting-point, which shows plainly the point of view from which his whole argument is to be understood, "*Postquam homines sibi persuaderunt omnia quæ fiunt propter ipsos fieri* (still harping on that string!), *id in unaquaque rê præcipuum judicare debuerant quod ipsis utilissimum, et illa omnia præstantissima æstimare a quibus optime afficiebantur.*" This is manifestly directed not against large theistic thinkers, such as Pythagoras, Plato, Socrates, Zeno, but against the most shallow and superficial class of vulgar utilitarians ; and, in fact, in the last paragraph he expressly says it is the ignorant "*vulgus*," and not philosophers, against whom his whole appendix is directed. Any other supposition, indeed, completely breaks down the boundary line between the lofty intellectual theism of the profoundest of Hebrew thinkers and the Pyrrhonism and scepticism of the most idle and quibbling of the Greek sophists. Nevertheless, we must honestly say that the very strong language in which the concluding paragraph of the appendix seems to make all moral and æsthetical judgments depend, according to the sentence of Protagoras, on the subjective judgment of the individual may have given only too ready a handle to the irreverent spirits of the age, to quote Spinoza, as the protagonist of their monstrous doctrine of a reasonable framework of effects without the inherent and indwelling action of a reasonable cause. But those who enter into the soul of Spinoza with a deep and reverent sympathy will never be led to interpret any individual polemical passage in his book in such fashion as to confound him with any class of sceptics and sophists, however clever. His constant drift is not to banish God from the world, but to banish human conceits from God's plan. His rejection of teleology, as vulgarly applied by certain shallow dogmatists of his time, is in its whole spirit and scope manifestly a rebuke to human impertinence, not an insensibility to divine wisdom.

(V.) The only other question on which a few words may seem necessary here is, whether we have any hint in the Mosaic account of the creation and the state of man in Paradise of the existence of an Evil Spirit or DEVIL as the author of Evil. Of course, historically, there is none ; that is, if we are right in interpreting the account of the fall as a theological myth ; nevertheless, it may be thought that the serpent in the myth may not be simply an allegorical figure, but an indication of a personal principle of evil, which afterwards appears on the stage of Jewish faith in a more distinct and less equivocal form. And here, as in some other theological questions, we must commence by standing on our guard against the very natural tendency in all

Christian believers to look on the Bible as a book presenting a consistent unity of creed from beginning to end, and not rather, as it manifestly is, in not a few essential points, a development from a less to a greater, and from a something unseen and unsuspected, to a something publicly displayed and emphatically acknowledged. Nor is it necessary that the development should always be,—as no doubt it has been in the main,—from worse to better; it is quite possible in the growth of Jewish, as of other opinions with regard to accessory and unessential matters, that there may have been a development from better to worse, from the silence of a wise ignorance to the profession of a presumptuous knowledge. Of this sort of retrogressive development, the acceptance of a personal Devil, or transcendental Author of Evil, as a part of the popular Jewish creed, is perhaps one of the most notable. Of such a malignant Power, beside and antagonistic to the divine goodness, there is not the slightest trace in the Pentateuch. The serpent in the mythus of the fall has just as much to do with the orthodox Christian Devil, as the Lucifer or Sun of the Morning, in Isaiah xiv. 12, has to do with the Pandemonian personage who, from the days of Jerome downwards, has appropriated that appellation. And as to call the evil spirit Lucifer was not an interpretation of the Lucifer meant in the prophecy of Isaiah against the king of Babylon, but only a new application of an old simile, so the identification of the Devil and Satan with the old serpent in Rev. xx. 2, is an adoption of an apt image,—nothing more. And when St. Paul, in 2 Cor. xi. 3, talks of the serpent beguiling Eve, whether he accepted the fall as a historical fact or as a theological myth, he does merely what Aristotle or Zeno might have done, when they quoted the Homeric sorceress Circe as turning her victims into swine, that is, degrading them from virtue into sensuality. Circe might be a fact or a fiction; what they used her for was to point a moral. In fact, nothing but the persistent vice of retrospective interpretation, so deeply seated in the bones of so-called orthodox theologians, could have led any sober thinker to introduce a counter Power of transcendental Evil into the theology of the Old Testament. The existence of such a power is altogether inconsistent with the absolute omnipotence of the Jehovah whom it was the national boast and special privilege of the Hebrew people to acknowledge; and had any such idea governed the writer of the book of Exodus, he could not possibly have talked as he does of God hardening Pharaoh's heart; but the Devil would naturally have been named as the author of this state of contumacious disobedience to the divine commands. And here we must note a curious coincidence between the extreme Hebrew monotheism and the polytheism of the Greeks. Neither the one theology nor its opposite could acknowledge a Devil; not the Hebrew theology, because the existence of such an adverse power implied a curtailment of the Divine Omnipotence; not the Hellenic theology, because the Homeric gods, as being radically elemental forces, and only by development moral forces, might be the authors of evil without contradicting their own nature. Not, of course, that either in Homer or Moses the guilt of sin is transferred from man to God; the great practical mystery of free will and moral responsibility in some sort still remains, only the Devil is not called in to explain the intrusion of evil into a fair world. And as the faith of Moses in this respect originally stood, so it remained deep in the Hebrew heart, so late as the days of Isaiah, who, in his prophetic vision of Cyrus (xlv. 7), loudly proclaims the absolute sovereignty of God in the sublime words, "I FORM THE LIGHT AND CREATE DARKNESS; I MAKE PEACE AND CREATE EVIL; I, THE LORD, DO ALL THESE THINGS!" And this, so far as I can see, was also clearly the doctrine of St. Paul, who, in his Epistle to the Romans, touching the deepest questions, makes no mention of the Devil; and if St. Paul required no aid from such a supernatural rebel against all good, his prominent appearance in our modern Calvinistic theology, based as it is on the metaphysical theology of the apostle, must be regarded as a superfluity, or rather an incongruity, a notion that has stuck to our creed by traditional accretion, not sprung out of it by organic virtue. Strangely enough, the only distinct mention of the Devil, as a historical personage, behind or within the serpent, as the author of the fall, occurs in a book which our orthodox Protestant Churches have combined to denounce as apocryphal. I mean, of course, the passage in the Book of Wisdom which runs thus :—"God created man for immortality, and made him the image of his own peculiar nature; but, BY THE ENVY OF THE DEVIL, DEATH ENTERED INTO THE WORLD."[1] We have here a distinct dogmatical assertion, leaving no doubt as to the faith of the writer, and perhaps of the age to which he belonged; but in the other passages of the Old Testament, as in the Book of Job and Zechariah iii. 1, which are adduced to prove the Hebrew belief in the modern Christian doctrine of the Devil, I can only see a dramatical figure, like Ἄτη in Homer and the Greek tragedians, which never attained to the dignity of a thoroughly incarnated and universally recognised cosmical personage. How far an acquaintance with the celestial dualism of the Babylonian and Persian theologies during the Captivity may have made the Hebrew mind in its latter stages familiar with an idea at war with its original character, I will not inquire; certain it is, from the vague and contradictory allusions to Satan in the historical books,[2] that the modern Devil had then acquired a certain position in the theological conscience of the nation. As to the modern Christian doctrine of the Devil, and the place which, by the tradition of centuries, it holds in the creeds of

---

[1] ὁ Θεὸς ἔκτισε τὸν ἄνθρωπον ἐπ' ἀφθαρσίᾳ, καὶ εἰκόνα τῆς ἰδίας ἰδιότητος ἐποίησεν αὐτόν Φθόνῳ δὲ διαβόλου θάνατος εἰσῆλθεν εἰς τὸν κόσμον. If St. Paul had held this dogma, or thought it of any consequence, he could scarcely have omitted to allude to it in Romans v.

[2] Contrast 1 Chronicles xxi. 1, with 2 Sam. xxiv. 1. The old idea of God as the ultimate author of evil prevails in 1 Kings xxii. 23. Here the lying spirit is, as he ought to be in a strongly monotheistic system, altogether servile and ministerial.

Christendom, it is no business of mine to discuss it here. I may only make the remark, in conclusion, that the framers of creeds in our Church Councils, from the third century downwards, have been a great deal too hasty in assuming that certain vague floating ideas in the popular mind, and which had incorporated themselves into the current language of the times, were to be considered as coming to us stamped with a divine sanction, and to be accepted in all seriousness as dogmatic propositions forming an inseparable part of the Christian creed. The Athanasian Creed, though in no wise remarkable for modesty, says nothing about the Devil; and, if he were omitted similarly in all the creeds and catechisms of Christendom, the omission would do no harm. The question of a personal Devil is a question of metaphysical curiosity, not of evangelical doctrine; and, so far as moral motives and moral judgments are concerned, his existence is, for all practical purposes, null.

THE END.

www.ingramcontent.com/pod-product-compliance
Lightning Source LLC
Chambersburg PA
CBHW031427230426
43668CB00007B/461